*Carrying
the
Torch*

Carrying the Torch

MAUD HOWE ELLIOTT AND THE AMERICAN RENAISSANCE

Nancy Whipple Grinnell

University Press of New England
Hanover and London

*Published in association
with the Newport Art Museum*

University Press of New England
www.upne.com
© 2014 University Press of New England
All rights reserved
Manufactured in the United States of America
Designed by Mindy Basinger Hill
Typeset in Adobe Caslon Pro

University Press of New England is a member of the
Green Press Initiative. The paper used in this book meets their
minimum requirement for recycled paper.

For permission to reproduce any of the material in this book, contact
Permissions, University Press of New England, One Court Street,
Suite 250, Lebanon NH 03766; or visit www.upne.com

Library of Congress Cataloging-in-Publication Data

Grinnell, Nancy Whipple.
Carrying the Torch: Maud Howe Elliott and the
American Renaissance / Nancy Whipple Grinnell.
pages   cm
"Published in association with the Newport Art Museum."
Includes bibliographical references and index.
ISBN 978-1-61168-495-7 (cloth: alk. paper) — ISBN 978-1-61168-496-4 (ebook)
1. Elliott, Maud Howe, 1854–1948. 2. Women authors,
American—Biography. I. Title.
PS 1588. G 75 2014
818'.409—dc23
[B]   2013022397

TO DAVE

*For his unwavering love
and support—and patience!*

CONTENTS

Preface ix
Acknowledgments xv

ONE 1

TWO 15

THREE 29

FOUR 42

FIVE 61

SIX 73

SEVEN 84

EIGHT 102

NINE 115

TEN 128

Notes 143
Bibliography 163
Index 169

Plates follow page 76.

PREFACE

IT WAS THE STRIKING PHOTOGRAPH BY BACHRACH OF THE BEAU-tiful yet formidable older woman that introduced me to Maud Howe Elliott, a historical figure at the Newport Art Museum where I arrived as curator in 1998. The portrait from 1928 shows her clad in black mourning attire, adorned with various medals, while through a veil her clear, intelligent and lovely eyes meet the viewer head on. A Pulitzer prize-winning author and recognized arts advocate in her day, Elliott was the co-founder of the institution that began in 1912 as the Art Association of Newport and is now the Newport Art Museum and Art Association. Interested in Newport's art history and a student of women's history, I had never heard of Elliott.

Maud Howe Elliott, like many of history's "lost" women, was respected and well known during her lifetime, which spanned almost a hundred years in the nineteenth and twentieth centuries. Elliott gained prominence as the literary daughter of two of Boston's great historical figures, Julia Ward Howe and Samuel Gridley Howe. Her first forays into the world of writing included art reviews and "letters" for the *Boston Transcipt*. She went on to author twenty-one popular books of fiction and non-fiction, as well as countless articles and stories. She shared the first Pulitzer Prize for biography with her sister Laura Elizabeth Richards, for *Julia Ward Howe, 1819–1910*. She visited artists' studios and lectured on artists of both sexes to a variety of American audiences beginning in the late 1880s in Chicago, where she played a prominent role in the woman's building at the World's Columbian Exposition of 1893. She firmly believed that the

United States was fertile ground for great art; she wrote "The best work with few exceptions, done by American artists has been done *in* America: Copley, Stuart, Allston, Hunt, La Farge, Fuller, Saint Gaudens, Alden Weir, Winslow Homer, George Inness have all painted at home."[1]

Elliott was not confined to the arts in her interests, however; she was a suffragist as well as a passionate supporter of Theodore Roosevelt, forming the Rhode Island Women's Progressive Party in 1912 and giving lectures across the nation in support of the 1916 candidate, Charles Evans Hughes. Elliott was also a journalist of stature, writing syndicated columns in a number of American newspapers and indeed, was often an investigative reporter. In a career that encompassed six decades, five wars and great social upheaval, Elliott used her pen, her voice and her persuasive personality to advocate for a progressive agenda of cultural and political reform.

Elliott's adopted city of Newport, Rhode Island, has long recognized her many cultural and civic contributions. When she died at the age of ninety-three in 1948, Maxim Karolik, the great patron of American art and benefactor of the Museum of Fine Arts, Boston, sent a letter to the *Newport Daily News*. He wrote, "I am not sure whether we all realize what the passing of Maud Howe Elliott means to us Newporters. I think she epitomized the cultural life of Newport…If we are interested in Newport as a progressive New England town, we must keep Mrs. Elliott's torch burning for our cultural life here."[2] Karolik, credited with influencing the renaissance of American nineteenth century painting in the twentieth century, recognized a kindred spirit in Elliott, who focused on raising not only Newport's, but the nation's consciousness about the importance of American art and artists. A strong adherent to the classical ideals of the Greeks and Romans, as well as the humanism of the Renaissance, Elliott believed that the American nation contained these same seeds of greatness.

Maud Howe was born in 1854, the fifth child of Julia Ward Howe and Samuel Gridley Howe. Her mother's name is familiar to earlier students of American history primarily for authoring the words to *The Battle Hymn of the Republic* during the Civil War and following that coup with decades of activism on behalf of women's rights, world peace and social reform. Her husband, Samuel Gridley Howe—nicknamed "The

Chevalier," "Chev" for short—was a Brown University and Harvard-educated physician, Greek freedom fighter, abolitionist, advocate for the physically and mentally disabled, first director of the Perkins Institution for the Blind and pioneer in education for the blind. An early opponent of tax breaks for the wealthy, he supported a progressive tax system and was considerably ahead of his time in social and political reform in all areas except one: women's emancipation, a fact which did not bode well for his marriage or family harmony.

With three older sisters married and one brother off to a prestigious scientific career in New York, Maud felt the family dysfunction more than the others, as she was left behind with an ailing father and absent mother. She struggled desperately with her identity during adolescence and well into adulthood, always seeking a mission in life. Endowed with many of the attributes that would make another nineteenth century young woman content, including beauty, charm, social standing and intellect, Maud instead flouted convention and developed an impetuous and spoiled nature that drove her parents to despair. Surrounded by suitors, she partied into the early hours of the morning, but showed little interest in settling down, prompting her father to worry about her "frivolity." After his death in 1876, Julia Ward Howe sacrificed her meager savings and took twenty-three year old Maud on the Grand Tour, ostensibly to find her a suitable and presumably wealthy husband. Samuel Gridley Howe had depleted his wife's fortune with his philanthropic schemes for liberal causes, but for two years mother and daughter managed to travel and visit, fortified by Howe's friendships with some of Europe's most celebrated literary, political and artistic figures, not to mention royalty. Howe herself was considered American royalty.

It was in Europe that Maud Howe Elliott found her calling. She was rapturous about her discovery of the world's great art in Holland, Belgium and Italy. The history, the pageantry and the culture of England and the Continent overwhelmed her senses and sensibilities. She dined with Robert Browning, sat for Edward Burne-Jones, yachted and toured with lords and ladies, went to church at Westminster Abbey and met the great politicians of the day. American beauties were in vogue, and Maud competed for attention with women such as the breath-taking Lily Langtry, then the toast of London. While seemingly European society was as enchanted with Maud as she was with it, the Grand Tour did not have the expected result for a young woman of breeding and beauty. On a train in Perugia, Italy, Elliott met the man who was to be her husband: a four-years-younger, bohemian, penniless artist from England. At the age of nineteen, the orphan John Elliott was with his traveling companion—an older English "bachelor" with whom the artist had an unusually close relationship. Maud Howe and John Elliott were married ten years after their introduction. They embarked on a productive and mutually beneficial partnership in which she traveled, wrote, and cultivated the arts—especially her husband's painting—and he lived mostly abroad, reaping the professional benefits of the Howe family's connections around the world. Beginning in the 1890s their home base was Rome, where they were surrounded by other expatriate artists and writers as well as the classical and renaissance ideals that so inspired Maud.

Maud Howe Elliott also spent a considerable part of her marriage visiting her mother and overseeing her business affairs, both in Boston and Portsmouth, Rhode Island, where the family had summered since the 1850s. All the siblings doted on their mother, but Maud had a particularly close relationship with her and seemingly felt herself the primary caregiver, which did not always sit well with the rest of the family. In 1910 Julia Ward Howe died, and the Elliotts returned permanently to the United States. After a period of bereavement and much consultation with other family members, Maud received the option to live at Oak Glen, the home in Portsmouth, Rhode Island, and the Elliotts resumed their lives: he worked on his art, and she supported them both by writing and lecturing. The biography of Julia Ward Howe, referred to as "The Life," was a family affair, perhaps sparking more controversy than inheritance matters, as the siblings quarreled over authorship issues, including whose names would be featured on the title page.

In her 1923 autobiography *Three Generations*, Elliott tellingly wrote, "From my first hour I was wrapped in a fragment of my mother's garment. If her mantle cannot truthfully be said to have fallen upon me, I have at least contrived to creep under a corner of it and it has kept me warm all my days!"[3] This tendency to think of herself as the heir apparent accounted for the flurry of causes that Elliott undertook shortly after her mother's death. She shouldered the banner of woman's suffrage, pursued so fervently by Howe, and embarked upon the cause of the Bull Moose, or Progressive political party, championing Teddy Roosevelt. And most ardently, Elliott brought her mother's unflagging resolve, energy, and organizational skills to form the Art Association of Newport. Like Howe, who founded Newport's Town and Country Club in the late nineteenth century, Elliott sought to cultivate people's minds and heighten their senses by exposing them to the arts and sciences.

In 1912, after Maud delivered a lecture to a discussion group in Newport on "An Artist's Life in Rome," the Elliotts were prevailed upon to form the Art Association of Newport with a group of like-minded citizens and artists. It was in Newport where Maud Howe Elliott's passion for the arts flowered; she drew upon her family's and her own significant circle of aesthetes, writers, artists, musicians, politicians, military men, historians and scientists to help the Art Association flourish with ongoing exhibitions, classes, programs, and lectures. While early twentieth-century Newport is often associated with an exclusive summer colony, opulent mansions, and a society of excess, Elliott's goal was decidedly democratic. She wrote, "Our strength lies in the fact that we are a truly representative association, including people of every age and every sort of income, that we welcome with equal cordiality all sorts and conditions of men, women and children, asking only one thing, that they come to us in the ... spirit of devotion to the cultivation of artistic endeavor."[4]

After her husband's death in 1925, Maud Howe Elliott summoned her resources and embarked upon the final chapter of her life. She continued to devote herself tirelessly to the Art Association, but began to travel with a new vigor, both in Europe and the United States, sometimes renewing old friendships but also attaining a closure of sorts for unfinished family business. She went to Greece to return Lord Byron's helmet, which her father had retrieved during the fight for Greek independence after the poet's death in 1824. Seeking warm winter weather, Elliott was an early "snowbird," visiting and writing descriptively about the people, climate, and customs of Florida, Jamaica, Panama, California, and the Southwest. She co-founded a second arts organization, the Society of Four Arts in Palm Beach, Florida. During these years she published biographies of her husband; her cousin, the acclaimed writer Francis Marion Crawford;

her uncle, the charismatic lobbyist Samuel Ward; and the classic book *This Was My Newport*.

If there was one constant refrain in the work of Maud Howe Elliott, it was expressed in one of her earlier lectures: "One of our greatest national mistakes is that art is a luxury, a thing by itself, which may or may not be cultivated according to the taste of the individual, or nation ... [The Pilgrim Fathers] came to this country bringing great ideals, and grave mistakes with them, the most serious mistake was a hatred and distrust of Art!"[5] She devoted her life to instilling a passion and respect for the arts in America that would embody the classical ideals of what she considered the greatest civilization—that of the ancient Greeks. The humanizing influence that Christianity introduced during the Italian Renaissance was also important to the development of American civilization. But by the time Elliott died in 1948, Americans had been through two wars and the Great Depression, and her urging to "keep the home fires burning for art" was losing its relevancy.

Over half a century later, the arts advocacy for which Elliott worked so hard is more alive than ever. As the Newport Art Museum celebrated its centennial in 2012, its mission echoed the vision of Maud Howe Elliott: to inspire "passion for the arts in diverse audiences through exhibitions and collections, arts education, historic preservation, and arts and cultural programming." At this time I feel sure her voice would once again be lifted to ensure that creativity and respect for artistic endeavor receive encouragement and support among the citizens. Personally, this is a story that I have been compelled to write after twelve years of getting to know and understand Elliott through her letters, her writing, her work, and a rather otherworldly coincidence. In March 1948, Elliott died and was laid to rest in Mount Auburn Cemetery, Cambridge, Massachusetts, while six months later I came into the world right down the street at Mount Auburn Hospital. It is up to future generations, now, to carry the torch for the arts.

NANCY WHIPPLE GRINNELL

ACKNOWLEDGMENTS

THE ADVENTURE OF DELVING INTO THE LIFE OF MAUD HOWE Elliott began at the Newport Art Museum, which is the institution that has allowed me to produce her story. My grateful thanks to Elizabeth A. Goddard, Executive Director, for her support and encouragement and to the Board of Trustees, who over the years have good-naturedly fostered my obsession with the founder of our institution. Making the book a possibility in a very substantial way was Elizabeth Prince de Ramel, and my thanks knows no bounds for her generosity in funding the project. Also, untold appreciation to Diane Wilsey, who made possible a month-long sabbatical and assistance in the curatorial department by Karen Conway.

From the beginning there have been many cheerleaders for this project. One of the earliest was Danny D. Smith, Archivist for the Yellow House Papers and the Gardiner Library Association, who has guided me through the special collections at the Gardiner Public Library (where was he when I was locked in at 5:30?) and entertained me with Howe and Richards family lore. Sue Horton, a former Board member at the Newport Art Museum and great Maud enthusiast, gave me her Maud books when she relocated to Florida many years ago and has remained interested and supportive of my endeavor. Ellen Liberman wrote a great article about the Museum and the prospective book in *Rhode Island Monthly* in 2002; twelve years later she is delighted to have the book come to fruition. Cora Lee Gibbs, Director Emeritus and Christine Callahan, former Executive Director of the Newport Art Museum were always encouraging. In Newport, George Herrick had encountered mention of

Maud through his research and Isabella Stewart Gardner connections, and has unfailingly provided access to his findings. Florence Archambault, a Newport historian extremely knowledgeable about Maud's political activism has generously shared her material. James L. Yarnall, Ph.D., has given me great professional guidance in our collaborative presentations about Maud in *Newport History, the Journal of the Newport Historical Society*, of which he is editor.

Numerous libraries contain archives relating to the Howe family, not to mention the Wards, the Chanlers, the Richards, the Halls, and on. Two have served as the major sources for this narrative. The John Hay Library at Brown University, where Elliott received an honorary doctor of letters in 1940, and where I received an MA in 2004, holds the Maud Howe Elliott Papers. I am not sure if the staff thinks I have another job (I do), as I have haunted their reading room for twelve years. I will miss the friendly help of Andy Moul, Ann Dodge, Alison Bundy, and Kathleen Brooks. The Yellow House Papers at the Maine Historical Society are just as important to Maud's story, as they contain almost seventy years of correspondence between Maud and her sister Laura Richards. My great appreciation to librarian Nick Noyes and staff Bill Barry, Jamie Kingman Rice, and Dani Fazio. I am grateful for the use of materials at Harvard's Schlesinger Library and Houghton Library. Bert Lippincott and Jennifer Robinson at the Newport Historical Society have always been helpful. At the Society of Four Arts, in Palm Beach, Florida, Director Nancy Mato has loaned their wonderful portrait of Maud and expressed enthusiasm for the project.

When I was working on my MA in American Civilization and Museum Studies at Brown University, I analyzed different aspects of Maud's activities under the guises of Women's History, U.S. History, American Literature and Art History, and I am grateful for the critiques and comments of faculty Barton St. Armand, Jane Gerhard, Mary Jo Buhle, and Robert Emlen.

Maud had no children, but she had nieces and nephews, and now has many great-nieces and nephews. Several have enthusiastically supported my research and progress. I am eternally grateful to Kate Stickley for providing access to Julia Ward Howe journal material. I met Rita Putnam at the memorial service for her aunt, Posey Wiggins, who herself was a remarkably accomplished woman, and the granddaughter of Laura Richards. Rita has been a great link to the Richards family. Three years ago Maud Fluchere and Zell Kerr, Florence Howe Hall's granddaughters, came to the Newport Art Museum to present us with one of Maud's medallions from Italy. In 2011 Carrie Minturn Kerr and her family brought us three wonderful artworks by John Elliott that her late mother, Zell, had felt should be at the Museum. In similar incidents the Museum has acquired Elliott's portrait of Julia Ward Howe from the late Rosalys Hall, another niece on the Hall side, and portrait of Maud by Mabel Norman Cerio, from Patricia Saunders. Maud would likely be very pleased that the Newport Art Museum has gathered these treasures, and we are appreciative to all Maud's relatives.

Scholar Miki Pfeffer of New Orleans, who is publishing a book on Julia Ward Howe's experiences at the New Orleans Cotton Centennial in 1885, has been unfailingly supportive and generous in sharing information. John Waters, who recently uncovered significant documentation on Maud and Jack's time in Chicago in his research on their friend, William Pretyman, was very thoughtful in sharing his findings. Federico Santi and John Gacher of The Drawing Room, in Newport, have shared their knowledge of Maud and John Elliott. I am indebted to Newporter Trudy Keen, who has efficiently combed through newspapers to find little gems of articles about Maud's activities. Mary Taft, also of Newport, has graciously invited me into her home, Lilliput, on Rhode Island Avenue, where Maud spent the last thirty years of her life.

Two women who have also followed their own passions into print and who have been great boosters of my work are my mother, Jacqueline Conant Whipple, and my daughter, Lucinda Conant Grinnell. There are two people who have dropped everything when I needed their help. Tara Ecenarro, my vastly knowledgeable curatorial associate at the Newport Art Museum, helped me pull things together with remarkable efficiency, thank goodness. And my significant other, David Sharp, has supported me in untold ways, for which I am forever grateful. We are all glad that Maud's story can finally be told.

*Carrying
the
Torch*

ONE

Maud with her venturous climbings and tumbles and childish escapes,
Maud the delight of the village, the ringing joy of the Hall,
Maud with her sweet purse-mouth when my father dangled the grapes,
Maud the beloved of my mother, the moon-faced darling of all,—
ALFRED, LORD TENNYSON, 1855

WHEN MAUD HOWE WAS BORN IN NOVEMBER 1854, HER FATHER suggested the Greek name of Thyrza for the beautiful baby girl—but according to older sister Florence Howe Hall, the "good Anglo Saxon name of Maud" prevailed instead.[1] Laura Elizabeth Richards, who was nine at her sister's birth, wrote that Maud's newborn personality did not immediately evoke more than the nickname "Polly"; it wasn't until Alfred, Lord Tennyson's poem *Maud* appeared in February 1855 that her name was clinched. In her autobiography *Three Generations,* Maud Howe Elliott fondly reminisces about her early childhood and the stories she had heard about her birth. In fact, Maud was born at a tumultuous time in her parents' marriage. Samuel Gridley Howe and Julia Ward Howe, wed since 1843 and the parents already of three daughters and one son, had considered divorce more than once. Howe, an enigmatic, moody, and domineering personality, was adamantly opposed to his wife's equally determined intention to write and publish poetry and to read it in public.

Nevertheless, Julia's collection of poems, *Passion Flowers,* was published anonymously in Boston by Ticknor and Fields in 1853. Her mentors in this endeavor included family friend Henry Wadsworth Longfellow, and yet Julia had kept her husband completely uninformed. The public immediately recognized the author and the startlingly autobiographical subject matter, which often seemed to cast aspersions on traditional roles of marriage and motherhood and to celebrate woman's independence. Samuel Gridley Howe (called "Chev" by intimates—short for "Chevalier") was enraged. In a letter of February 1854 to her sister, Annie Mailliard, in Bordertown, New Jersey, Julia wrote how distraught he was: "The Book, you know, was a blow to him, and some foolish and impertinent people have hinted to him that the Miller was meant for himself—this has made him almost crazy.... He has been in a very dangerous state, I think, very near insanity."[2]

It seems that Maud was the cost of reconciliation. Julia had written again to her sister Annie that she was postponing her visit. "[Chev] was in such a state of mind that it would have been unsafe to leave him. I have been able to calm and sooth him, somewhat, and he now promises that I shall leave on the first of March for any length of time agreeable to you."[3] The resulting pregnancy was documented in a letter to her sister Louisa Crawford, begun in July 1954 and completed five days before Maud's birth on November 9.

> I see from your letter that you have learned a fact of which I have not written to you, that of my approaching confinement. You ask whether I am glad or sorry. I can scarcely trust myself to speak of it, so bitter and horrible a distress has it been to me. You recommend ether—my dear Wevie, my mental suffering during these nine months nearly past has been so great; that I cannot be afraid of any bodily torture, however great. Neither does the future show me a single gleam of light. I shall not drag this weary weight about with me, it is true, but I cannot feel that my heart will be any lighter. I dread to see the face of my child, for I know I cannot love it.[4]

Ironically, Maud became her mother's adored child and cherished companion.

For his part, Dr. Howe believed that bearing children and caring for them was the duty of a married woman, and furthermore, that the long months of pregnancy and pain of childbirth were nature's way of preparing a woman to be a loving mother. Upon Maud's birth in the "Doctor's

Wing" at the Perkins Institution for the Blind, in South Boston, he wrote to his friend, educator Horace Mann, "We have in fact another daughter; that makes five new banyan branches, binding the old trunk down to earth. The delivery was such as to rejoice the hearts of strong-minded women and physiologists. Bravely every day up to the last, and twice a day, did the mother exercise in the open air." Although he was not physically present during the delivery, nor for much of his children's early childhood, as a physician he seldom hesitated to enforce his opinions of healthful practices.

The arrival of baby Maud coincided with the beginning of Julia Ward Howe's literary reputation, and she published several more works during the 1850s. Although her husband remained controlling and complaining, Julia had a newfound self-confidence, and a simultaneous resignation to her role as wife of a celebrated and egotistical man. In her letters to her sisters, Julia opened up about her marriage, childbearing, and resulting depressions. When her daughters were compiling their mother's letters for her biography, Maud wrote in her own diary, "Beyond belief interesting. She seems to be like an opal flashing fire always, but sometimes violet wrath, red despairs, rosy hope & blue hope and tender everlasting green of constancy to her own flesh and blood. They explain her more than anything. They explain myself nearly as much. Laura says that the blackest time of all, was before my birth. These tremendous depressions, these supreme elations, are all here, stamped in my poor little being, deep, deep! The temperament of genius is not a comfortable thing to possess without the genius that is its only excuse for being."[5]

Despite her depressions, which could have been hormonal swings or mood disorders, the Howe children remembered their mother with delight. She was fun. She laughed a lot. She tended to their wants and needs with unflagging good humor. She composed lullabies for them. She gave them nicknames: Dudekins, Fo-Fo, Tommy, Wolly, Polly, Duchess, and more. Certainly, Laura, who became famous for her children's nonsense rhymes, did not inherit this knack for silliness from her father—although he was a practical joker in his youth. Julia Romana, the oldest Howe child, showed her early literary aspirations, writing plays performed by their parents and editing *The Listener*, a weekly periodical about their school and family activities. At the age of ten, Julia Romana wrote about the birth of Maud: "A very curious little animal lies on the editor's table this week."[6]

And Maud certainly had gentle memories of her mother. In her autobiography she recalls eating wild cherries at the family's summer home in Lawton's Valley, Rhode Island, and being admonished by her mother, "If you eat those cherries again, I shall slap your hands with this stick." The next day Maud approached her mother with berries in her mouth, carrying a stick. Instead Julia kissed and hugged her. She remained a steadfast comfort to Maud and her siblings, soothing and reassuring, despite spending her free time publishing poetry, editing abolitionist newspapers, or learning Hebrew, all of which she did during Maud's early childhood.

The Perkins Institution was home to the blind, the deaf, and the "feeble-minded," but the characteristic most remembered by Maud about her birthplace was the "triumph of architectural splendor" of the staircase with its polished mahogany rail, spiraling downwards five floors to white marble floors below. Both its magnificence and its danger appealed to the little girl. Her brother, Henry Marion Howe, called "Harry," got in trouble for sliding down the banister. The building, formerly the Mount Washington Hotel, located in South Boston, was the family's intermittent home for several years. Originally named the Mount Washington House, a description of the day informs us that the structure was "sufficiently elevated to command a view of the harbor of Boston and its numerous islands and also of the city, with its capitol towering above every other edifice; and likewise of the adjacent county with its mansions, steeples and villages reflecting back the morning sun and showing in all directions the most abundant proofs of the generosity which has attended them since the departure of the British forces."[7]

Samuel Gridley Howe was fifty-three when Maud was born, already the father of four, and thoroughly absorbed in his humanitarian and abolitionist work. She wrote that her first distinct memory of her father was of waking one Christmas morning to find him holding her new baby brother, Sam, who wasn't born until she was five. She also recalled feeling abandoned by her mother at this new birth.[8] Growing up surrounded by blind children was not the traditional proper Bostonian upbringing. It must have affected the little Maud profoundly; her sister Laura wrote that

Maud was given a beautiful doll with glass eyes, which she proceeded to poke out. She covered the empty sockets with a ribbon, in imitation of the blind little girls she had been taken to speak with the previous day. Laura Bridgman, the blind, deaf, and mute girl who came to the Perkins Institution in 1837 when she was seven, was taught to read and write by Dr. Howe and became an international media sensation. Maud often attended the weekly "exhibition days" at the Institution, when prospective funders came to observe the blind youth demonstrate their proficiency at reading Braille—printed by Dr. Howe's press—singing and playing musical instruments, all accompanied by a blind organist.[9]

In his prime Samuel Gridley Howe was a magnetic presence and a tall, handsome man with dark hair and flashing blue eyes. He had first impressed Julia Ward while riding on a black steed. Howe seemingly identified with his horses, which were always fast, black animals named Breeze or Blast[10] who often bolted, leaving others stopped in their tracks. Howe's friends as well as his horses were mighty; they were "statesmen, soldiers, philanthropists, men of action whose time was too precious for long visits, but who came and went with a certain tense purpose."[11] His closest friend, Charles Sumner, was a United States senator and fervent abolitionist whom all the Howe children remembered with trepidation. He strongly disapproved of Julia's career. Unitarian minister Theodore Parker was inspirational to both Chev and Julia, and indeed wanted to take baby Maud home to his childless wife, as the Howes already had three daughters. Horace Mann, who, like Parker, died in 1859, was a partner in educational reform in Massachusetts with Chev. Thomas Wentworth Higginson, a strong abolitionist and supporter of women's rights, moved from a close relationship with Chev to being a supporter of Julia's beliefs.

Impressed as they were, both friends and family were also witness to Howe's black moods and fierce temper. One of Julia and Chev's oldest friends, Henry Wadsworth Longfellow, wrote in his diary in 1845 that Howe seemingly had lost his enjoyment in people and felt that his life was slipping away.[12] Chev frequently suffered from headaches, chills, and fevers during which he lay in agony in a darkened room, ministered to by his family who crept around waiting for their vibrant father to once again spring into action. Daughter Laura wrote, "I do not remember his ever being irritable with us children; yet he was not a patient man. He did not suffer fools gladly; he rent them in pieces and went on over their trampled bodies."[13]

All the children recalled their father's restless nature. Both in his professional and private life, "He wanted little rest; four or five hours' sleep was enough for him; more than that was 'wanton murder of time.' He cared nothing for recreation in the ordinary sense of the word; but change was the breath of life to him."[14] Often that change was unsettling for his wife and family. When his two oldest daughters came of churchgoing age, he insisted that Theodore Parker's services were not "reverent" enough for their religious education. Julia was very distraught with this decision, but soon attached herself to another great Unitarian minister, James Freeman Clarke. Chev's need for change also meant that the family moved around constantly. The Howe family folded their tents like Arabs, wrote Flossie, who also recalled that Laura's beau Henry Richards would come calling and find that the family had moved.[15]

In 1845 Chev had purchased a colonial farmhouse on six acres of land adjacent to the Institute in South Boston; this property sloped gently down to the harbor. There he constructed additions to the house that included a huge new wing and conservatory, a greenhouse and a bowling alley. This home was christened Green Peace, by Julia, and Maud recalled the interior: "a cabinet from the Palace of the Popes at Avignon, purchased by our parents on their wedding journey, together with the Roman cabinet and the oak and ebony *prie-dieu*, and brought home from Europe to set up housekeeping in South Boston; this is the year 1844, before the craze for old Italian furniture had struck our country."[16] Outside was a sumptuous garden of fruit trees and flowering plants. Unlike her memories of events, Maud's flair for capturing details of remembered décor was flawless.

The other family home recalled lovingly by all family members was "the Valley," or Lawton's Valley, in Portsmouth, Rhode Island. In 1852 the Howe family had spent the month of August in Newport, at a boardinghouse known then as Hazard's House, overlooking Easton's Beach. There they gathered with friends: Charles Sumner, George William Curtis, as well as Henry Wadsworth Longfellow—"Longo"—and his wife, Fanny, their children, and her brother Thomas Gold Appleton. In his jaunts between South Boston and Newport, Chev discovered and purchased another rundown farmhouse in a secluded, wooded area twelve miles from Newport. According to his wife's memoirs, the purchase was made "without much deliberation," at the behest of Alfred Smith, "a well known real estate agent, who managed to entrap strangers in his gig, and drove about with them, often succeeding in making them purchases of some bit of property in the sale of which he had a personal interest."[17] Not surprisingly, Alfred Smith was the real estate magnate who developed Bellevue Avenue in Newport.

Julia wrote, "We found it a wilderness of brambles with a brook which ran much out of its proper course."[18] Dr. Howe proceeded to transform the wilderness of brambles into an idyllic summer retreat; the brambles gave way to green grass, the brook was confined by flat stones. He added on to the main house and converted a small gristmill into a guest/playhouse, overlooking a wooded gorge replete with waterfalls cascading onto sun-dappled rocks, all meandering down to Narragansett Bay. For the children it was magical, as Maud wrote:

> The great rock formed the grand staircase to the slate parlor at the tip top of the hill. It had a carpet of fine gray moss patterned with orange lichen, and side wall of juniper trees whose gray-blue berries served to fill our dolls' dessert plates. The cups and saucers were made of oak leaves pieced together cunningly with bits of stalk. A little lower to the right was the back stairway and the kitchen, with the most perfect oven hollowed from the side of the rock that the heart of child could desire. Here we bake the juniper berries, served in fairy feasts.[19]

Julia Ward Howe had been used to suffering in silence as the family was "plucked up from a beloved house and set down somewhere else, for weeks or months as the case might be."[20] Chev rented out Green Peace as the Howes' activities centered more on Boston proper, and from 1847–1850 home was 74 Mount Vernon Street on Beacon Hill in Boston. During the 1850s the family seemingly alternated between Green Peace, the Perkins Institution and Lawton's Valley. A favorite home recalled by all was 13 Chestnut Street, also on Beacon Hill, a rented house designed by Charles Bulfinch in which they lived during the early 1860s. Whatever the reason for Chev's compulsion to move so often, he seemingly had little regard for Julia's and the children's needs to have a home where they could put down roots. Julia came to love Lawton's Valley, where she was able to do most of her writing, and where the children found some stability. Maud spent her first fourteen summers there.

Maud's memories of her earliest years were so hazy that in her autobiography she referred to that period as "The Twilight of the Gods." Her illustrious parents came and went, her surroundings constantly changed; her older siblings were off to school. The shadowy figure of John Brown later haunted her memory, along with such legendary early family acquaintances as Florence Nightingale and the Marquis de Lafayette. Far more intelligible characters in Maud's recollections were "the Owls," a name invented by the Howe children to describe their mother's friends: Henry James, Senior, a fearsome bearded man with piercing eyes; the Unitarian clergyman William Rounseville Alger, said to have never used a word of less than five syllables; Edwin Whipple, an essayist and lecturer who actually resembled an owl; and Elizabeth Peabody, the great educator and reformer, whose experimental kindergarten Maud attended. Peabody's brother-in-law, Nathaniel Hawthorne, also had an educational influence on the young Maud; it was in his *Tanglewood Tales* that she was first introduced to Greek mythology, an interest that would inform her life's work. One person who remembered *her* was writer Nathan Dole. "I recall some function at your mother's. But as the sun puts out all the stars, the memory of you utterly dims every other detail. I can see you as distinctly as if you were before me now, not another soul among all the guests can I remember. You were an extremely—oh dear me—words are so banal to use in characterizing the loveliness of a happy girl. I wish I could say you were 'wicked looking.' That would be more pepsome, but no, it is a vision of radiant girlhood."[21]

Maud was six years old when Fort Sumter was fired upon in April 1861. Her "Memories of the Civil War, 1861–1864" was published in 1943 during the Second World War as a brochure to benefit the Newport Chapter of the Red Cross. She begins her "memories" by recalling visits with her father, a founder of the U.S. Sanitary Commission, to the newly established military hospital in Portsmouth Grove, Rhode Island, a rehabilitation facility for injured soldiers, efficiently run by Katharine Wormeley of Newport. The horrors of war were seemingly lost on a sheltered eight-year-old who recalled running away with Eddie Bowker from the nearby Redwood estate to the grounds of the Portsmouth Grove hospital and being promptly sent home. At Lawton's Valley Maud remembered hosting her friend Edith Andrew's father, who happened to be Massachusetts Governor John Albion Andrew, a force for the North in the Civil War and friend of Abraham Lincoln. Andrew supported the Emancipation Proclamation, as did the Howes, and advocated for blacks in the military; he was instrumental in forming the 54th Massachusetts Regiment.

Although Samuel Gridley Howe was a monumentally important figure in the abolition movement, as well as in the formation of the U.S. Sanitary Commission and work with the Freedmen after the War, it was an act of his wife that is the family's most celebrated accomplishment a century and a half later. As legend tells it, Julia Ward Howe accompanied Chev, Governor Andrew, and Reverend Clarke to Washington, D.C., in November 1861. Before dawn a sleepless Julia rose to pen the words to the tune *John Brown's Body*, now celebrated as *The Battle Hymn of the Republic*. That deed apparently failed to impress Maud at the time, as she couldn't remember hearing about it until years later.[22] She did recall the anguish on her father's face upon learning of the murder of President Lincoln.

A personal tragedy in the Howe family likely had a more profound effect upon Maud than the Civil War. In May of 1863, her little brother, Samuel Gridley Howe, Jr., died of diphtheria at the age of three years. The family was devastated. As Laura wrote, "My father never recovered fully from this blow; my mother, many years younger, and of more resilient temperament, though stricken equally low, was able to rise sooner."[23] Perhaps also Julia was able to express her grief—in her diary, her letters—unlike Chev who internalized it. Laura and Maud remembered little Sam laid out on a marble table, surrounded by flowers, covered with their mother's crepe shawl. For Maud, eight at the time, Sam's death further isolated her from her older siblings, who played in pairs: Julia and Flossy, Harry and Laura. She wrote, "I was now left an odd number. The elder children seemed much older ... they were all precocious; I was the reverse."[24]

The result was that Maud was left more to the company of adults and family friends, who in her mother's case, embraced the culture offered in Boston. Julia Ward Howe ensured that her children would not be denied the opportunity to hear live performances of music, to attend ballet and theater, as she was. Her mother had died shortly after giving birth to her eighth child when Julia was five, leaving her distraught father to retreat into a harsh Calvinistic religion that forbade his children any social life outside of the home. Maud was captivated by the imaginative and dramatic world of the theater. She grew up wanting to be an actress. She loved pageantry and music. She often danced the night away, according to her mother's memoirs.

Maud's love of pageantry can be traced back to the Fourth of July celebrations on the Boston Common, attended by her family before they departed for Lawton's Valley. The parade featured Antiques and Horribles, torpedoes and firecrackers, the band playing a lively Yankee Doodle; the ascending giant balloon with its straw basket underneath, the parade of the Ancient and Honorable Artillery Company and concluding with the glorious fireworks display over the Common. Samuel Gridley Howe considered this festive show of patriotism to be an important event for his children; he was not born until after the War for Independence, but he was a great believer in fighting for individual freedoms.

Another "festival of patriotism" that Maud remembered well was the National Sailors' Fair held at the Boston Theater in 1864. Similar to the U.S. Sanitary Fairs held as fundraisers during the Civil War, the Sailors' Fair raised money for a home for seamen disabled in the Civil War. For ten days the Theater was transformed into "a wonderful hive of varicolored bees, all 'workers,' all humming and hurrying."[25] The Howes' contribution to the Fair effort was *The Boatswain's Whistle,* the event's daily newspaper, edited by Julia Ward Howe. The logo of the boatswain was designed by artist William Morris Hunt.[26] The newspaper included a message from President Lincoln and poetry and prose by the leading liberal thinkers of the day. It was Maud's job to sell copies of *The Boatswain's Whistle.*

The Boston Theater, with its curtain depicting Italy's Lake of Lugano, imparted to Maud an early taste of Italian scenery. Her father's friend Orlando Tomkins owned the theater, and his brother, Joseph Howe, owned stock in it and allowed Julia and her children to use his seats for matinees. Edwin Booth was the marquee idol of the day, a handsome, talented actor whose Hamlet became legendary; all the Howe girls were in love with him. Maud first saw him in *The Iron Chest* at the Boston

Theater in 1857. When Booth attended a Howe gathering on Chestnut Street in 1862, Beacon Street society turned out to see him; the inherently shy actor, however, retreated to the corner of the room with eight-year-old Maud to make shadow puppets on the wall with a rabbit made from his handkerchief.[27] Although Maud was the baby in the family, she often stole the show.

"True servants of Apollo" is how Maud described the builders of the Boston Music Hall in 1852. Designed by family friend George Snell, later to add an addition to Newport's Redwood Library, the Music Hall was a favorite destination of the young Maud and her considerably older companion, John Sullivan Dwight, director of the Harvard Musical Association and founder and editor of *Dwight's Journal of Music*. A Howe family intimate, Dwight had been a Unitarian minister, part of the Brook Farm commune and the Concord circle of literati that included Ralph Waldo Emerson and Oliver Wendell Holmes. Most important to Maud and her sister, Laura, Dwight taught them to love music. Like the offerings in the Boston Music Hall that Dwight had a hand in building, classical music was his choice, and he and Maud attended concerts as well as rehearsals for all the major works of Bach, Mozart, and Beethoven.[28] As much as the Music Hall itself, Maud remembered its "Great Organ," commissioned by the committee led by Dr. Jabez Baxer Upham in 1857, built by E. F. Walcker and Company in Germany, and transported to Boston in 1863. The design firm of Herter Brothers in New York finished the case. Its magnificent installation was not lost on Maud: "For months we watched the slow upbuilding of the organ, seen the golden pipes unpacked, tested, and laid in a row on stage. Now everything was in place, the mouths of the painted singing women seemed ready to breathe out music. A pair of mighty colossi bore the weight of the massive front on their bowed head[s] and shoulders."[29] Maud accompanied her mother to the dedication for the great organ, where the actress Charlotte Cushman read a poem by Annie Fields, wife of the publisher James Fields.

At that dedication Julia Ward Howe whispered to her daughter, "Crawford's statue seems to be listening to the music."[30] She was referring to the bronze statue of Beethoven, sculpted by Maud's uncle Thomas G. Crawford, the late husband of Julia's sister, Louisa. Crawford had been an American neo-classical sculptor who resided in Rome. He was originally from New York, where coincidentally in his apprentice days for marble craftsmen John Frazee and B. E. Launitz, he had carved the marble fireplace mantels in the home of the young Julia Ward Howe. While drawing from plaster casts at the National Academy of Design in New York City in the 1830s, Crawford had discovered the classical sculpture of Italy. In Rome he studied under the great Danish sculptor Bertel Thorvaldsen, observed the sculptures in the Vatican, and dissected cadavers at the mortuary, before commencing a successful career making copies of antique sculptures and portrait busts.

The sculpture that made Crawford's reputation was *Orpheus and Cerberus,* a marble recreation from Greek mythology of the poet who enters Hades in search of his lover Eurydice, and in the process lulling to sleep the three-headed dog Cerberus. In 1839 Charles Sumner saw the plaster model in Rome and proceeded to raise funds for a marble version to be installed in the Boston Athenaeum. *Orpheus and Cerberus* arrived in Boston in 1843 and in 1844 was the center of the first solo exhibition by a sculptor in the United States. Sumner, being Samuel Gridley Howe's closest friend, surely invited the newly married Howes to this event. In 1856, a year before his premature death from a cancerous tumor, Crawford's six-foot-tall Beethoven was installed in the Boston Music Hall. Later, when Maud first visited Italy in 1877, she studied the plaster casts of her late uncle's work.

Art was important to the Howe family; there were always pictures on the walls in their residences. Maud acquired a love of art at an early age, and it was stimulated by her surroundings. While Julia Ward Howe's intellectual prowess has been the subject of much study, little mention has been made of her knowledge of art, acquired through the art patronage of her father. Samuel Ward was a prominent figure in the New York world of banking; as a partner in the firm of Prime, Ward and King, he helped secure a loan of five million dollars from the Bank of England to enable American banks to resume specie payments, and established the Bank of Commerce, of which he became president. In 1835 Ward built a large brick home for his family at Bond Street and Broadway, known as The Corner, and added a wing that housed the first private picture gallery in New York. It was his "special pride. The children might not mingle in frivolous gayety abroad, but they should have all that love, taste and money could give them at home; he filled his art gallery with the best pictures he could find. A friend (Mr. Prescott Hall, lawyer and a summer resident of Newport), making a timely journey through Spain bought for him many valuable pictures, among them a Snyder, a Nicholas Poussin, a reputed Velasquez, and Rembrandt. It was for [Julia's father] that Thomas Cole painted the four pictures representing "the Voyage of Life."[31]

Cole's *The Voyage of Life* indeed was commissioned for Ward in 1839. Cole wrote, "I have received a noble commission from Mr. Samuel Ward, to paint a series of pictures, the plan of which I conceived several years since, entitled *The Voyage of Life*. I sincerely hope that I shall be able to execute the work in a manner worthy of Mr. Ward's liberality, and honorable to myself. The subject is an allegorical one, but perfectly intelligible, and, I think, capable of making a strong moral and religious impression."[32] Although the many biographies of Ward's famous daughter emphasize his strict demeanor and Puritanical distrust of frivolity and the performing arts, he was actually a big supporter of visual arts and education. Among his accomplishments he helped to found the University of the City of New York, secured proper accommodations for the collections of the New York Historical Society, helped to found the Stuyvesant Institute, and was active in improving conditions for New York City's poor.

Ward was prescient in his appreciation of the young Thomas Cole, who was to become an iconic figure of the Hudson River School. Ward seemed to feel a kinship with Cole's desire to "unite artistic excellence with subjects of high moral and religious character." Unfortunately *The Voyage of Life* was not yet completed at the time of Ward's death in November 1839. Ward's heirs (presumably Julia's older brothers Sam, Richard, Marion, John, and Henry) were initially agreeable to the completion of the series and Cole's desire to exhibit it publicly (as Ward had been), until the intervention of the estate's executor, Thomas S. Huggins, who demanded half the proceeds from such an event. Cole was angry and reportedly concerned that the paintings, upon their completion in the fall of 1840, were "lying around on the floor, uncared for." Cole proceeded to paint a second series of *The Voyage of Life* in 1840–41. The first version was sold to the American Art Union in 1848, from where it devolved into several private collections before becoming part of the Munson-Williams-Proctor Institute in Utica, New York, in 1955.[33]

Although both her grandfather and *The Voyage of Life* were long gone when Maud visited the Bond Street residence on a trip with her mother in the 1860s, she marveled at the windowless gallery, lit from above. From her mother she heard stories about artists who frequented the premises in the 1820s and 1830s. Robert Weir, the portrait painter and father of American impressionist Julius Alden Weir, was a friend of Ward and had painted his portrait; Weir became most famous, however, for illustrating a moment in Clement Moore's "The Night Before Christmas." Miniatures survive of the Ward children, painted by the early Newport painter Annie Hall.

Samuel Gridley Howe also collected art, notably a set of engravings of Greek temples, remembered by both Laura and Maud. They hung in his study: The Parthenon, the Temple of Victory, the Erectheum, the Acropolis. So it was for a young girl surrounded by great thinkers, radical activists, and cultural mavericks, that the confluence of Greek and Roman culture, Renaissance ideals, and noble artistic thoughts molded her mind. As she wrote, "A copy of the Greek Clytie stood on the stairs; I loved her so much that on going up to bed, after having kissed all the family goodnight, I would pause and, if nobody were looking, reach up and kiss the cold lips of the marble woman."[34]

TWO

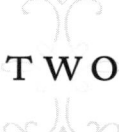

> Thirteen years ago my dearest Maud was born in this very room . . .
> She was a beautiful child, but not a very happy one. I regard her with anxiety.
> Her passions being strong, her intellect one that resists training, I mean of the
> ordinary kind. God bless her and make her good and happy when I am gone.
>
> JULIA WARD HOWE

MAUD HOWE DID NOT SUFFER THE PERILS OF ADOLESCENCE gracefully. As she entered her thirteenth year, she showed a characteristic petulance as she wrote to Laura:

> A Happy New Year. I is [*sic*] so lonely without anybody. Flossie [*sic*] is at David's and Julia is at the blind all the time, our papa is so lonely, but there is no good in telling you that while you are talking with delightful Mr. Church and forgetting entirely the folks at home . . . Mama had about 50 calls on New Year's Day, stupid John K . . .[1]

She continued in this vein, writing to her mother in February 1867:

> Dear Mama, I write to you because I am so lonely. Flossie and Mr. D have gone to the theatre and papa gave the other two tickets to the servants. I don't know where Julia has gone. I wish you would come back for I am perfectly miserable. Nobody seems to care anything about me. My head and my eyes ache so I must stop writing. Love to Laura. I am your very unhappy daughter.[2]

Things did not improve when her parents and two siblings embarked on a seven-month European tour in March 1867. Samuel Gridley Howe again felt the call of Greece, where he wished to come to the aid of Cretan citizens who were fighting the Turkish insurrection, and he convinced his wife to go along. Laura, age seventeen, and Julia, twenty, accompanied their parents on this European sojourn, which also included visits to England, France, Italy, Germany, Switzerland, and Belgium. Nineteen-year-old Flossy remained at home to attend to her new fiancé David Prescott Hall; Harry to pursue his sophomore year at Harvard; and Maud in the company of Flossy and the redoubtable Miss Paddock, the housekeeper. Flossy's recollections of her charge were not kind: "Maud was in her thirteenth year—a handsome child of generous and noble impulses, but of an impetuous disposition that made her at times difficult to deal with. 'Old Splendid' was the name given her by a dressmaker to whom we were all attached. 'The stormy petrel' was another nickname."[3] In her autobiography Maud recalled how she "bitterly resented being left behind," and upon the family's return in the fall, she was again desolate that her older sisters all received silk dresses made in Paris; she was deemed to be at that awkward stage where she might quickly outgrow a dress! Soon consoled with photographs of Greece and Italy and artifacts from some exotic locales, Maud devoured the stories of the family's travels, in particular their visit to the Paris Exposition of 1867.

Julia Ward Howe published her reminiscences of the trip in a book called *From the Oak to the Olive; A Plain Record of a Pleasant Journey*. The book clearly shows Howe's artistic sophistication; her commentary verged on art criticism, although she disparaged art critics of the time; they being "wordy and ignorant, praising from caprice rather than from conscience."[4] Instead, Howe valued an artwork's originality, its technical finesse—she astutely disapproved of over-restoration—its expressive qualities. For the curious reader she defined chiaroscuro, deplored the plundering of antiquities, and discussed John Ruskin's *The Stones of Venice*, to further understand the architectural mysteries of that city. Mother and daughters toured the Louvre, the Vatican, the Sistine Chapel, the Farnesina Palace, the Catacombs, the Naples Museum, Pompeii, the Palazzo Pitti, the Uffizi, Venice's Academia delle Belle Arte and Cathedral of San Marco, the Parthenon, Munich's Pinakothek and Glyptothek, the

Museum at Zurich, and finally the wonders of Rubens at the Cathedral of Antwerp.

Howe's intention on this trip, aided by *Murray's Handbook*, was to somehow transfer her own awe and respect for the masterpieces of Western art, particularly in Italy, to her daughters, referred to as "the neophytes." However, in her characteristically philosophical prose, Howe acknowledged that following the recent tragedies inherent in the Civil War and its aftermath, art history paled in comparison. "And now I must confess that, after so many intense and vivid pages of life, this visit to Rome, once a theme of fervent and solemn desire, becomes a mere page of embellishment in a serious and instructive volume."[5] Howe observed how the absolute power of the Catholic Church was destroying Rome, resulting in a city where poverty and a lack of education were almost insurmountable, democracy did not exist and the upper classes lived much too extravagantly. She noted that her home on Boylston Place would easily fit into the largest room of the Palazzo Odescalchi, the quarters of her sister, Louisa, now remarried to expatriate painter Luther Terry. As for Laura, her reminiscences of the trip included relatives, friends, and festivities, but no paintings! It remained for Maud to unequivocally embrace the visual culture of Europe.

Julia Ward Howe was able to connect better with the American artists who worked in Rome, although she really could not understand why they would abandon their own country of opportunity. She visited the foundry where the bronze sculptures of her late brother-in-law, Crawford, were cast, as well as the work of American sculptors Emma Stebbins, Harriet Hosmer, Randolph Rogers, and Joseph Mozier. She went to all their studios in Rome; Hosmer's work left Howe unmoved—"vapid and pretentious," "statues like marble silences."[6] She was also critical of Rogers and Mozier: "Both have considerable skill, neither has genius." Even her friend, the illustrious sculptor and leader of the American art colony in Rome, William Wetmore Story, did not escape her discerning eye; after visiting his studio Howe found him "greatly improved, but not yet a great original artist. His *Medea* frowns from without, not from within."[7]

Howe was most appreciative of the painting of her friend William Morris Hunt of Boston and Newport, who at the time of her visit was in Europe. Hunt's work was included in the Universal Exposition in

Paris. She observed that his paintings there were not placed to advantage, but on a later visit to his studio, she admired "much beautiful work. His genius very versatile. Two landscapes from Normandy very individual and charming. Portrait of C. F. Adams. Study of an Italian girl—even a scarlet cactus, beautifully painted."[8] Hunt was the earliest artist remembered by Maud. The "storm of long gray beard, aristocratic hawk-like nose and piercing eyes" made a mighty impression on the young girl when she and her mother visited the family at their farm in Readville, Massachusetts (now Milton) during the Civil War.[9] Hunt had married Louisa Dumaresq Perkins, a Boston Brahmin whose grandfather was Thomas Handasyd Perkins, the early benefactor of the Perkins Institution for the Blind. Louisa was an old friend of Julia's. Hunt's signed lithographs of *The Bugler, The Violet Seller,* and *The Woman at the Fountain* hung in the family's Green Peace home. The impact of Hunt's influence as a teacher and an early appreciator of the French Barbizon School left lasting impressions on Maud.

Undoubtedly Julia Ward Howe's early recognition and appreciation of American artists were catalysts for Maud Howe Elliott's lifetime of advocacy for this group. In the early 1860s Julia had often taken Maud to call upon her friends at the Studio Building, on Tremont Street in Boston, which housed artists' studios open to the public on Saturday mornings. Its roster included Hunt, architect George Snell, painter Benjamin Curtis Porter and art dealer Seth Vose, whose business had begun in Providence. Howe likely also passed on to Maud her idea that American artists needed to study the "high art" of Europe in order to become better artists, and in fact was prescient in her idea of a public art museum, the first of which would open as the Metropolitan Museum of Art in 1870.[10]

While Maud's interest in the arts was not to flower for a few more years, Julia Ward Howe's interest in the issue of woman suffrage took root soon after her European trip. Chev sold Lawton's Valley around 1867, and the Howe family spent the summer of 1868 in the "Stevens cottage near Newport,"[11] where Julia's friend the Reverend Charles Brooks invited her to read some of her essays in the Unitarian Church parlor on Sunday afternoons. The reactions of the audiences varied, with one woman declaring "This is the way I want to hear women speak"; another, reportedly the socialite Mrs. Paran Stevens, left indignantly when Julia, offering her thoughts on idle rich women, said, "If God works, Madam, you can afford to work also." Mrs. Stevens later invited Julia to call and was very conciliatory.[12] Julia's newfound power to stir audiences resulted in an ever-widening circle of invitations to speak on philosophical, political, and social matters; in 1868 she presided at the first meeting of the New England Woman's Club, an organization devoted to women's activism, of which she served as president almost continually from 1870 until her death in 1910. The culmination of Julia's new awakening was the formation of the New England Woman Suffrage Association, also in 1868, with Julia elected as president.

Samuel Gridley Howe supported woman's suffrage, but he did not support his wife speaking in public. His early protests reverberate throughout Julia's journals and his own letters. He wrote to daughter Laura in 1869, "Everything is going on as usual here. Flossy continues to improve. Maud is overflowing with health and spirits and is very darling and good . . . Mama goes out a great deal, but working too a great deal at home. Alas! Dear Wollie, she will break herself down in the service of the Bohemian who makes a cat's paw of her genius; you must try when you come home to make her give up the papers — or she will give up the ghost."[13] The daughters also resented their mother's absence, with Julia noting in her journal the crying or arguments that often accompanied her leaving. In 1870 Julia went to Vermont on a suffrage campaign, leaving Chev to note: "We are like sheep without a shepherdess."[14]

Conversely, Julia often showed irritation at almost everyone in her journal from this time. "Very angry with Chev for changing the heating apparatus without consulting or even informing me. A most unnecessary and inconvenient measure, a feature of his mania for such changes."[15] Chev, now approaching seventy, summoned up enough energy to once again uproot the family; in 1868 he sold the house at 19 Boylston Place and bought another at 32 Mount Vernon Street, the last abode where the family was to live all together. He also purchased a new summer home in Portsmouth, Rhode Island, called Oak Glen, which for some of the family never quite measured up to the magical Lawton's Valley. In addition to her complaints about her husband, Julia worried about daughter Julia Romana's strange behavior, which manifested itself in social ineptitude and depression. She was upset that Flossy's future in-laws, the Halls, were not happy about the impending marriage, apparently hoping for a more affluent daughter-in-law to boost the family's coffers.[16] And Julia was very concerned about Maud's constant physical ailments, her stubborn resistance to conformity, and her flighty behavior.

"Maud in pursuit of pleasure under difficulties," was how Chev described her behavior in a letter to Laura, the one daughter who was a comfort to both parents.[17] As a reaction to the discord at home, in about 1869 Maud discovered the world of society and escaped as often as she could to visit friends, a pattern that continued well into the 1880s. Maud, like her mother, loved social gatherings, but while Julia's were usually socially constructive, Maud's were just plain frivolous, in the opinion of her father. She received "sundry invitations" and attended party after party, staying out late and pouting when things did not go her way. At one party Maud was giving, the economizing sister, Flossy, told her that she could not have ice cream, it was too expensive; Chev came to the rescue by making homemade ice. He did not approve, however, of this trifling existence, expressing his misgivings often: "Maud pursues her school course, though I am sorry to say, she is getting prematurely fond of outside excitement."[18]

In 1871 Maud's desire for outside excitement was exacerbated by the exodus of her three sisters and brother from the household. On December 30, 1870, at home in a quiet ceremony Julia Romana married Michael Anagnos, who had returned with the family from their trip to Greece to become the doctor's secretary and later the director of the Perkins Institution. Julia Romana, her father's favorite, the little girl so delighted at the birth of baby Maud, who read to her all of the Waverly novels, was essentially now a stranger to her sister. As Maud wrote, "She was the intimate of my childhood, but I remember a curious withdrawal the moment my feet touched the threshold of girlhood.... When I braided my tawny mane and 'put up' my hair like a big girl, I lost something that had been an intrinsic part of our relationship."[19] The departure of Laura was a bigger blow, although she and her husband Henry Richards, an architect who was a Harvard classmate of brother Harry, were moving next door to Green Peace after an extended European tour. Laura and Henry married at the Church of the Disciples on June 14, 1871. Flossy and her intended, David Prescott Hall, a New York lawyer whom she had known since they were children playing at Lawton's Valley and Vaucluse, were married at 32 Mount Vernon Street in November 1871. Brother Harry graduated from Harvard in 1869 and went on to do graduate work in metallurgy at MIT, beginning a distinguished career in his field. He married Fanny Gay in New York in 1874.

One of Maud's first forays onto the national stage was a trip to the White House in April 1871 with her father. Chev was meeting with President Ulysses Grant to discuss annexation of Santo Domingo (now the Dominican Republic) to the United States. Chev wrote to Laura, "Dear old Maud dined with me at the White House yesterday and Mrs. Grant begged me would I let her come and stay with her Nellie! So today I escorted her bag and baggage and left her in the presidential mansion."[20] Santo Domingo was the last great cause in Samuel Gridley Howe's life. He disagreed with his old friend and more liberal colleague Senator Charles Sumner, who considered Chev's (and others') interest in Santo Domingo tantamount to U.S. imperialism. Chev saw the country and its poor inhabitants ripe for Americans to introduce education and health care—and he liked the climate, even considering building a house there.

Consequently, in February 1872, the Howe family—Chev, Julia, Maud, two cousins and one friend—left New York in a blizzard on the steamer *Tybee*, twelve days later to enter the harbor of Santo Domingo. Maud marveled at the emerald and turquoise water and inhaled the sweet smell of tropical flowers and fruit. For a two-month stay, the Howes brought "trunks, bandboxes, tables, chairs, beds, mosquito nettings and a grand piano."[21] Apparently Julia was not to be without her music, even though her stay was abbreviated, as she was to leave the family for a long-planned trip to London, the culmination of two years of activism for a women's peace conference. Julia called upon mothers the world over to join together to promote peace, hoping to unite forces in a women's peace conference. After Julia departed Santo Domingo, the remaining group sailed to Cuba before returning to Boston.

Maud was an astute observer of Santo Domingo's people, customs, politics, food, and flora. From a perspective of fifty years she wrote, "This, my first experience of foreign travel, was doubly precious because I was thrown so much with my dear father. During our four months absence from home we were together constantly. He taught me how to travel, to take the open road with an open mind." Chev's feelings on the trip were different; he wrote to Laura, "Since your mother's departure I find it rather hard to hold in the girls, who with Mrs. Quackenbush are stark mad after the young men whose acquaintance we have made. It is a bad school I find for dear Maud and I would get her away if I could, but we must wait over until the next month's steamer when I will gladly go back to dear old Boston and never venture into the tropics again with four tinder boxes in charge." And later, "I left Santo Domingo with Maud and her flirtatious friend Derby a fortnight ago; am on my way home. Miss Paddock has them in charge; thank the Lord for my deliverance."[22]

The young Boston socialite Lucy Derby emerges as a friend and co-conspirator in Maud's social life in the early 1870s. Derby, three years older than Maud, was the daughter of a prominent lawyer whose family resided on Charles Street in Boston. Undoubtedly inheriting some of her father's persuasive powers, Derby was to champion many reform causes, including leading the Girls Club of Boston for a decade and advocating for the arts and letters. Maud was often part of the festivities at the Derby household, particularly when the English comedic actor Edward Askew Sothern was present—a personality so memorable that his photograph was included in Maud's autobiography. Derby later described the mayhem at a typical dinner party—practical jokes, "mesmerism," and magic tricks with "Miss Howe still under the influence"; later at the theater Sothern would favor the ladies with a special performance.[23]

Aside from an escape from her parents' querulous home life, Maud's youthful love of frivolity and inclination for fine living were likely inherited from her Uncle Sam Ward, the beloved older brother of Julia. Just as she had revolted against her strict, Calvinistic upbringing by encouraging her children to enjoy music, dance, theater, and a social life, her brother had learned to cultivate the good life when he moved to Paris at the age of nineteen, ostensibly to further his mathematical studies. Called home to enter the family banking business, Sam Ward found that his talents and heart lay elsewhere; and his peripatetic career included investment debacles, the gain and loss of a gold mining fortune and a successful period as a lobbyist in Washington, D.C., before leaving the country amid scandal. Julia wrote, "He became known as King of the Lobby, but much more as the prince of entertainers."[24] Sam Ward's marriages hardly fared better, with the early death of his first wife Emily Astor and the desertion of second wife Medora Grimes. The Astor family went to great lengths to keep Sam away from his one daughter Margaret, and two sons by his second wife died young and largely unknown by Sam. In spite of his shortcomings as a businessman, husband, and father, Ward was a jovial man, generous to a fault, and the world's most loving and loved uncle. Upon another visit to Washington, D.C., in 1875, this time with her mother, Maud wrote, "We stayed at Wormley's, hard by the lodgings of Uncle Sam Ward, who now brought me, instead of sugar plums and playthings, visitors and invitations."[25] According to Laura, he also gave Maud diamonds and sapphires.

While Oak Glen at Portsmouth was the center of family activity in the summer, the city of Newport had long held associations for Julia and Sam Ward. As children in the early 1830s they summered at the George Bailey farmhouse, leased by their mother's mother, Sarah Cutler. Later owned by the Norman family and now restored as the hub of the Norman Bird Sanctuary, this house was filled to overflowing with the Cutler family's southern and northern relatives, who included Julia's first cousin, Ward McAllister, later to become famous as the beau monde's arbiter of social mores. He recalled, "Well do I remember my Uncle Samuel Ward and Dr. Francis of New York, building bonfires on Paradise Rocks on the Fourth of July and flying kites from Purgatory."[26] In 1837 Julia and Sam's father became convinced of the healthful benefits of Newport for his motherless children and bought an elegant home at the corner of Bellevue Avenue and Old Beach Road, becoming one of the first New Yorkers to make Newport a permanent summer residence.[27]

When Maud first developed her "social consciousness," in the 1870s, the tone of Newport society was distinctly French, similar to her Uncle Sam, who "was rather French than American in appearance and manner, sparkling, effervescent, full of laughter, motion, gesture."[28] Maud's memories were of a summer colony in the "wooden" age — when the architecture was wood, rather than stone and marble. "In the afternoon, society took its drive up and down Bellevue Avenue from five to seven. The horses, harnesses, carriages, lap dogs, ladies and toilettes were the handsomest money could buy. While I admired the style of it all, the artificiality fretted me, and after a few days of Bellevue Avenue I was glad to scurry home to Portsmouth ... and go for a tramp."[29] Unlike the quiet days of her mother's antebellum Newport, when boarding houses offered accommodations to genteel Southern plantation families, Maud's memories of Newport in the 1870s recall the increasing importance of wealth, social standing, and keeping up appearances.

Maud may have deplored the "artificiality," but she did enjoy the social life, to which she was introduced by family friends such as Mrs. Charles H. Dorr.[30] The Dorrs, later to be staples of Bar Harbor Society, spent the summer of 1870 in Newport and Maud stayed with them. Julia, now dealing with an ailing husband, the birth of grandchildren, and an ever-widening circle of commitments involving her causes, seemingly overcame her guilt for leaving her family so often by indulging the whims of her youngest. Her diary from the early 1870s frequently cites chaperoning Maud and her friends' parties and excursions as well as spending money that she didn't have for Maud's wardrobe.

Both in Boston and Newport Maud was surrounded by admirers. Laura wrote, "Maud was in her early bloom of her great beauty, and was much beset by suitors of every age and degree. They hovered about Green Peace; the general atmosphere was one of high sentiment. This was in the early seventies, remember." Maud sang in those days and the suitors brought the songs of the period and left them on the piano, heavily underscored.[31] Her father was more caustic. "Maud is rather sad and disappointed by the early closing of the gay season; although she has the consciousness of having been the leading belle and beauty; and although some of the wounded ducks linger about the town hoping to meet her and two or three of the bolder ones drive out to see her, in spite of the risk of finding her engaged with 'one of the other fellers.' She has been hard pushed I think and somewhat distressed but very wisely she has resolved not to engage herself until she becomes of age."[32] Samuel Gridley Howe apparently tolerated one young man, Gorham Bacon, more than most. "Gorham Bacon has been telegraphed off the coast, and is expected here within three days. He is a very constant admirer of Maud and is rather more to my mind than any other of her followers. He is thoroughly American: simple, straightforward; honest and industrious and above all has a warm affectionate nature; which is above all other things the most important for happiness in the married state. Her other admirers are men of fashion; who think that to shine in society is the chief end of life."³³

Maud was a statuesque beauty, with dark hair and her father's piercing blue eyes. Her mother commented upon one occasion "she looked like a rosebud, brilliantly beautiful."³⁴ Benjamin Curtis Porter was a portrait painter and frequent guest at Howe social gatherings. Porter entered his first portrait of Maud into the National Academy of Design's Exhibition of 1877, prompting a response by a review in the *Art Journal:*

> Benjamin Curtis Porter of Boston made his mark in New York by sending the Academy Exhibition of 1877 his *Portrait of a Lady with Dog*. No previous or subsequent work of his is so noteworthy as this in quality. The lady stands leaning gracefully upon the back of a high chair on which is seated a pertinacious staring full-blooded pug dog, whose ugliness is in eloquent contrast to the refined and classic beauty of the woman. The motive of the representation had the disadvantage of being considered by some spectators to be a little stagy. Other persons preferred the dog to the woman; others still like the attitude of the woman best of all; but the picture as a whole met with popular and academic representation.

Apparently dissatisfied after some of the comments, Porter painted a second full-length, very elegant seated portrait of Maud in 1877. Clad in a sumptuous pale yellow silk dress, Maud competes with no dog for attention, as she stares regally at her audience and gives credence to her reputation as one of Boston's reigning belles.

Another family social connection was cousin Maddie Ward, Uncle Sam's daughter by his marriage to Emily Astor, who attained New York Knickerbocker society status in 1862 when she married U.S. Congressman John Winthrop Chanler. In 1873 they built a mansion in Newport overlooking Easton's Beach, called "Cliff Lawn."³⁵ Maud, eighteen at the time, recalled, "My first grown up party was the cotillion ball my cousin Maddie gave as the housewarming of Cliff Lawn. It was an evening of enchantment. My partner was an Adonis for looks, a Mercury for lightness of foot. His name? Lost in the mists; but I remember his profile, and the lingering pressure of his hand when we said goodnight."³⁶ Even as a starry-eyed young woman, she compared her paramours to Greek gods.

Samuel Gridley Howe's health had been declining for years and Julia had attended to him as well as she could, accompanying him once more to Santo Domingo in 1874, playing interminable games of whist at Oak Glen and spending time with him at his beloved Green Peace. When the city of Boston began making preparations to put a street through Green Peace, Julia convinced the authorities to wait. Chev had grown increasingly moody and anxious as the end neared, prone to violent fits of behavior that surely upset the entire family. He seemingly had a catharsis shortly before his death, with the revelation to his wife that he had been unfaithful earlier in their troubled marriage. Julia was disturbed, but wanted a peaceful end to their life together. A photograph from 1873 shows a happy Chev with his first grandchild, Alice Maud Richards, on his shoulders; Laura, her husband, and their two young daughters had also been keeping Chev company at Green Peace. Maud, in true form, associated the year of her father's death, 1876, with the year of the Centennial Exhibition in Philadelphia.[37] Chev died on January 8, 1876. Grief-stricken at first, by the day after her husband's funeral Julia was self-possessed enough to write in her journal: "Began my new life today. Prayed God that it might have a greatly added use and earnestness."[38]

The family dynamics changed drastically upon the death of Samuel Gridley Howe. In the summer of 1876 Laura and Harry Richards and their now three children moved to his family homestead in Gardiner, Maine. Harry's architectural career had gone nowhere except for the considerable home improvements to both Howe homes in Boston and Portsmouth, with little remuneration from his father-in-law,[39] and he had the opportunity to join his brothers at the family's paper mill business in Gardiner. Maud found a new niche as protector and secretary to her mother, whose reputation had by now eclipsed her husband's. In his will, Chev left his money to be divided among his four daughters; although Julia's inheritance had almost entirely been lost or squandered by her husband and male relatives, Chev had a hard time believing Julia would be in dire financial straits.

Uppermost on Julia's mind was the welfare of her charming but high-maintenance daughter, Maud. Julia's journal reflects her financial concerns: "Paid music for Maud's party, $33 and gave Maud $18 to pay for current finances . . . Was discouraged about expenses, my funds being nearly out and Maud having a bill at her dressmaker's of $105, besides other charges." When Julia did receive a bit of a windfall from her family business concerns in New York, she wrote, "Very thankful am I, and very desirous to spend this money better than I usually do. I determined to keep an account of my expenditures and especially of the money which Maud causes to run away so swiftly."[40] A wealthy husband for Maud was likely the hope of family members. However, surrounded by suitors as she was, and indeed having been ardently pursued by numbers of men, including one José Maria Gautier in Santo Domingo, she clearly, at age twenty-one, had her reservations about marriage.

Education was also a stumbling block, as noted by all family members with observations about Maud's lack of purpose and her obstinacy. Flossy remembered Maud calling her teacher a fool and throwing an inkbottle across the schoolroom. On her 1867 European trip Julia Ward Howe had written to her daughter Maud, "I hope to have you abroad with me someday and should have been glad to have had you with us all these days. You will be better able to enjoy such things when you are older, and have more education."[41] On Julia's next trip to Europe in 1872, she again wrote Maud, "Darling, of more importance still is your education. Now are you hoping to regain the time slot for your studies this winter? You will have to make a great effort; you're your dear, wonderful little self. You will have to resolve, not reluctantly, but patiently, to do some regular work every day at music, languages and solid reading. Music will be the seeds of culture which in your later life will give you great pleasure, when the things which please you most now will have lost much of their charm."[42] Patience was not part of Maud's temperament; in her autobiography she acknowledged that her learning did not come from sitting in classrooms, but rather in experiencing the life surrounding her.

The Centennial Exposition in Philadelphia in 1876 was one such learning curve. Maud went to Philadelphia to visit friends Ida and Alice Cushman, who having lost their mother, lived with their aunt Rebecca Wetherill in a grand house on the Main Line. The girls' father was miniature painter and engraver George Hewitt Cushman, who took the trio to the Art Gallery at the Centennial where Maud studied the European paintings. The art excited her enough to want to become an artist. Her immaturity and spoiled nature continued to surface, however, as indicated by a letter she wrote to her mother, "My dear little mama, I am so homesick for you today. I wonder if you are missing me, doubtful—you have I suppose Laura and her children with you, as well as Julia, all more to you then I. Well, it is doubtful when I shall come, perhaps this week with Flossy, perhaps not till the next—I am out of money—utterly. Cannot stir to the Centennial or anywhere till I have some more. I think 10—say 12 dollars would be enough please send—immediately. I hate to ask you for money—what can I do. Goodbye, give my love to any of the family who care for it—Maud."[43] The plaintive note struck by Maud in her letters from ten years earlier has not changed perceptibly. It remained for a grand tour of Europe to bring Maud Howe to her senses.

THREE

My dearest Laura, ... Have you been to Holland? Have you seen Paulus Potter's bull? Rembrandt's Night Watch? Gerrit Dou's lovely pictures? Bewitching Frans Hals? Quaint Jan Steen, dreary Hobema—and other of the delightful Dutch pictures? I forget whether you have or not, but you can imagine what a delight they were to us—Full well til we came to Antwerp and then lost every other remembrance of art in the presence of the Great Masters.

MAUD HOWE, LETTER TO LAURA ELIZABETH RICHARDS

ON MAY 21, 1877 MAUD HOWE AND JULIA WARD HOWE SAILED ON the Cunard steamer *Parthia* for London, by way of Liverpool. Funds for the trip had been raised by Julia's lecture tour to the Midwest the previous fall, at last raising Maud's awareness of the family's dire financial circumstances. Maud accompanied Julia on part of the western trip, charming the conductor on the locomotive from Milwaukee to Chicago. Julia enjoyed visiting states such as Kansas, where Chev had bought land when they visited in 1857. Kansas had good schools and a lower cost of living, and Julia briefly fantasized on the entire family relocating there to live in comfort and relative affluence—probably dismissing the idea upon visualizing Maud settling in Kansas. According to family lore on Laura Richards' side, the European Grand Tour was undertaken to find a rich husband for Maud.[1] However, Julia's letters reveal another side of the story, her wish for Maud to be happy, educated, and "in good time settle, married or single, into such a way of living that will suit you."[2] Julia also adored her youngest daughter, who was fast becoming a vital companion.

In their biography of Julia Ward Howe, Laura and Maud wrote of the trip, "Throughout the journeying which followed, our mother had two objects in view: to see her own kind of people, the seekers, the students, the reformers and their works; and to give Maud the most vivid first impression of all that would be interesting and valuable to her. These objects were not always easy to combine."[3] The journey's first stop in London only emphasized the different priorities of the two travelers. Julia delved into religion and politics; she spoke at the Unitarian Association annual conference; she then attended a meeting on modern Greek and went to Parliament to listen to the controversial advocate for Home Rule of Ireland, Charles Parnell. Maud remembered the ladies' gallery as being "hot, crowded, uncomfortable and screened like the musharabeah window of an Egyptian harem." More to her liking was the round of "dinners, dances, garden parties, races of boats, of horses; matches of cricket, of football; 'shows' of pictures, flowers, vegetables, dogs," it being the height of the London season.[4] While Julia filled her days with meetings, writing, and lectures, by evening "she bravely watched the dancers foot it through the livelong night, and drove home by daylight with her 'poor dancing Maud.'"[5]

Settling in the bohemian Bloomsbury, the two were immediately immersed in London's liberal political and Pre-Raphaelite artistic world. Both Julia and Uncle Sam Ward had many contacts in British society and politics. Maud recalled that in England, unlike the United States, statesmen were vital ingredients at a successful hostess's dinner. Most of their friends were "Gladstonians," and Maud and Julia were visiting London just prior to William Gladstone's reelection as prime minister. Lord Rosebery, the "adopted nephew" of Uncle Sam as well as Gladstone's campaign manager, was one of the facilitators of their visit, inviting the two to lunch shortly after their arrival. Sam's friend Lord Dunraven, later to own the America's Cup contender *Thistle*, took them yachting and to the Derby. Lord Houghton, another old friend of Sam and Julia, was part of the group of aristocratic literary figures they saw frequently. The younger Henry James was often Julia's escort to events; Maud was wary of him, "fancying that he was 'studying' me for copy."[6] They went to church to hear the radical theologians of the day: Stopford Brooke, who was to leave the Church of England for Unitarianism; Moncure

Conway, an American abolitionist who left Unitarianism for socialism; and the more conservative Arthur Stanley, Dean of Westminster Abby.

The height of the Aesthetic Movement was reached in 1877. Maud observed that the "cult for beauty was unlike anything I have ever known before or since."[7] Uncle Sam's friend Edmund Yates was editor of the *World* society journal, a forerunner of today's London tabloids chronicling the lives of the beautiful people. In London "professional beauties" were the rage—their photographs were for sale along with those of actors and royals, and crowds converged upon them as they emerged into public view. Apparently a photograph of Maud was appropriated for sale with those of the other beautiful young women.[8] At one banquet Maud was seated on one side of the visiting Ulysses Grant, with Lily Langtry, the "Jersey Lily," on the other. In fact, Maud was once mistaken for Lily Langtry in New York.

This cult of beauty prevailed in the art world as well, where the Pre-Raphaelites were challenging the ruling order of the Royal Academy. The Grosvenor Gallery, founded by Sir Coutts Lindsay, opened in 1877, its owner expressing a newfound confidence in "art for art's sake." James McNeill Whistler was one of the stars of the opening, the others being Sir Edward Burne-Jones and Sir George Watts. Whistler, who Maud was to recall as "a vain fop, dressed to kill," exhibited his tonalist "arrangements" and "nocturnes," while Burne-Jones transcended the earlier Pre-Raphaelite concerns with detailed, glowing surfaces to create more moody, romantic paintings. Watts sought to uplift his audiences with allegorical paintings; Walter Crane's classical and literary subjects were very ethereal.[9] Maud recalled that her sympathies in 1877 were with the Pre-Raphaelites and John Ruskin with their "more finished" work; but later revised her opinion, calling Whistler an immortal who created masterpieces.[10]

George Howard, the Earl of Carlisle, was an artist, friend and patron to the Pre-Raphaelites, who escorted Maud around to the museums and also exhibited his work "with the rebels" at the Grosvenor. He wanted Burne-Jones to paint the lovely Maud. She wrote, "From the first sitting I knew I was not up his alley. He went on with the painting to please Howard, but it was no good. I was not his type. He finally put me on one of his large decorative panels, where a row of nymphs disport themselves."[11]

Maud also had an introduction to the Arts and Crafts movement when she was introduced to William Morris in Burne-Jones' studio. "He wore aesthetic clothes, a coarse blue linen shirt, and tan colored tweed suit. The effect of his get up was that of a great gentleman masquerading as an artisan."[12] Marie Spartoli Stillman was both a Pre-Raphaelite painter and a model, married to the English critic William Stillman. She became a lifelong friend of Maud's after their meeting in the 1870s, likely in London, where Marie exhibited her work at the Grosvenor Galley; her most favored themes drew on Italian literature. She later came to the United States to visit Maud in Newport and show her work at the Art Association of Newport.[13]

In July 1877 the Howes left London. Holland, Germany, Switzerland, and France followed, with exclamatory letters from Maud to her sisters, delighting in the artistic treasures and customs of these countries. The prisons at The Hague were most interesting to Julia, but she also was rewarded by seeing Maud's awe of and interest in the Rembrandts, the Rubenses, the Van Dycks in Amsterdam. They proceeded to Prussia, where Julia's sister Louisa was visiting her daughter Annie, who had married the Prussian Baron Erich von Rabe and lived in Lesnian, in German Poland. These relatives had very little use for Julia's reform efforts and were instead concerned with formal appearances and preserving a feudal system of class division. Louisa beseeched Julia and Maud to travel first class, something both unaffordable and undesirable to them; they connived to go second class to a nearby city and switch to a first class car when they were as close to their destination as possible. The Baron and Julia sparred about his belief in "the excellence of war" and preference for dueling. More at home in Switzerland, Julia attended the Geneva Congress, called to protest the legalizing of prostitution in England. Here was a subject close to Julia's heart; it allowed her to emphasize the importance of education for women to enable them to be on equal footing with men, with well-paying work open to them, and not fall victim to prostitution through economic need. Surely Maud was garnering a new perspective on woman's roles on this trip.

"October found the travelers in Paris, the elder still intent on affairs of study and reform, the younger grasping eagerly at each new wonder or beauty."[14] Frederic Passy, a social economist, befriended Julia and made possible visits to the French Parliament and the French Academy of Arts, where they were able to observe those ensconced in this last bastion of French Academic painting. More memorable for Maud was the visit to Gustave Doré, an artist whose popularity far outdistanced his reputation with art critics. Julia admired the passion and angst in some of his religious and literary paintings and illustrations, while Maud observed his modeling of a great Bacchanalian vase being prepared for exhibition in the 1878 Exposition Universelle—a piece later referred to derogatorily as "Doré's bottle" by William Wetmore Story, then U.S. art commissioner. After Doré's death in 1883 Maud would write an article on him for the *Boston Transcript*. The two travelers were to return to France the following summer, but in November 1877 they again packed up and headed south to Italy.

Turin, Milan, Verona, Venice, Bologna: Maud and Julia climbed to the top of cathedrals, plumbed the depths of tombs of the Scaligers and discovered the Bolognese artist Elisabetta Sirani, a painter about whom Maud was later to lecture. A letter from Julia in Milan to her daughter Julia Romana emphasized their visits to the schools, which were largely very effectively run by women; she wrote of Italian politics, voicing her opinion that the Italians were not so interested in the freedom of their people as were the French, but were united in their dislike of the Germans.[15]

The two arrived in Rome in time to spend Christmas dinner with the Terry family—Louisa, Luther, their children Arthur and Daisy, as well as Maud's cousin Francis Marion Crawford. The Terrys lived in an apartment in the Palazzo Odescalchi, an imposing brick and stone building with a central courtyard, designed by Bernini and located on the Corso. Maud wrote, "Rome, the old enchantress, held me enthralled from the moment St. Peter's dome floated before my eyes like a faint blue bubble on the far horizon."[16] Louisa Ward Crawford Terry's importance as a grand dame of the American art colony in Rome was only enhanced by the elegance of her surroundings. She kept an open house, and one artist remembered the Terrys' drawing room as "even more of a cosmopolitan meeting place than the Storys',"[17] referring to the group of American artists surrounding sculptor William Wetmore Story at the Palazzo Barberini. As the wife of the late sculptor Crawford—and probably as the sister of Julia and Sam Ward—Louisa's salon drew elite Italians of all political persuasions and had a distinctly more international flair than the Storys'. Maud noted, "It appeared to me that the two serious things in life from the Palazzo Odescalchi standpoint were society with a small s and art with a big A."[18]

In Rome Maud found a cause célèbre: the grandeur, the pageantry, the arts, all such a contrast to the austerity, the seriousness of purpose that eclipsed her family life in Boston. Frank, or "Fritz," Crawford, the same age as Maud, introduced her to Roman antiquity as well as the splendors of Christendom. Although Protestants at the time, Crawford and two of his sisters were later to convert to Catholicism, so overpowering was the ritual, the array of magnificence present in the Church. Crawford, brought up in Europe with a three-year stint at St. Paul's School in Concord, New Hampshire, was a romantic protagonist for Maud. Very handsome—"some people thought him like the famous bas-relief of Antinous at the Villa Albano"[19]—and worldly, with a magnificent singing voice and a flair for languages, he seemingly had no real goals in life. Maud played the devil's advocate, encouraging her cousin to return to the United States and find a profession. Perhaps sensing a kindred spirit, Maud wrote to Laura in a letter: "Now you must be very patient with Fritz, whom I have come to love dearly for at first he will seem a most aggravating creature, with rather superior ways. He has lots of faults, is vain, conceited, intolerant and inconstant to work . . . Rare with young men of his education and life, for our sex, puts women on a pedestal and I am sure has never helped one down from that pedestal. A most docile creature, if you do not let him know you are leading him, he feels an influence immediately and yields to it, but must not see the rein."[20] Maud had a project, and this desire to motivate and initiate change and activism in others, a characteristic particularly relevant to her future marriage, was taking shape.

As for Maud's future endeavors, in the winter of 1878 she began to study with an Italian artist known for his landscape painting in the naturalistic style of the Barbizon School. Giovanni Costa, a romantic figure who was also a revolutionary in the Risorgimento, the fight for Italian independence, had a following among English and American artists, as well as the Macchiaioli, a group of modern painters. He had studied with Corot, imparting to Maud the great artist's preference for poetic, tonal landscapes that conveyed a mood. She left for class before breakfast, learned to prime a canvas and put the colors down.[21] As she told it, Maud's artistic career was temporarily cut short when in February 1878 she came down with Roman fever, a form of malaria that was the curse of the American traveler. By spring she was on the mend and Julia, Frank, and Maud went to Orvieto. The return of good health enabled Maud to appreciate the Fra Angelico and Signorelli paintings, the Etruscan tombs, the scenery and her cousin's delight in sharing the simple Italian ways. They ate macaroni and drank wine and Crawford sang Italian folk songs, accompanying himself on the guitar.

This recuperative journey included visiting Florence and Perugia, where Maud met the man who was to become her husband. John Elliott and his friend, Frederick Shakerley Kemp, were returning to England after spending time in Rome. It was a stormy evening and the travelers were all disembarking from the train to board the omnibus and travel to the Hotel Brufani. For the nineteen-year-old aspiring artist, an orphan who had been born to Scottish parents in England, and the twenty-three-year-old woman of beauty and pedigree, it was — as she recalled it fifty years later, allowing for a bit of romantic embellishment — an instant attraction. "Suddenly a sword of rosy lightning split the inky blackness of the sky, and for one breathless moment it was bright as day. I saw Jack's face, and he saw mine for the first time in that flash ... It is May in Perugia, the hedgerows are fair with wild roses, the air is sweet with honeysuckle and I am looking into his eyes."[22] However, it was a pot of tea, a less romantic talisman, that sealed their fate. In an irritable voice — a characteristic that Maud should also have taken to heart — Jack complained about the hotel's tea and Maud rushed to retrieve their traveling tea basket with good strong English tea. The four travelers saw Perugia and Assisi together and appreciated each other's tastes so much that they met each other numerous times in the next year.

The summer of 1878 saw a return to Paris, where the Exposition Universelle opened in June; Maud found it very inferior to the Philadelphia Exposition of 1876. Family friend and sculptor William Wetmore Story, also the art commissioner for the United States, was highly critical of the American government's performance at this event. In Maud's later lectures on American art she sympathized with Story's concerns, stating that the sum allotted to the department of fine arts was "ridiculously inadequate," that sculpture was prohibited, that the total number of artworks in oil and watercolor was 143 and lacked examples of Gilbert Stuart, Washington Allston, and William Morris Hunt, among others. Maud thought Story to be overly strident, but his refrain struck a chord with her that later became her lament as well. Story reported, "As a nation if we do not profess to look down upon art, at least we utterly neglect it. It forms no portion of our education and in the public representative bodies, a lamentable ignorance prevails. The great National Academy or Museum of Art exists to confer honors and awards, to educate students or to improve public taste. All the academies and museums that exist are private and local in their character, limited in their means and unsupported by the nation. Art is heavily handicapped in America. The notion of our government is that it must manage for itself, without means or opportunities of study and culture. It depends for its support on private patronage solely. And develop itself as it may in the cold shadow of neglect. One might as well expect the highest literary culture without libraries and schools."[23]

One American work that was included in the Exposition Universelle was Benjamin Curtis Porter's final portrait of Maud, painted in 1877, prompting a Darius Cobbin of the *Boston Evening Traveler* to note Porter's "power of combining magnificence of color with chaste design and elevated feeling." Maud wrote to Laura from St. Malo, "Porter's last has attracted much notice, much blame, much praise—Mrs. Dorr does not like it, nor does Story, but he likes nothing, but others declare it remarkably well painted. Rather the general opinion is that it is much older than I am—since coming abroad I might have made my future as a model—as seven artists, all have standing, all have requested that I sit for them—and some sculptors and I have refused them all and have only been obliging to three boy students, the two Storys and the English fellow traveling with us—the first two made two caricatures which were not meant to be caricatures and the third boy is doing something very clever; I am sitting for him as I write—he works doubly hard poor fellow. For on the success of this, his first attempt, depends on whether he will be allowed to follow art, for which he has a great talent, or . . . if the powers that be think he succeeds his friend will send him to Paris to study—this is all no vain glory but I thought it might amuse you."[24] Of course the "English fellow" was John Elliott, by September very much a part of Maud's life. In fact, he often preceded her arrival at the next destination.

The late summer of 1878 was spent in Normandy and Brittany, exploring the picturesque seaside towns, often meeting up with acquaintances from home making the Grand Tour. In Dieppe they reclined on the beach under red umbrellas with the Storys and by night demonstrated American dance steps for the locals. Maud, always the madcap, swam in her bathing costume of blue flannel trimmed with white short sleeves as far out as she could, "with the gentlemen."[25] It was in Quimper that John Elliott, now familiarly "Jack," designed a little white cap for Julia, based on local Breton costume. Naturally enough these frivolous happenings were conveyed back home in a series of letters to Laura, who was bearing her fourth child in the glamourless surroundings of Gardiner, Maine. "Kiss the little howling bundle of joy for me" and "I have sympathized with your troubles, poor old thing, this winter," were typical of the flippant comments Maud often sent. Naturally enough all three sisters were growing resentful of Maud's commandeering their mother for such a long time and wanted them to come home.

Maud, however, was having the time of her life, and she let loose on Laura her misgivings about returning, in a telling letter that conveyed her unhappiness when at home.

> . . . about our coming home, or rather our *not* coming home. I am sorry that you and Flossy are so much troubled about it. But I think mama must have told you, that she made the decision, without any pressure on my part, in fact you could not have been more surprised than was I, to learn it—In making it, she of course thought a great deal of me, but also, I think of herself. She is very anxious to go to Egypt and she would have gone this winter I think, had it not been for my illness—you know how quickly she adapts herself to new surroundings—she has enjoyed everything as fully as much, and I sometimes think *more* than I have. Her energy and enthusiasm are unlimited. We should have come home in the autumn—well, what then—mama would not have wished to leave

Boston, and yet how would we have lived there, on the little that we have to live on. Your home, which you have always made a home to me, would be inaccessible to me for the winter, for with this affliction of the heart, I can never again, I fear, endure such a cold climate—Julia's doors, or rather her husband's, have never been open to me, and poor dear Floss, cannot give me the hospitality she would like to—what remains then—a couple of rooms over the club, and in Boston, which of all places in the world, I detest—Rather a gloomy prospect—for my separation from you and Floss, would be as great, in everything except miles, as it is now—I have suffered so, morally, physically, that it is well I should have a little more time before I go back to the scene of it all. And yet, you all remind me, that mama is as much yours as mine. I feel this and do not wish to take more than my share of her precious life, for myself alone. But remember she is *my all*—my home, my protector. You have your husband, your children, your home—and mama is all this to me. It is not that I do not gladly share this with you, but you know that at home none of us have the larger part of her interest and society. It all goes to the infernal club away from us, but I honestly think she is much happier and less excited and restless than she was at home.[26]

In Egypt they lunched on the summit of the Great Pyramid on roast quail, fresh rolls and *pate de foie gas*, accompanied by iced champagne. They were feted by the European community in Cairo led by General Charles Pomeroy Stone, chief of staff to the reigning monarch, Khedive Isma'il. Maud, Julia, and cousin Julia McAllister visited the Khedive's harem where they found three Egyptian princesses clad in silk and brocade, dripping in diamonds, who were intensely curious about the American women and expressed amazement at the unmarried status of Maud and her cousin. Maud was the perfect foil for the exoticism of the Middle East, practiced at smoking the chibouk pipes, enchanted by her Egyptian guide Hassan's "patina of bronze," and delighted to dance the night away at the Abdin Palace ball, clad in the latest Paris fashion. "Behold me on this lovely Sunday afternoon, floating quietly along the Nile," Maud wrote to Laura.[27] Her mother's view of the Nile River inspired deep introspection as she trod upon the land of the biblical characters she knew so well and walked in the path of Jesus in the Holy Land. For this expedition they scaled steep precipices by horseback on their way to the Dead Sea, and encountered Bedouin bandits and storms of locusts.

Maud's irreverent take on the trip to the Holy Land is preserved in a letter to Laura:

> Behold it has come to pass that Julia which is the mother of Maud, and McCallister which is the cousin of Julia, passed through the land of Goshen, ever the land where the three sages set sail in the boat, where of is made a tub and passing through the canal which is called Suez took passage on a ship to cross the waters even unto Jaffa, which is the port of that city called Jerusalem And then went them men, unto the number of two, Henry, whose surname is Cooper and William, which is called William Franke, known as the C.C. which meaneth Captivating Captain. These five passed over the waters which lie between Egypt, the land of Pharoh unto Jaffa. And there was mourning among them and wailing in their midst and gnashing of teeth what they should have left behind the flesh pots of Egypt, which is the land of milk and honey—And there was woe among the tents of Cairo, in that the aforesaid had gone from them these seas devastating in the halls of Shepherds that knew their shadows no more—And lo in the afternoon of the same day, they departed southwards for the city which is called Jerusalem. And Julia, whose surname is Ward took with her daughter Maud and she who is called McCallister and departed shaking from her feet the dust of Jaffa. The women entered even into a chariot and these men that went with them were even upon horses. And so they departed carrying with them figs which are golden—and so endeth the first journey in the land of the Philistines. 1st Epistle to the Galatians.[28].

The last leg of their Middle Eastern journey found the travelers passing through Beirut, Cyprus and Constantinople, on their way to Greece. Even then the area was filled with unrest; the Turkish sultan was afraid to come out of his "kiosk of a palace" for fear of being shot, and only did so to go to the mosque. Turkish officials were often rude to the Americans, and Maud and Julia spent their time under the protection of Admiral and Mrs. Frank Higginson, who arranged for Navy beaux for the girls and lots of festivities. The Higginsons accompanied the Howes to Athens, a destination that was significant for the wife and daughter of "the American hero of the Greek Revolution."²⁹ Their welcome included a roast lamb banquet with the Cretan chieftains expressing gratitude for Dr. Howe's efforts on behalf of Greek freedom. They also consorted with Dr. and Mrs. Heinrich Schliemann, professional (and controversial) archaeologists who were excavating the Acropolis, finding untold treasures that were then carried off to share with "the civilized world." While Julia Ward Howe had embraced a progressive education for her daughter, guided by Friedrich Froebel's philosophy, Maud recognized that the hands-on education she received on this trip was ultimately far better.

In February 1879 mother and daughter headed back to Rome, where Jack Elliott awaited. He had become fast friends with Louisa Terry and a frequent guest at the Palazzo Odescalchi. It seems obvious from Maud's descriptions of the young artist that he was very different from the macho, "manly" type of man such as her father, her brother-in-law "the Skipper," or the Navy men she admired. A "pretty page" is how she described him to Laura: "for he is just like Thackeray's ballad 'Ho! pretty page with the dimpled chin.'" In another letter she wrote, "He is a graceful beautiful creature, like a Donatello [sculpture], — he is a charming draftsman and makes lovely sketches for me as we go along—He has wonderful deep hazel eyes and a mass of black wavy hair, a big beautiful mouth just in the shape of a Cupid's bow, filled with white teeth. He is a great lover of Shakespeare, and I have learned the whole part of Juliet, which we often rehearse together—He is at present directing your envelope—But of him do not oh sister, read to inquiring friends—only because things sound so different far away."³⁰ Jack was devoted to Julia, attending to her when she was not feeling well; he took care of their creature comforts, advised them on their dress, and although he did not particularly enjoy receptions, was the perfect escort to the theater, which he adored. It happened that Maud was selected to portray the Greek goddess Aspasia in a tableau at the German Embassy in Rome, in celebration of the Emperor's birthday. Her costume had to be just so, and Jack created a pattern of Greek design which he himself threaded into the tunic.³¹

By the time the travelers came back to London for their last leg of their adventure, Maud had a thorough knowledge of the artistic and architectural wonders of the western world and their origins in antiquity. She was in awe of the art spirit that flourished in Europe, the importance of art to the daily life of the people and felt that American artists needed such recognition in their own country. In their second London season, Maud, Julia, and Jack visited the opening of Burlington House at the Royal Academy, at the time headed by the "perfect old poppycock," Frederick Leighton. But, she reminded her new artist friends, "London owed its Royal Academy to an American painter, Benjamin West, who induced the King to grant the charter to the Association for which he was president twenty-eight years."[32] Thus began Maud Howe's mission to build recognition for American art and enrich the lives of citizens in the process.

FOUR

I am glad to find that I can do something with literature.
With journalism I have more natural sympathy. I like the excitement
and stimulus of knowing that the printer's devil is waiting for me. I have
corresponded all summer with the *New York Tribune*, and have had opportunities
of other journalistic engagements. But journalism is wearing to the nerves. I have
already suffered for the efforts I have made in it, and though I feel the power in
me to rise in that profession, I shall make first a strong push for a footing
in literature, as a freer and more agreeable profession.

MAUD HOWE LETTER TO SAM WARD

SOON AFTER THEIR ARRIVAL BACK IN NEW ENGLAND, IN JULY OF 1879 Maud and Julia went to Oak Glen, in Portsmouth, Rhode Island, where they usually remained well into November. Oak Glen was now a matriarchal house, and Julia referred to herself as "Mistress of the Valley." Although she still found her "precious time" to work, she also fed, housed, and entertained her growing family. The grandchildren, at present, numbered seven.[1] Flossy, who lived in Scotch Plains, New Jersey, regularly brought her brood to Oak Glen for the entire summer; the Richards family came from Maine for shorter visits. Louisa Terry and her daughter, Daisy, on their way to visit third sister Annie Mailliard in California, spent part of the summer at Oak Glen. Samuel Gridley Howe had never appreciated music or dance, but now the house resounded with the sounds of Julia on her Chickering grand piano, brother Harry's smooth tenor, and Maud's guitar rhythms. Then they rolled up the rugs and everyone danced. The focal part of summer evenings was the "open air parlor in the shape of a semi circle, set about with a close tall green hedge and shaded by the ancient spreading boughs of an ancient mulberry tree," referred to as the Green Room.

After Maud returned from the Grand Tour, apparently without matrimonial prospects, the extended family seemed to feel that she was destined for spinsterhood, and if that were to be the case, what would she do? Following up on her time with Costa in Rome and some further study in Paris, and likely inspired by the many sketching expeditions in which she had recently participated on the continent, Maud seriously considered becoming an artist. Prior to her leaving for Europe she had been avidly painting on china and tiles, a popular hobby for genteel young ladies at the time. From Laura in Gardiner, Maine, in 1877:

> And with us at this time is Maud, our Maud the Duchess, who paintith upon china with brushes and with scarlet and blue and purple; in so much that I, being even such as I am, and . . . which being interpreted means the Empress, are moved to do likewise, wherefore there is weeping and lamentations in the household even among the maidens thereof, Bridget weeping for her cups and saucers and would not be comforted because they were all dashed over.[2]

In 1879 Maud enrolled at the School of the Museum of Fine Arts, Boston, where she spent the fall semester mostly studying anatomy under Frederick Crowninshield.[3] Art careers for young women of means were acceptable, even encouraged as a profession for those who did not become wives and mothers. Gilded Age women flocked to art schools and by the turn of the century represented one third of those aspiring to professional art careers. But it did not take long for Maud to realize her shortcomings as an artist. "I had learned that it is not enough to feel the love of beauty, the yearning for artistic expression; an artist must have art in his fingers as well as in his soul." She left a legacy of a few "passable flower paintings."[4]

Intermittently, Maud entertained the idea of going on the stage, having been encouraged by the great Italian actors Tomasso Salvini and Adelaide Ristori. Uncle Sam Ward wrote to Julia, "What do you think of her studying Ophelia and Desdemona as Salvini suggests? She is a splendid creature, and I doubt her being happy in single cussedness. She has a lively memory and knows how to use her splendid eyes."[5] During the 1880s Maud often was called upon to participate in *tableaux vivants,* or living pictures in which costumed figures posed in a theatrical still life. Julia's journal notes that in April 1880 Maud made two of the best at Mrs. W. B. Richards': *Das Mädchen auf der Fremde* and the Duchess of Devonshire.[6] A stereopticon slide portraying her in Grecian costume, taken by A. D. Handy of Boston, likely commemorates one of these occasions. In one of her later theatrical performances, in New Orleans, she was applauded and buried in flowers![7] Maud undoubtedly received little encouragement from her very proper siblings in the pursuit of the theater.

During the winter of 1879–80 Julia and Maud rented two rooms in Benedict Chambers, a boarding house on Spruce Street in Boston, which certainly did not keep them in the style to which they were accustomed, never mind the disruption caused by visiting friends and relatives. Julia fell and severely tore the ligaments in her knee in the fall of 1880.[8] To the rescue came Uncle Sam Ward, at the end of his career as an influential lobbyist, and recently the recipient of an unexpected but welcome windfall in the amount of a $3,000 monthly allowance and an additional sum of $750,000 from railroad stock profits.[9] Now sixty-six, Sam wrote to his good friend Longfellow, "My dear Longo, Thank you for your always affectionate greeting. There is nothing more certain than that I have been the object of some supernatural intervention, yet I sometimes think it is a mockery to be made rich just as I am going off the stage. But, there are nieces and nephews and sisters whom the windfall will make, in fact has made, happy."[10] And so, after moving out of his Brevoort Hotel basement quarters in New York City and into an elegant apartment near Washington Square, he turned his attention to the rest of the family, telling Maud and Julia to start looking for a house in Boston. In the meantime he put them up in a furnished residence at 129 Mount Vernon Street, where they moved in November 1880.

With Julia forced to curtail—slightly—her activities, Maud recalled a happy family time during the early months of 1881. Joining them was her charismatic cousin, Frank Crawford—now called Marion, come to Boston to study opera with Georg Henschel.[11] After strumming his guitar throughout Italy, studying Sanskrit at the University of Rome and

Harvard, and editing the *Indian Herald* in Allahabad on the Ganges River, Crawford was still undecided about a career. Louisa Terry feared her son to be a "rolling stone" and mustered the family forces on his behalf.[12] Maud introduced him and his half sister, Daisy Terry, to Boston. "We are gay, gayer, gayest. The two Marion cousins taking in Boston society like young ducks to a pond." At the same time she fancied herself the family accountant, taking on the bookkeeping duties for which she had received minimal training from her exasperated father. She began serious house-hunting, writing in the same letter to Laura, "The house business has been as you may imagine, fatiguing, as I have been over every house in the West End that is for sale, have seen real estate agents, assessors, experts, etc. 'til I am weary of them all."[13] In April 1881 Uncle Sam made possible the purchase of the home whose address would resonate through the annals of the Howe family: 241 Beacon Street.

The culture of "neurasthenia" was rampant in late nineteenth-century America,[14] and Maud's anxiety and melancholy played into this national fixation. Julia's journal indicates how worried she was about "dear Maud," and sent her to three different doctors, noting that they agreed on "her peculiarities of constitution."[15] Not helping matters, Julia noted that "[Maud] does not enjoy young children," and in the spring of 1881 both Laura and Flossy were again pregnant. Laura suffered from morning sickness, and Maud wrote:

> I was very disappointed at [not] coming to you, and as I need not tell you the reason however don't think me an unsympathetic beast, I am sorry because I feel you are not strong enough just now for the exhaustion which you must necessarily undergo and also selfishly because I shall not see you for so long. For I should not be good for you now until you are much stronger and I more settled. Perhaps in June I will come to you if you are strong and frisky. I can't bear to think of you keeled up on the sofa, with those kids kicking about over you, tiring your poor head.[16]

Laura's reply:

> I had hardly hoped to hear from you, for I knew you would be troubled. Sweet, you may or may not ever know the happiness of seeing children of your own about you; but it should give you some idea of what that happiness

is, that in the midst of this pit of torment where I now lie, I can lift a feeble voice and thank heaven for its goodness in blessing me once more ... You must not think the children tumble over me. They are so careful and tender, and even Julia says "Poor mama tick? mama bet-tah!" In gentlest tones.[17]

Flossy's fourth child was due in June 1881 and she was coming to Oak Glen for the birth, an event that Maud apparently wanted to avoid.

Uncle Sam's solution was to send Maud for a visit out west to the San Geronimo Ranch—the home of the Mailliard relations—for which Sam had recently paid off the mortgage. He had also brought Annie Mailliard east so that all four siblings could celebrate Julia's sixty-second birthday, the last time the remaining Ward siblings were to be all together. Maud accompanied her aunt back to California and for their seven-day journey Sam arranged gourmet meals of roast chicken, tongue in aspic, a perfect ham, *pâté de foie gras, marrons glacé,* fresh rolls, then graham loaves—sublimated black bread that had not grown stale in the seven days—and peaches, pears, and apricots were followed by grapes, bananas, dates, and figs. A huge bottle of rose water was provided for swabbing the face when passing through the badlands, where the alkaline water was held to be bad for the complexion.[18] Maud's keen eye recorded the adventure: "We have plunged into the wide, wonderful waste of prairie. Oh the great endless stretches, how wonderful they are, broken by the distant herds of cattle, the poor cabins of the squatters and the white bonneted wagons of the emigrant trains ... !"[19] The two made a detour to the Mormon community in Salt Lake City, Utah, Maud to interview Emmeline B. Wells, editor of the *Women's Exponent*, about "pluralism" in marriage. Wells, an ardent suffragist, was embraced by the radical National Woman Suffrage Association, but not the moderate American Womens Suffrage Association, which Julia Ward Howe had co-founded. Julia's letter to Maud jokingly hoped that the Mormon men would not detain Maud in their territory.[20]

Daisy Terry had visited the ranch the previous summer and referred to it as her "Californian Exile,"[21] but Maud enjoyed the summer's stay and wrote home with a reporter's flair about such topics as the Chinese labor question (the Chinese Exclusion Act was to be passed in 1882), the red dust that forced their carriage to drive at a snail's pace, the incredible redwood trees. Artistically observant as always, she noted the "Bierstadt oak," which the painter had loved, and the beautiful Chinese bronzes and embroideries she saw in shops. "An artistic nation, their sense of color is unsurpassed, though in drawing the Japanese outrank them."[22] Maud's mood must have at least temporarily lightened, as Laura's letter of July 14 to Uncle Sam notes the "return of her buoyant spirits which seemed quite to have left her at one time."[23] Julia's letter of August probably did not make Maud homesick, as her mother described life at Oak Glen: "a storm, warm then cold weather, all the children had diarrhea." A second letter from Julia was far more insightful:

> What am I going to do with you next winter if you continue to have nerves and the like? I fear my darling, that you will never [thrive] in New England. The atmosphere here is all "go"; I am so thankful for the beautiful time you have had in California! Your letter in which you tell me about San Francisco . . . was delightful. And you are wrong about matrimony. You might marry a poor man, because you could help him so much. Have had a dear letter from Jack. Can't write anymore today.[24]

It seems that Jack Elliott might have been part of the reason for Maud's melancholy. Elliott was keeping in touch with the Howe family and had come to visit in the summer of 1880.[25] Born in 1859, Elliott had been orphaned at a young age, but used his considerable wits to educate his younger brother and infiltrate the literary and theatrical world of London in the 1870s. From brief mentions in Maud's biography of her husband's early life, one learns that he was a disciple of the English poet and novelist George Meredith, as well as of Karl Blind, a German revolutionary turned English writer. Somewhere along the road Elliott encountered Edward Shakerley Kemp, a "confirmed bachelor"[26] two decades older than Elliott whose father had been an English land developer and Parliamentarian and left him a modest estate. The two lived and traveled together, enjoying the theater, the art world and museums, and were on their way to Rome when they met up with Maud and Julia in the spring of 1878. After the departure of the women, Elliott continued on in Rome, ingratiating himself with the Terry family and the Storys, and becoming particular friends with Marion Crawford and his half brother Arthur Terry. Likely taken under Julian Story's wing in Paris in 1879, Jack studied at the Academy Julian, associating with the expatriate American art colony there. But it was in Rome where Jack felt most at home; he belonged to the International Artists Club, through which he was introduced to his "master," Don José de Villegas, with whom he began to study. From afar, Maud became increasingly intrigued with this dark, brooding young artist who, unlike most of the young men who wooed her, was willing to sacrifice all worldly goods—or most of them—for his art.

In the fall of 1881 Maud, her mother, and Marion Crawford moved into the well-appointed 241 Beacon Street. Uncle Sam continued his largesse and was a frequent visitor; although he was never able to find the discipline to nurture his own career, Sam was very successful at planting the seeds for success in others. He was intrigued by his nephew, whom he had not seen in years. Both cultivated men in the European mold, Sam had early lost his sons and Marion had lost his father; it seemed natural for them to form a close bond. As Marion entertained Julia and Sam's literary friends—Longfellow, Oliver Wendell Holmes and Thomas Gold Appleton—with tales of his exploits in India, his gifts as a storyteller became readily apparent, and Sam strongly suggested that literature was to be his nephew's path. Sam turned his lobbying skills to Marion's career, giving dinner parties in which he cultivated William Henry Hurlbert, editor of the New York *World,* Thorndike Rice, editor and owner of the *North American Review,* George Jones and Charles de Kay of the *New York Times* and Jeannette Gilder of the *Critic.* "Uncle Do," as Aunt Annie's husband Joseph Mailliard was known, had grown up in Bordentown, New Jersey with the Gilder family and arranged introductions to Jeannette Gilder's better-known brother, Richard Watson Gilder, editor of the newly established *Century Magazine.*[27] Marion Crawford certainly had the backing for his soon-to-be-successful literary career.

In her autobiography Maud writes that she yielded to "the inevitable family calling of literature": in other words, it was rather a last resort. When Julia sat "scribbling" upstairs in their new home, and Marion sat downstairs in the reception room writing reviews for the *Critic* and other articles, it was only natural for Maud to take up her pen. With cues from her mother, in 1882 she began to write "letters" or columns for the newspapers, being at different times the Newport correspondent and the art correspondent. Her uncle's New York connections helped; Whitelaw Reid, editor of the New York *Herald,* critiqued her style:

> General remarks about Newport have been written by everybody for the past 20 years. What we want now is a newsy picture of Newport life, day by day, or of that part of it which the general public wants to hear about — social matters and the chit-chat of society must therefore be largely the staple of such a Newport letter as is suitable for a daily newspaper . . . Naturally we want the social matter as good, natural as possible. At the same time we do not want it to degenerate into adulation. There is an occasional tendency, against which I am sure it is needless to caution you, to set up one of two rather vulgar New York people as the demi-gods of Newport. I have always been especially puzzled to comprehend how that changling cad, Mr. Belmont, got the prominence in anybody's mind that some of the Newport writers seem to give him.[28]

Maud wrote a column called "Newport Breezes" for the *Boston Transcript.* Her miniscule checks often sufficed to buy cigarettes and postage for Marion, who would promptly return the loan when his check from the *Critic* arrived. While Marion was writing erudite book reviews and essays, Maud was often reporting on frivolous events, and a letter from Uncle Sam chastised her for being impatient:

> I quite agree with you that it is wrong to fritter away one's mind upon reports of fashionable nonentities, but remember this gives you dispatch and readiness with the pen and that is an important function in your authorship. You have plenty of time before you, and your granaries are capacious for lots of mind stores. You must read more and read thoughtfully. Discipline of the mind is best attained as in your dear Mother's case, by making yourself a daily task, to read attentively some sound book — not a French novel.[29]

Interestingly Marion did not read much at all; he happened to have a facility with words and languages, and it was probably a purely sexist reason that Sam chose to encourage his nephew in his career more than his literary nieces. Maud wrote, "He looked the whole bunch of us over, as a stock raiser looks over his thoroughbreds, and picked Marion for winner . . . he put his money on Marion." There is some argument as to whether it was Sam or an editor from Macmillan who gave Crawford the advice of writing about his time in India, a move that was to result in the sensationally successful novel *Mr. Isaacs*.[30] Crawford began the book in New York in the spring of 1882 and continued it in Boston, mostly working in the reception room at 241 Beacon. His encouragement came from his relatives, but also from a fairly new acquaintance, the elegant heiress Isabella Stewart Gardner, known as Mrs. Jack. Gardner came into Crawford's life soon after his breakup with Mary Perkins, the daughter of Thomas Handasyd Perkins, Jr., with whom he had mistakenly considered himself affianced. Mrs. Jack, a close friend of the Howe family, was married and fourteen years older than Crawford, but he was drawn to her regal nature, her cosmopolitan lifestyle, and her love of fine art and culture acquired by a European education. For her part, Crawford was a young Adonis, anxious to be educated at her feet.

Mrs. Jack was known to the Howe family as "Kepoura," the Greek name for Gardner, designated by Maud's brother-in-law, Michael Agnanos. Maud's earliest memories of Gardner included seeing her at the old Harvard Music Association Thursday matinees at the Boston Music Hall in the mid-1870s, escorted by her three orphaned nephews.[31] Maud was in awe of Gardner's Worth gowns, her pearl necklaces and her travels; in fact Maud and Julia's trip to the Middle East was likely inspired by Gardner's descriptions from her 1874 pilgrimage. A mutual interest in fine art was also a catalyst for their long friendship; Gardner bought her first painting in 1873, a "modern" Barbizon work by Emile Jacques.[32] But in 1882 there loomed a threat to the Howe-Gardner relationship, when Marion Crawford's friendship with "Belle" Gardner took on a note of impropriety. No stranger to gossip and speculation, Gardner was not concerned that people talked about the amount of time she and Marion spent together, their trip to New York to look at art, their summers together at her Beverly home. Even the worldly Uncle Sam voiced a note of concern in a letter to Julia, "I don't know what will be the outcome of his present *affaire du coeur*. It seems to stimulate him to great efforts—But is this stimulus a healthy one?"[33] In any case, there is little doubt that Gardner's steadfast encouragement and advice helped Crawford publish two very successful novels in a short period of time.[34]

Maud's first novel *A Newport Aquarelle* was published anonymously in mid-1883 by Roberts Brothers, the firm that had recently produced

Julia's *Modern Society*. The book did not have the critical acclaim of *Mr. Isaacs*, but a blurb in the New York *Tribune* noted, "Something of a sensation has been created at Newport by the appearance of a novel . . . The story is accepted as a lampoon on a well-known banker, on a lady of especial prominence in Newport society and on an unobtrusive gentleman who has devoted himself for thirty years to his own amusement and Newport society. This book is generally considered ungracious in its lack of appreciation of the social worth of some of Newport's most entertaining summer residents."[35] The thinly disguised characters supposedly represented Newport banker August Belmont, society leader Mrs. Paran Stevens, social arbiter — and Maud's own second cousin — Ward McAllister, and finally, femme fatale and actress Mrs. James Brown Potter (Cora Urquhart). No wonder the book was anonymous!

Laura was aghast:

> Duchess, You *must* let me know at once, what the word is about the book. If it is absolute denial, well and good; only I must have your authority for it. I don't suppose it will be of much use, as it seems to have been instantly traced home. And do let me know what people say about it in Newport. Harry and I are both delighted with it . . . Harry says I go about clucking infinitely prouder than if I had laid the egg myself! And of course I am! It is a thoroughly bright, charming delightful book my pretty! After seeing and reading it, I beg to withdraw my approval of the Advertiser's notice; I now consider it hoggishly insufficient. And oh how lovely the binding is. Oh dear, I am so happy over it! But I tremble too, for your pen is oversharp, my dearest child, just like your little naughtily two-edged tongue and you should not talk so about Boston if you mean to live there.[36]

On the surface *A Newport Aquarelle* was a parody of social mores and manners in Newport society, characterized by an analogy to the ancient world when Maud wrote: "[Newport] is really sort of a modern Pompeii where all the rich Americans come to play at taking a rest."[37] The book offered historically significant descriptions of local color: tennis and partying at the Newport Casino, horses and their trappings at the polo fields, the unobstructed view to Conanicut Island and Fort Dumpling, picnicking at The Glen. But lest one think the *Aquarelle* was a frivolous work, its autobiographical nature revealed a dark side of Maud that was only hinted at in the family correspondence. Through her twenty-five-year-old heroine, Gladys Carleton, beautiful but without fortune, a New Yorker recently returned from touring Europe with her mother, Maud provides insight into her own feelings of vulnerability, of being unlovable, of her conflicting desires for independence and acceptance, of whether to marry for money or love — or not at all. As Gladys walks by herself in Lawton's Valley and sits "overhanging the waterfall, looking down into the deep pool," she contemplates suicide. "The burden of her life seemed too great for her to bear, and she wept for the emptiness of her lot, of her heart. . . . Why should she not die now? How easy would it be to slip down from the great rock and lose herself in the oblivion of the black pool, with the white foam dancing above her? Who would care much? . . . No one would really miss her. Her mother would grieve a little while, but the other daughters would soon receive the share of affection which the shallow parent had given her."[38]

All the attention on Marion Crawford's success undoubtedly affected Maud's ever-fragile feelings of self-worth. Was her significance only in her beauty? All the biographies of Julia Ward Howe refer to "the beautiful Maud" or characterize her as petulant and problematic. While Uncle Sam was unsure about Maud's calling, he was quite cognizant of her appearance and used her company to his advantage in his business dealings: "I spent three hours with President Arthur who inquired after Maud most particularly." Unsurprisingly to his family, Sam's finances again took a turn for the worse, as he became involved in a questionable scheme to develop a resort at Long Beach on Long Island. He often requested his sister Julia's presence, wearing her black velvet and lace and her mother's diamonds to lend an air of respectability to his ventures,[39] and he just as often asked Maud to join him. Maud freely admits that she was drawn to "Sam's glittering circle as a moth to a candle," but that he did seem a bit conflicted and thought maybe she ought to be "at home working soberly at her writing."[40]

The life at Newport certainly gave Maud fodder for her fiction, but it also provided her with an opportunity to create a picture of a vibrant community, not in paint but in words. In her recollections of authors she had known, her description of the visiting Oscar Wilde is memorable. Wilde, the "apostle of aestheticism," was introduced into New York society in January 1882 by Sam Ward, by way of his London friend, Lord Houghton. Sam was not necessarily looking for notoriety; he respected the accomplishments of the flamboyant literary figure whose accoutrements included a sunflower worn or carried. In a letter to Maud, Sam described his guest: "His make-up is very extraordinary, long black hair hanging to the shoulders, brown eyes, a huge white face like the pale moon . . . , a white waistcoat, black coat and knee breeches, black silk stockings and shoes with buckles. Until he speaks you think him as uncanny as a vampire."[41] Wilde wanted to meet Julia and when he was in Boston was invited for a spur-of-the-moment luncheon, with Marion Crawford, Mrs. Jack, and Julia Romana among others. Julia had first gone to church to deliver a sermon, prompting the frantic Maud to meet her at the door chiding her for leaving her to prepare for the event.[42] Wilde came to Newport in May and again in July, when he spent two days at Oak Glen, to deliver a lecture at the Casino. Maud was not present for either event. Nevertheless, a society column printed a paragraph announcing the engagement of Oscar Wilde and Maud Howe. This was telegraphed to European newspapers, much to the annoyance of Julia and the shock of the family in Italy.[43]

At Oak Glen hung the "classic fragment of two sculptured masks of the comic and the tragic muses," a device used at the meetings of the Town and Country Club. In 1871 Julia Ward Howe established this club to explore the natural treasures offered by the island, apart from the social ones. She recognized that many of Newport's summer visitors were men of science who could enlighten citizens about the area's habitat: "Flowers in season, fish while the waters are warm and clear, rocks while those who can explain their wonderful record are among us." A talk by Maria Mitchell on the planet Jupiter, a lecture on botany at the Paradise Rocks, and a sailing adventure were planned. Literary and artistic offerings would also be part of the club. Maud attended many of the meetings of the Town and Country Club, perhaps enjoying the games of charades and performances most, but learning to appreciate the natural world from marine biologists such as Alexander Agassiz, who took the group to Castle Hill to speak on fishes and deep sea dredging, or Colonel George Waring, who did much work in conquering yellow fever and arranged a field trip to his model farm. The founder of the Massachusetts Institute of Technology,

William Barton Rogers, summered with his wife in Newport and was active in the club's administration, as was fellow abolitionist, feminist, and author Thomas Wentworth Higginson, although he had criticized Julia for entertaining Oscar Wilde. Maud remembered the literary greats who visited: Mark Twain, Bret Harte; the artists and architects John La Farge, William Trost Richards, Richard Staigg, Richard Morris Hunt; and of course the women: Helen Hunt, Kate Field, Sophia Louis Whitwell, Emma Lazurus; and many other prominent Americans. In 1881 Marion Crawford spoke on Italy, but he annoyed Julia by disparaging the current liberal government of which she approved. By the mid-1880s Maud was herself a featured speaker at the Town and Country Club, lecturing over the years on art and literature abroad.

Maud graciously acknowledged her cousin's talents and even reviewed his two books for the *Boston Transcript*. In April 1882 she wrote an article published in the *Transcript* describing an operetta, *Lord Buncombe's Daughter*, with music by Timothy Adamowski and lyrics by Julia Ward Howe,[44] that was so well written it was misattributed to Crawford by a New York *World* editor. It was then syndicated in the *World*, with a congratulatory note to Maud from Uncle Sam: "I rejoice in a success which will make your pen more sought for. I think that meditation and the pressure of practice have improved your style and imparted a grace and ease which only your sex possesses the charm of."[45] Alas, Uncle Sam's frequent admonishments and glamorous lifestyle in New York were soon to be history, as he departed in haste for England in the dark of night, on the advice of his lawyers in November 1882. He had lost his entire fortune and more in the Long Beach scheme and was fleeing from creditors, with a note to Julia to keep mum about his whereabouts. The family was devastated.

Not far behind Sam Ward was Marion Crawford, whose plans for a trip to Japan and India with Belle Gardner and her husband were dispatched in short order. Marion wrote to his mother, "I have suddenly decided to abandon the Japan scheme and to spend the year with you."[46] From Julia came a note to Maud, "You are not, darling to say one word to anyone about Marion's departure. I will explain the reasons why. He has determined to go to his mother. The other party will wish him to go to Japan. He has his reasons for wishing to keep very quiet about his movements.

I am very thankful that he has decided as he has. Cannot say more on paper. *Mum* is the word," and "Marion has now decided to sail on the *Florio* steamer on May 12. I have had some worriment about his plans, but am very glad the Japan trip has been given up, at least by him."[47] Marion Crawford left for England in early May 1883, to join Uncle Sam. Upon his arrival he wrote to Maud. "I must heartily thank you and more truly than I can put into words, for your brave and great help in this trouble. I know that without you the whole thing would have fallen through, and I am most truly grateful."[48] Despite speculation that Crawford and Gardner had a sexual relationship,[49] there is no extant evidence to prove that they had more than a romance based on mutual admiration and intellectual rapport. It seems likely that something or somebody made Crawford realize the error of his ways. Indeed, he wrote to Uncle Sam not to disclose his whereabouts to Gardner and that "there is a time in life when certain things must stop and I think the time has come."[50]

Maud's role in this Victorian melodrama is less than clear. Her romantic nature likely found the relationship a bit titillating, but pious Julia made her see the impropriety of the situation. Maud went to stay with Gardner to "get her through," and ostensibly to keep her from following Crawford. The initial plan for the journey had been for Julia and Maud to accompany Belle and Marion — husband Jack Gardner was not planning on going.[51] Instead, Maud had to content herself with letters from Gardner, describing in detail every locale she visited, from Japan, China, Indonesia and India. Gardner notes repeatedly how glad she is to hear back from "Bacchante," "Beautiful girl," "My dear, dear friend." She writes at the end of 1883, "Goodbye for this year, dear. Be a good girl for the next one, and be ever a friend to me, and may we have many happy days together in the year that is before us." And in March 1884, "How I wish I were in the Boudoir, with you on the little chair opposite to me, and that it was a real talk that we were having — not one of those one-sided things."[52] While she inquired after Crawford and the publication of his fourth book, *To Leeward,* which she wanted Maud to send her,[53] she also asked about the publication of *A Newport Aquarelle* and commented favorably on the subject of her next novel — about California. And as the book progressed, she wrote "I do hope your book will bring in returns of money untold and fame and reputation of the very best kind."[54] From these letters it is obvious that the two were close, that the scandal had not ended the friendship, and that Gardner respected Maud's writing abilities as she had Crawford's. Upon the Gardners' return in July, Julia noted in her journal, "Received a visit from Mrs. Jack Gardner, who has wondrous things to tell of her year and a half of globe-trotting. She carried Maud down to Beverly at 2 pm."[55]

The San Rosario Ranch, the novel that Gardner hoped would make Maud rich and famous like her cousin, was published in late 1884. It was based on Maud's visit to the San Geronimo Ranch in California, but as one reviewer noted, there was not really a ranch, there were no animals mentioned, and the men were not ranchmen; there were artists and lovers, living for a time on the ranch![56] The hero, an artist named John Douglass Graham, seemed to be partially based on Marion Crawford. "The first rays of sun . . . touched his thick brown hair, giving it a glint of bronze, shone on the wide white forehead, flashed into the eyes and showed her for an instance a stern profile, exceedingly beautiful." Graham, educated in Europe, had his studio in San Francisco and lived in a tower on the ranch, part of an old Spanish mission. He had been burned in love and did not want another woman distracting him from his art, but had second thoughts upon meeting the exquisite young Millicent Almsford, born of American parents in Venice, Italy, where she was raised. Carrying a dark secret, she has recently arrived on the ranch visiting the owner, her half brother. The plot not only involved romance and intrigue, but murder and morality. Millicent, it turned out, to escape her father's new wife in Venice, had run off and married, only to find that her new husband still had a wife. Graham finds this out by mistakenly reading her diary—he finds he has been betrayed by a wanton woman! Other recognizable characters included the Shallop family, whose elaborate lifestyle in San Reale came from success in the gold mines; Mrs. Shallop, like the wife of Uncle Sam's benefactor James Keene in Newport, preferred the simplicity of the old days.

The reviewer was correct in noting that *The San Rosario Ranch* was not about ranch life. It was about the old world and the new, about materialism, about culture, and about art. When Millicent arrives at the ranch she wails, "I belong to the land of my birth, where the present is beautiful with the splendors of the past. . . . I hate it, this land, where you all strive for money, not for art."⁵⁷ Both the main characters are conflicted about what is important in life. Millicent's feelings undergo a "radical change ... She was now awakening to the stirring reality of the present and felt dimly that to be an heir to the glories of the past was but a part of living—an inheritance which affects us less than the actual doing and striving of our own times."⁵⁸ Maud's most vivid descriptions were reserved for the artists "of our times": Graham and his fellow artists' studios, the paintings on the easels, artist models (one of whom turns out to be the dastardly murderer of the family servant), the dilemma of painting stifling portraits versus the glorious natural surroundings.

Maud also dealt with gender issues in *The San Rosario Ranch*. Graham identified with machismo, with deerslaying and rough living: "Evil to him appeared abstractly as a female element in the world; and the great qualities of nobility, abnegation and heroism in his eyes were masculine attributes only."⁵⁹ That said, Millicent, an avid swimmer (like Maud herself), saves his life as they swim together in the Pacific. When Graham suddenly disappears from the surface, Millicent dives towards the bottom of the ocean, pulls him up, and orders him: "Put your hand on my shoulder—so, and I will swim below you. Her voice was hoarse and shrill as that of the screaming seagulls. He could not speak, but looked toward the shore as if he would have her save herself and abandon him to his fate. 'No, no!' she cried. 'I *will* save you,' and placing his hands on her shoulders, struck out bravely toward the shore."⁶⁰ But Graham, like Marion Crawford, wants to put women on a pedestal; he does not want to see them as fellow human beings and thus he cannot accept the flaw that he sees in Millicent's deception. However, in her story Maud often has the last say:

> It would have been better for him if he could have learned the lesson which all wise men learn if they live long enough,—that women are neither angels who stand immeasurably above men, nor inferior beings whose place is at their feet, but human like themselves, full of good and faulty instincts and with all their imperfections, the God-given helpmates of man.⁶¹

The San Rosario Ranch, at which Maud labored until it threatened "to swallow [her] up soul and body,"⁶² was received with praise from Laura. Maud often consulted her author sister on her writing and they had argued over the ending, Laura apparently hoping Graham and Millicent would live happily ever after. Maud argued that with the two marrying each other the moral of the story would be lost: "If Graham does not have remorse [for choosing his art over a deceiving woman] where's the moral? Try to think of something but babies and answer me this as you feel."[63] Laura thought the end result was "noble, beautiful, so all I had hoped and expected! The *Aquarelle* was a short flight, a trying the wings with but uncertain fluttering; this is a strong upward flight, with steadfastness in every stroke. You have won your place, my darling, and you need not now have any fear, for it must be secure."[64] Marion Crawford was tactful, but more critical, giving Maud examples of her over-flowery and sometimes ungrammatical language, but most insistent that she use less description and more conversation. The book was noticed in the press and Maud's stature as a writer was definitely elevated.

In the fall of 1884 Julia Ward Howe began preparing for her role as chief of the Woman's Department of the New Orleans Cotton Centennial. Maud was to accompany her mother to New Orleans in December where she was superintendent of the literary division, meaning that she established a library of books by and for women. The six months spent in New Orleans were fraught with problems and controversy, as funds promised for the women's exhibits were not forthcoming, many southern women resented a northerner taking charge — especially one who had written the Civil War anthem for the Union — and the press was less than kind to them. Julia's organizational skills rose to the occasion, however, and Maud was of course enamored by the festivities, Mardi Gras, the balls, the men — "and lovers! Never so many before. At present two safe old married men (old and fat)" who plied her with "bonbons and cakes of soap." Maud had many "lovers" in her life, as did the heroines of her stories, but her definition of lover did not involve physical love. Furthermore, she wrote Laura that her frivolous descriptions were merely for her sister's amusement, and that her work interested her. At the conclusion of the Centennial Maud arranged for the donation of the 1,400 books in her assembled library of women writers to be donated to the Southern Art Union's library, so that they would remain a collection and be useful to the community. She presented the books in "loving remembrance of the long winter of labor and of pleasure."[65]

The Cotton Centennial was the second of three World Expositions that had a profound effect on Maud's life's work. The bringing together of like-minded people, in this case established and emerging writers, was central to her experience in New Orleans. Julia, with Maud's input, started a group of aspiring writers called The Pans, which included two women who were to become successful authors: Grace King and Elizabeth Bisland. Maud prepared a paper on Nathaniel Hawthorne that she read to the group. Two of the esteemed literary figures of the day to visit with The Pans were Charles Dudley Warner and Joaquin Miller. Miller, an eccentric known as "the Poet of the Sierras," molded himself in the frontier image and introduced the Howes to Buffalo Bill, while Warner, familiar to Maud from the Town and Country Club, was a writer and humorist in the vein of his friend Mark Twain. Not invited by The Pans, but brought to the Howes under cover of darkness, was the New Orleans novelist George Washington Cable, controversial for his realistic portrayals of Creole life and racial injustice. Julia's practice of never letting her husband or her friends tell her who she should or should not associate with was having an influence on Maud, who was increasingly comfortable with those persons who did not quite fit the mold—both in her personal life and her novels.

John Elliott did not fit the mold of the respectable suitor, the able provider, or the romantic hero. But he was persistent in his efforts to win over Maud, and in December 1886 she wrote to Laura,

> You will be surprised and I fear a good deal troubled to learn that Jack has come out again, bent on marrying me, and seems likely to carry his point this time. I am sorry sorry that you can't be glad, and so please don't bother to write me anything about it for you couldn't write from your heart and I should feel the effort you would make to say something kind. Only wait until you see him and don't burden your heart or Harry's against him. He isn't a little black beast, he is a true-hearted creature, the only man who has ever really loved the best me. I am full of peace and hope, and the black gulf seems to be all shut over and gone.[66]

Although their romance was long-distance, Maud and Jack had their go-betweens. Jack had endeared himself to Julia both in their initial encounters and in the correspondence they kept. Julia likely recognized that at age thirty-two, Maud should probably commit herself to this devoted man. Uncle Sam Ward, before he died in Rome in 1884, had become attached to Jack and his bohemian enclave of artists—in fact, Sam fit right in! Jack painted a portrait of Sam that is one of the best things he did.[67] One of Sam's letters to Jack indicates the artist's dogged pursuit of Maud: "Commend me to the dear Villegas both, and fag away with your brush, eye and brain until you forget there is such a thing as a woman in the world."[68] The rest of the family members were not so sure. And outsiders were quite blunt: Belle Gardner's husband Jack wrote his brother, "I am disgusted, because he hasn't a copper—He is an Englishman, a painter, and has lived most of his life in Rome—has been in love with her for eight years. I believe they are going to try and live in Boston, at first, and he hopes to get work—house decoration if nothing better offers."[69]

As for Maud, after deliberating for years, she in fact had summed up her feelings as early as 1883 when she wrote in a passage from *A Newport Aquarelle:*

> Now, you have a heart, and were meant to love something and somebody besides yourself. Suppose the man whom you marry is not your young ideal; what of that? All men are troublesome comforts, but it's a great thing to have a companion of your own time, whose interests are one with your own and who will go with you through life.[70]

FIVE

> I could say to any young man or woman at the beginning of the career
> of an artist—"go to Paris to study your profession but come back to America
> to practice it." The best work with few exceptions, done by American artists
> has been done in America: Copley, Stuart, Allston, Hunt, La Farge,
> Fuller, St. Gaudens, Alden Weir, Winslow Homer,
> George Inness have all painted at home.
>
> MAUD HOWE ELLIOTT

IN MARRYING JACK ELLIOTT, MAUD MADE A CONSCIOUS DECISION to forgo the life of Proper Bostonian society, to put work above leisure, and to actively promote the importance of art. Jack Gardner continued his disapproval of the match: "Maud Howe had a pretty wedding and looked very handsome. She had a number of presents and was very pleased with them, but they were neither so numerous nor so handsome as they ought to have been and nothing like what they would have been if she had been or married rich."[1] The ceremony took place at 241 Beacon Street with longtime Unitarian family minister James Freeman Clarke presiding. The wedding and the dress were "startlingly original," as promised by Maud, who "in queenly loveliness stepped forth," emerging from a bamboo curtain parted by nieces Rosalind Richards and Carrie Hall, wearing a gown of white grosgrain satin with duchesse point lace, covered by a tulle veil. The wedding guests stood under a bower of palms and laurel designed by Mrs. Jack and the groom. The couple proceeded to the vocals of *Integer Vitae*, a Horatian ode with lyrics for this occasion by John S. Dwight, Boston's sage of music:²

> With songs of delight, with garlands most bright
> With blessings and prayer salute we the pair
> Whom love shall enfold with a circlet of gold
> These fetters so fine art of metal divine
> May they bind to a peace that shall ever increase
> May they pledge to a faith that is perfect til death.
> To Hymen³ we sing, let the glad echo ring
> Let the strophe resound and good wishes abound.
> Hail Hymen! God Given for Earth and for Heaven.⁴

Maud and Jack went to New York for a brief honeymoon. The city was the center of both the academic and avant-garde American art world, and Maud, initially through Uncle Sam's contacts, had become very familiar with the Tenth Street Studios, the National Academy of Design, and the Metropolitan Museum of Art, founded in 1870. The home of Mary Cadwalader Jones at 21 East Eleventh Street was a hub of artistic importance where Marion Crawford had been especially welcome. As a child Marion had known Mary in Italy. Mary was the wife of Frederick Rhinelander Jones, brother to Edith Wharton; she was a good friend to John La Farge and held weekly Sunday luncheons that Crawford often attended, as did Maud when in New York. There she dined with such other habitués as John Singer Sargent, Augustus Saint-Gaudens and La Farge, "with his strange myopic eyes," at a "table with its fine linen cloth, sparkling crystal, ancient silver . . ."⁵ Another New York haunt frequented by La Farge, St. Gaudens, and architect Stanford White was the carriage-house home of editor Richard Watson Gilder and his wife, the former Helena de Kay, an artist said to have been the muse of Winslow Homer. It was in their studio home on Fifteenth Street, years before Maud and Jack were part of their salon, that a plot to unsettle the National Academy of Design came into being.

Maud's newspaper letters and columns had been focusing increasingly on the arts. "Much of my *Transcript* work was art reviewing. Among other artists, this brought me in touch with John La Farge, Augustus Saint-Gaudens, Albert Ryder, and Charles Walter Stetson. I was one of the first writers to cry aloud the excellence of the work of these and many another American artist, and was, in consequence, *persona grata* at the studios."[6] Work by these and other artists who had absorbed "foreign" influences—looser brushwork, sketchy drawing, indistinct compositions—was sometimes rejected by the strict jury for the National Academy annual exhibitions. Both Julia and Maud Howe were champions of the more "poetic" and natural style, espoused by the paintings of their friend William Morris Hunt, and his sometime student in Newport, La Farge. In 1875 Helena Gilder, Hunt, La Farge, and others staged a *salon des refusés* at the gallery of Daniel Cottier; two years later this same group formed the American Art Association, whose name changed to the Society of American Artists, in 1878.

One of the biggest advocates of this modern approach to art was *New York Times* art critic Charles de Kay, brother of Helena. Their mother, Janet Drake de Kay, was an old friend of the Howes, a guest at Maud's wedding, and the widow of a naval officer who had fought for Greece's independence along with Samuel Gridley Howe. Janet de Kay was likely one of many who provided entrée for Maud into New York's art world. In 1883 Maud had noted: "To New York to see Mrs. de Kay. There was the fall opening of the Academy of Design, there was the opening of the great Metropolitan Opera House—all of which I was asked professionally to see and report on."[7] Charles de Kay wrote poetry as well as a novel titled *The Bohemian: A Tragedy of Modern Life;* most passionately he championed an artist more bohemian than most—Albert Pinkham Ryder. With de Kay, Maud visited Ryder in his third-floor studio in a Washington Square brownstone. The artist, from New Bedford, Massachusetts, was stirring up controversy with his moody, poetic paintings of shadowy forms, but, according to his critics, he totally lacked drawing skills. Maud recognized that in Ryder's case it was his use of color and thick glaze—not detailed drawing—that imparted the design and the mood and "gave an almost enameled look to his pictures." At the time of her visit in 1883, *Pegasus* was on the easel, a celebrated work that was later dedicated to de Kay.[8] Maud wrote that she was one of Ryder's early discoverers and acquired his *Macbeth and the Witches:* "I have the pleasure of living with one of Ryder's moonlight scenes, a strange picture rich and fantastic as a vision form of hasheech. The moon is rising between two black hills. The sky is darkly blue, and the river which runs toward you through the middle of the canvas is suffused with the golden moonlight. In the side of the stream is a mounted horseman and in the other are dimly seen the figures of three dancing hags. It is the moment when Macbeth crossing the dreamy heath meets the weird sisters."[9] Unfortunately Maud sold the painting before it "was recognized as a gem of great price."

Another artist favored by de Kay for his rich tonal color and softly contoured, moody landscapes was Charles Walter Stetson, from Providence, Rhode Island. De Kay wrote that "an individuality of the finest caliber was gradually asserting itself among American colorists," that Stetson "was a colorist bold beyond the ordinary," and that "pictures such as he paints are the horror of all well-regulated academical artists . . ."[10] Maud knew Stetson both in Boston and later in Rome, and she regularly visited his studio and exhibitions. Stetson, like Maud, was insecure about his profession, and after an exhibition at the Boston Art Club, he was thrilled that Maud had written about his work in the *Boston Transcript:* "Mr. Stetson's *Beggar in a Pleasure Garden* is especially admired, both for its rich coloring and poetic composition." The exhibition was a success, the painting was sold "thanks to the enthusiasm of Maud Howe Elliott, one of the first persons to recognize Stetson's 'genius'"[11] In 1884, in order to lighten their mood on a dismal day, Julia and Maud visited a Stetson exhibition at Noyes and Blakeslee in Boston and bought "two small watercolors, very cheap. Maud's cost $10 and mine $15."[12]

George Fuller was an artist who epitomized the "poetic" in his figurative landscapes, who expressed an internal response to the natural world rather than an ordered external perspective. Moreover, he was a thoroughly American artist who after an early career as a National Academician had been painting away in near obscurity on his farm in Deerfield, Massachusetts, content to work from his "Mistress Nature, above all else." Lucy Derby had taken Maud to visit Fuller when he reappeared on the art scene in Boston in 1876, after the failure of his farm. Maud used Fuller's story in her later lectures on "showing our love for art" to emphasize the true artistic temperament:

She [Lucy Derby] was determined to find out who this George Fuller with his glorious misty color, his golden warmth, his originality, his unconventional and striking manner might be. She kept up her search and finally got at these facts concerning George Fuller. He was no fledgling artist just back from Paris, with the method of such and such a master sticking out all over his work, he was an American painter, fifty-four years of age, who from his eighteenth year had devoted himself to art. These were rather staggering facts to our young enthusiast, but she had faith in herself, she knew that she was not mistaken, and that if this man had painted for nearly half a century without recognition, he was still a great painter, one of the few men of original artistic genius our country has produced. [He had traveled to Europe] . . . When he came back to the United States in 1860 he did not do the thing we are so sadly familiar with, set up a studio in New York and engage a corps of trumpeters to announce to the world how many orders he had and what a great price he was paid for his work!—no he went quietly back to the old homestead at Deerfield . . .

Lucy Derby had established a long friendship with Fuller, had brought her "rich friends" to buy his work, had encouraged him in his devotion to his art. The moral of this story was to support our American artists, as Derby had "shown her love for art to a noble end."[13]

This rapt respect for artistic genius and integrity is a characteristic of Maud's art writing: definitely flowery, but building public appreciation for American art. These stylistic tendencies also make it possible to attribute with some sureness many of the "art notes" in the *Boston Transcript* and other newspapers, which did not usually provide bylines in the 1880s. A review of William Picknell's landscapes at Williams and Everett is almost certainly Maud's: "Boston cannot too earnestly congratulate herself that her rising generations of new artists can maintain her traditional renown. The sturdy, unfaltering technique, the realistic delineation, the perfection of detail in either of the two great canvases [of Picknell's], are of the best modern school; but beyond and above all that are the genuine artistic motive and feeling, the elevated tone of the true priest's of Nature's worship, which no school can impart, but which must be inborn and nourished by the atmosphere of refined and earnest love of nature and truth, such as is breathed in Emerson's pages."[14] Emerson was Maud's favorite writer.

Maud was prescient in her appreciation for John Singer Sargent. "John Sargent that daring painter with whose work [by which] we have been dazzled and puzzled, is unquestionably one of our strongest men. His techniques in color, his tremendous dash and go procedure produce a great impression on the beholder. His portraits are unequalled."[15] In her artist reminiscences Maud later wrote that Benjamin Curtis Porter was eclipsed by John Singer Sargent as a painter of Boston society women. It was in 1888 that Sargent returned to New England from London to paint, among others, Isabella Stewart Gardner, to whom he had recently been introduced by Henry James. Sargent told Maud that he always painted the face in his portraits at one sitting, but that he had painted and scraped out Mrs. Jack's face nine times before he was satisfied.[16] The portrait was very controversial for its décolleté, and hundreds of people crowded into the St. Botolph's Club to view it.[17] Julia Ward Howe thought that the portrait, subtitled "Woman—An Enigma," had "great artistic merit and great faults of taste," and that it was, like other Sargent portraits of women, much too brazen.[18] By the late 1880s Gardner was friend to American artists, notably Sargent, Whistler, and her special protégée, Dennis Miller Bunker. Bunker, who had been taken in tow by Porter to meet "the *grand monde* of Boston" and see "gallons of the blue blood of Beacon Street," likely met Gardner at the same time he met Maud, whom he characterized as "a delightful and sympathetic person . . . she is solid on St. G [Saint Gaudens] and likewise on Thayer, so I naturally froze to her at once."[19] Bunker and Sargent were fast friends, painting in Europe together before the former's untimely death in 1890. In 1939 when she published her earlier notes on artists she had known, Maud correctly noted that Sargent was out of favor, but his time would come again.

Maud began incorporating artists into her fiction in the mid-eighties. "Flower o' the May," published in *Godey's Magazine*, told the story of Mrs. Janderson, a rich, unhappy widow from Denver. "She had no friends, she said, and for the last six months she had no lovers . . . 'I am growing old, 38 at my next birthday, waist measures two inches larger than last winter, gained 15 pounds.'" Indeed, "Poor Mrs. Janderson! These griefs were real enough to her; and without doubt, many another woman is suffering from just such troubles. At the same moment, women too, who like Mrs. Janderson, have had locked up in some back closet of their inner consciousness griefs of a deeper and darker nature than such mere surface troubles as increasing bulk, larger circumference and a lack of suitors." To take her mind off herself, she responds to an ad in the newspaper about purchasing an artist's work:

> Mrs. Janderson knew nothing about art. In Denver, where she had passed the last fifteen years of her life, it is not yet considered necessary to have the names of some half dozen of the more prominent French painters at the tip of one's tongue, nor to discourse familiarly of the comparative merits of Corot or Rousseau. She had not formed an opinion for or against Whistler or the French Impressionists and could not have told the difference between a Burne-Jones and a Millais. Such works of art as hung in her house had been put there along with the carpets and furniture by a fashionable decorator. She had never to her knowledge seen an artist. This gave a spice of romance to her charitable intention of benefiting the poor man, to sell his pictures to pay his rent. She was anxious to do a kind action, and glad that in doing it she was about to enter an unknown and interesting sphere.[20]

The "poor man" is instead a young woman of about twenty. May Flower — the name pinned on her cradle when she was left at the orphanage — is a bohemian artist who brings sensitivity, warmth and true meaning into the barren life of Mrs. Janderson — who coincidentally had an illegitimate baby approximately twenty years earlier! May Flower, symbolizing the beauty and benevolent nature of art, adds balance to the affluent but empty life of Mrs. Janderson.

"Flower o' the May" also shed light on Maud's family life and her parents' marriage. Mrs. Janderson "had quite enough of love, long and long ago. And enough of marriage too, for that matter. Ten years of most unblissful wedded life had given her a decided distaste for matrimony."[21] "Unblissful wedded life" is certainly what Julia Ward Howe had endured for many years, as the wife of the egotistical Chev. When Mrs. Janderson's lawyer advises her not to adopt May Flower in case of inheritance problems if she remarries, she answers, "I shall not marry again, Mr. Browne, . . . I shall not give up the full control of my property. It was too well earned for that." Julia was forced to earn a paltry living from lecturing for the rest of her life because her husband had been able to control — and spend—her fortune. And it becomes a little clearer why Maud married a man who lacked the magnetism and forceful personality of her father—two characteristics that she herself possessed in abundance.

Atalanta in the South, published in 1886, was a romance based on Maud's six-month stay in New Orleans. In the novel she tackles northern and southern relations following the Civil War, class distinctions, gender issues, interracial love, murder—and art. At the heart of the story is Margaret Ruysdale, a young sculptor who is trying to fulfill her father's lost hopes of artistic glory. Stuart Ruysdale, a northerner, had been an artist with a mission: "to nourish that love of the beautiful which is latent in the hearts of men, and to develop sculpture, the greatest of the arts, in his native country, from which he held that all that is best must be evolved, and into which it cannot be imported."[22] The Civil War ended his dreams when he lost his right arm and maimed his body in combat. Father and daughter have now come to New Orleans for his health; she, having studied in Europe, is at work on a sculpture of the elusive mythical Atalanta. Immediately Margaret is surrounded by suitors and subterfuge; shall she chose the respectable French doctor Philip Rondolet, or the more intriguing Creole adventurer Robert Feurandent, who models for her sculpture? Both men, friends since childhood, have been involved in a mysterious subplot involving a beautiful mulatto sister, a duel to the death, and a missionary priest in the woods. Atalanta, symbolizing Margaret's persona, was a mythic Greek woman who, although feminine, struggled with gender roles and had a conflicted relationship with her father, King Iasus. Margaret, having received her first commission, realizes that she is more than a tool for her father's frustrated aspirations: "All was now changed. Her individuality must play its part, she would be held responsible for her work, and her brain alone must direct her hand. For the first time in her life she felt the creative force in herself." Notwithstanding several ethical dilemmas, she also chooses the more unconventional man for her husband.

This idea of the artist as a nonconformist, as true to him- or herself, as above crass materialism, was an ever-growing theme in the art world, a reaction to the indecent display of wealth and ostentatiousness seen so often in New York and Newport among the new robber barons. Maud's diary showed her awareness of this idea, where she noted that Frank Lent's essay on "Success in Art" divided artists into two lots—those who strive for popularity and those who paint for art's sake. Artists face a forked road: one side leads to glory, the other to prosperity. In his novel *The Bohemian: A Tragedy of Modern Life,* Charles de Kay created a community of artists similar to the ones who sought out his sister and brother-in-law's salon in Washington Square. Maud concurred: "It is the curse of American life that most of us try and serve both God and Mammon.... The increase in luxury is largely responsible for this.... Disastrous as this course is to all men whose work is intellectual, to the artist it is suicidal! How many brilliant starts we see made among our young men who begin their career fired with enthusiasms and how few there are like Fuller who reach the full growth they were destined to reach. The moment a man admits that there is a commercial side to his art he puts his neck into the millstone that will drag him down into mediocrity—he best go hang himself; or earn his living as Fuller did as a farmer, or Thoreau, by making lead pencils, anything rather than prostitute his art by using it for potboiling!"[23]

No doubt the romantic notion of noble but poor artists was attractive to Maud. Of John Graham, the artist protagonist of *The San Rosario Ranch,* she wrote: "The painting of a picture was to him of more importance than its sale; the conception of a work more than its accomplishment. His enthusiasm was apt to wane as his picture neared completion."[24] As for Margaret Ruysdale, "it would be hard to imagine a person to whom the possession of wealth was of less importance."[25] And so in her own nonfiction life, Maud rationalized her marriage to a poor but honorable artist, despite having had affluent and formally educated suitors galore. She was now married to "a true-hearted" soul; she considered it her duty to support Jack in his artistic inclinations, to soothe his doubts and insecurities, to nurture his genius. Time was to test this vision of her husband, but as a young newlywed, she was in awe of the possibilities. Jack had a red chalk drawing of an "ideal head," actually a portrait of Maud surrounded by honeysuckle and hawthorn blossoms done shortly after they met. Maud used her contacts with Joseph Millet (brother of the artist Frank), who owned a printing business, to reproduce an edition of the drawing on fine paper. In the accompanying advertisement, Maud wrote, "It is characteristic both of Jack and the printer that no reference is made ... to the price of the print."[26]

Maud began to explore the idea of money as the root of all evil in other writing: a story called "Phil Owens—A Life Sketch,"[27] and a novel *Mammon* (later published as *Honor*).[28] *Mammon*, set in Washington Square, in New York City, involved greed and corruption among Wall Street brokers, land speculators, mining officials, not to mention a society that "worshipped not the God of the Christians, but the God of Mammon." This time the heroine, Honor Greyerston, was not an artist but a musician, who is jilted by her fiancé when her father loses his fortune on Wall Street. In her loveless marriage to her father's stockbroker, she holds salons where she admits "a few painters, men and women, who in her eyes were real artists."[29] Apart from a morality tale, *Mammon* offers a glimpse of a world that Maud knew: she draws from her Uncle Sam's misfortunes, the mining descriptions enhanced by her brother, Harry Howe, a nationally prominent mining engineer; the Ward family's financial ups and downs in banking, and her own experience in the literary and artistic salons of New York City.

As her fourth out of five novels, however, *Mammon* signaled the beginning of the end for her romantic fiction. Maud, now married and approaching forty, seemingly had a grasp on her life's work, and she was less inclined to write about young heroines who were filled with doubts, torn between true love and money, and rootless in a hostile world. And she also became a bit discouraged with some of the critical reviews of her novels. Her cousin Crawford had initially told her with *The San Rosario Ranch*, that she needed to have less description and more character development through conversation. Now Ernest Rhys, an English editor, who had enjoyed the imaginative flights of fancy in *Atalanta in the South*, implied that in general, and specifically in *Mammon*, Maud used so many adjectives that she often hid her "native turn of expression. Anyone can accumulate adjectives; no one can write like Miss Maud Howe when she is at her best—terse, idiomatic and facile." Rhys told her that Hastings Delavale, a character in *Mammon*, was "too superlatively handsome: 'every attitude he took had the classic beauty of the Greek ideals.' Angels and devils—you idealize them both too much, I imagine, for modern fiction."[30]

But one more novel offered Maud the chance to draw from her experiences in Europe, to depict beautiful and idealistic young heroes and heroines and to impart her belief in the power of art. In *Phillida*—a name of Greek origin—Maud contrasted the life of the idle rich, in the persona of one extremely handsome Sir John Lawton of Lawton's Manor, with the low-key, bohemian existence of his cousin and best friend Armydis, the artist. Coming between the two is Phillida, a young American beauty, brought up on a ranch in the West, cultured and educated, who falls passionately in love with Sir John, undeterred by his marriage to another woman. Armydis, although he has inherited a modest amount of money, works hard at his craft: "Armydis was awake and at work an hour before the usual time of rising. By noon he had put in a good day's stint."[31] His colleagues in his studio are the Italian sculptor Gino and the painter "Rakescrape, a poor devil of an artist." Unshaven, reeking of pipe tobacco, this character was perhaps based on Albert Ryder. Phillida and her relatives plan a visit to see these "real Bohemians"; she asserts that artists are the most interesting people in the world.[32] Taking a leaf out of Maud's own story, Phillida tells Armydis, with whom she develops an easy rapport, "I have always wanted to be a painter . . . I think I have it in my soul, but not in my fingers."[33] Ultimately, Sir John turns out to be a cheating cad who sails off on his yacht, only to meet his end in a disaster at sea, redeeming himself by giving the last life preserver to a young Egyptian boy. Phillida, meanwhile, has realized that it was Armydis she has loved all along, and the two find happiness together.

There were a number of influences that ultimately led to Maud's transition from fiction to nonfiction writing. Undoubtedly she was frustrated by Marion Crawford's succession of bestselling novels. Ernest Rhys pointed out that Maud was perhaps not introspective enough to write good fiction; "I am afraid you have not time or artistic stimulus enough in the restless world of American life, with all the social distraction that can't be escaped. The work of Hawthorne shows the value of a certain seclusion."[34] She also witnessed her sister Laura attain great respect and popularity for her children's stories and nonsense verse. Another literary influence in her life was Margaret Deland, a close friend and novelist who achieved a sensation in 1888 with her first novel, *John Ward, Preacher*. Deland's fiction dealt with social and economic issues, and Maud read all her books. "I rarely knew what my sisters, my mother, or Crawford were writing, and more rarely read their books when they were published. With Margaret the case was different. Here were deep, unsuspected springs of prejudice and tradition. Southern and Middle States instincts—her people had been slave owners—unlike any I had ever known."[35]

Deland set a standard for Maud. She was a married woman who was not afraid to succeed on her own merits. She had a supportive husband: "Lorin Deland was one of few men who did not resent his wife's greater reputation. He did not mind being spoken of as 'the husband of Margaret Deland.' He was far prouder of her than she was of herself."[36] Deland was a liberal Unitarian who advocated for unwed mothers and atheists in her writing; she worshipped Julia Ward Howe, to whom she was introduced by Maud's old friend Lucy Derby. In many ways Maud's consciousness was being raised about the role of women, about suffrage. Julia notes with glee in her journal how Maud changed her mind about the militant suffragist and women's advocate Mary Livermore, whom she had previously been "prejudiced against."[37] Maud's portrayal of women artists in her fiction was the beginning of her advocacy for them. Subsequently she began to realize how the right government can affect change and progress on many levels.

It was at this time of Maud's awakening interest in the cross-pollination of art, literature, women's rights and progressive politics that she and Jack found themselves relocated to the dynamic city of Chicago. Jack had actually been carrying out a commission for interior decoration in Chicago during the months prior to their marriage. This was a ceiling mural and frieze titled *The Story of the Vintage,* for the new Potter Palmer mansion on Lake Shore Drive, designed by Henry Ives Cobb. This commission put Maud in touch with Bertha Honoré Palmer, the master organizer who was to head the Woman's Department at the upcoming World's Columbian Exposition to be held in Chicago. Palmer opened doors for the Elliotts among the elite of Chicago society, and Maud found herself entering the lecture field, seemingly the ideal vocation for a woman of great presence, oratory power, dramatic flair, and a message of the importance of the arts to society.

SIX

The greatest art the world has ever known is the Greek.
The greatest period of Greek art was in the time of Pericles . . .
Under the reign of Pericles peace was restored to Athens . . . Mankind
reached its greatest intellectual development. The race was in its prime, steeled
to any task by its hardy, vigorous youth, strong in body and mind.
Out of the glorious peace rose up those monuments of art
before which we kneel today.

MAUD HOWE ELLIOTT

THE CITIZENS OF CHICAGO WERE ELATED WHEN IT WAS ANNOUNCED in 1889 that the World's Columbian Exposition would be held there. The city had bounced back after a disastrous fire in 1871 and now it would be the site of this extravaganza of nationalist pride, a chance to show the world just how advanced was the civilization of the United States. Director General George Davis spoke: "The ceaseless, resistless march of civilization westward—ever westward—has reached and passed the Great Lakes of North America . . . what we are and what we possess as a nation is not ours by purchase, not by conquest, but by virtue of the rich heritage that was spread out beneath the sun and stars . . . by the gift of the Infinite."[1] The chief of construction for the Exposition was Daniel H. Burnham. He was to project the ideal city, a harmony of beauty, classicism and order. Fittingly, the bevy of neoclassical palaces came to be called The White City. The Exposition became controversial for The Midway, the carnival-like display of people of different ethnicities—treated as savages or exotics—from around the world. But the fair also brought together women in a slightly less controversial contingency, one in which Maud was to play a role.

Setting the stage for Maud's accomplishments in Chicago was the commission that her husband had received from Bertha Honoré Palmer, the wife of successful dry goods merchant Potter Palmer. She had hired the firm of Herter Brothers, fresh from their decoration of William H. Vanderbilt's home in New York City, to oversee the décor of her mansion being built on Chicago's newly developed Lake Shore Drive. Herter Brothers, under Christian Herter, had been known for their furniture and fine craftsmanship, but by the 1880s they were also commissioning painters and paintings; how they became aware of Jack Elliott is not clear, but it was likely through a Howe/Ward connection in Newport or New York. In November 1886 Jack received a letter from Herter Brothers commending him for his dining room ceiling design *The Vintage,* and letting him know how pleased Mrs. Potter was with the work. It was at a dinner party at the Palmers that guest William Pretyman, an adventurous English artist and decorator, saw and admired the dining room mural. He chatted about it with his dinner partner, Jean (Mrs. John B.) Sherwood, a women's activist who put him in touch with the Howes, and Pretyman invited Jack to come work for him in Chicago.

Although Jack had been pursuing his art in Rome, the heart of the Christian world, the influences in his decorative work were decidedly pagan. Maud attributed his festive theme of the Dionysian rites to his recent participation in the art festivals at Cevara, an enchanted town of grottoes on the Roman Campagna, to which the artists paraded while clad in togas, playing pipes (Jack played a mandolin), and presumably drinking wine. The mural involved laughing cupids gathering the grapes and making the wine. Pretyman had arrived in Chicago in 1887 with his beautiful American wife, Jenny, and daughter, and he invited Maud and Jack to live with them in their new residence. They soon retreated to the suburb of Lake Forest, a bit cooler in the summer than Chicago but thirty miles removed. Jack now had to commute to a Chicago office building where Pretyman had outfitted a studio. After doing some religious drawings for a prospective church project, Jack began work on *The Progress of Love,* a series of decorative panels for the Perry Smith house, as well as "several other canvases, executed under the lash of Pretyman's strong will and finished little to Jack's satisfaction." Pretyman apparently ran a tight ship, and it was not to Jack's liking, or as Maud put it, "Jack was a sensitive artist with more of poetry than of business in his make-up."[2]

Maud, however, found Chicago inspiring: "I belong to a lunch club, very select—in fact I am one of the select women of Chicago! Begorra!" Maud protested (a bit too much) that she was forced to perform "the great society act" for Jack's business prospects; it was probable that like her mother she found the round of luncheons, receptions, and visits very stimulating for her own self-worth and aspirations as well as those of her husband. "I am considered a success ... I believe. Hectic! The most hectic, breathless life I ever led—but in many ways delightful."[3] She entered the lecture field, launching a series of talks on literature in the spring of 1889 at the "very swell" George Armours, of meatpacking fame. She spoke on "Literature of New England," "Our Southern Literature," "The West in Literature," "The Metropolitan School (New York)," "Has America Produced a Poet?," "English Poets," "English Novelists," "France in Literature Today," "Dawn of Russian Literature," and "Contemporaneous Russian Writers."[4] Like a nervous stage mother, Julia stopped in Chicago on her way back from her own lecture trip in April 1889 and observed, "Maud's performance was very good. She read with great spirit some scenes from *Taras Bulba* and her own comments on various Russian authors were in my opinion, very creditable. I could not help being very anxious for her only through a natural instinct."[5] Maud spent the summer of 1889 in Newport, and gave the lecture on southern literature to Newport audiences for a meeting of the Town and Country Club at the home of Mrs. James Van Alen.[6]

By 1890 Maud was finding her place in the American Renaissance, that period in which America would create its own unique art and architecture based on prototypes from the past. Thus her insistence in her novels, critical writing, and now her lectures that American artists study from the classical ideals of Greece and Rome, and also of the Italian Renaissance, but come home to create a national art. She explained this in a series of lectures delivered to elite Chicago audiences in the fall of 1890: "The Growth of Art," "Foreign Art in America," "Our American Artists," and "The Ethics of Art."[7] Her reasoning was that these native American artists would be better able to interpret their own familiar landscapes, and have a greater sympathy and understanding with portraying American genre scenes. To strengthen the profession, Maud emphasized the need for national standards in the instruction and exhibition of American art. She expressed her view that "there is too much getting the opinion of Europe—we must 'strike' for the opinion of our own—we must educate the public. We must root out the popular and establish the exclusive. We must teach our buyer what to buy—that lesson lies with the artists. We may write lectures, patronize an exhibit, but it is the artist who must reform art, and give it its true place and dignity. We can help a little but what a very little!"[8]

One of the ways Maud helped was to visit artists' studios, museums, collectors, and dealers. She noted in her "to do" list for the month of January, 1890, during which she was staying with her mother in Boston, "See the Art Museum in Boston. Quincy Shaw's pictures at Athenaeum!; Visit Sears pictures; Ask Mrs. Jack—Mention bas relief; See Metropolitan Museum; Vanderbilts; See studios of all possible painters: St. Gaudens, Ryder, Sargent, Shirlaw, Chase, see picture dealers and exhibitions; Cottier. Art periodicals."[9] In one of her lectures she offered her thoughts on the Metropolitan Museum, which she said "is very sure to possess in time a fine collection of works of art. The foundation of a famous collection has been laid here, and [although] the museum still contains much that it could better dispense with, it is on the whole a most encouraging place for lovers of art to visit."[10] She emphasized that it is our civic duty to embrace art and artists, citing Henry Marquand, a financier, Newport neighbor, art collector, and later president of the Metropolitan Museum, as "one of the most intelligent and public-spirited citizens who ever served the cause of art." Marquand apparently acquired and donated the original Luca della Robia maiolica altarpiece to the museum, while having a replica made for his own house. "The spirit which prompted Mr Marquand to give the original to the people, while keeping a mere copy for his own delight, does not need my comment or praise." Maud encouraged her audiences to makes sacrifices for art's sake. "Go without wine and buy a beautiful statue. Go without a fine dress and buy a good picture. Study the works of art that you possess or that your friends possess. A good picture, like a good person, grows dearer and dearer the better we know it."[11]

PLATE 2.
Laura and Maud, 1885. The Yellow
House Papers: the Laura E. Richards
Collection, Gardiner Library Association
and Maine Historical Society, Coll.
2085, Record Group 10B

PLATE 1.
Maud, stereopticon slide by
A. D. Handy of Boston showing
her in Grecian costume, c.1880. The
Yellow House Papers: the Laura
E. Richards Collection, Gardiner
Library Association and Maine
Historical Society, Coll. 2085, Record
Group 15A, F.20

PLATE 3.
Samuel Gridley Howe with
granddaughter Alice Richards, 1873.
The Yellow House Papers: the Laura E.
Richards Collection, Gardiner Library
Association and Maine Historical
Society, Coll. 2085, Record
Group 34, F.5

PLATE 4.
The Howe children, 1869, Harry
and Laura standing, Flossy and
Julia Romana, middle, sitting, Maud
in plaid, below. The Yellow House
Papers: the Laura E. Richards
Collection, Gardiner Library
Association and Maine Historical
Society, Coll. 2085, Record
Group 34, F.5

PLATE 5.
Maud, on "Golden Special" train, campaigning for presidential candidate Charles Evans Hughes, 1916. The Yellow House Papers: the Laura E. Richards Collection, Gardiner Library Association and Maine Historical Society, Coll. 2085, Record Group 15A, F.20

PLATE 6.
Julia Ward Howe at work, 1900s. The Yellow House Papers: the Laura E. Richards Collection, Gardiner Library Association and Maine Historical Society, Coll. 2085, Record Group 10A

PLATE 7.
Maud, 1928. Photograph by Bachrach,
Newport Art Museum Archives

PLATE 8.
Maud, from a crayon drawing by Benjamin Curtis Porter, 1870s. Reproduced from Maud Howe Elliott, *Three Generations*

PLATE 9.
Miss Maud Howe and Her Dog Sambo, 1876, by Benjamin Curtis Porter, reproduction used to illustrate her article "My Friends, the Dogs." Portrait deaccessioned from Corcoran Gallery of Art, present location unknown

PLATE 10.
Portrait of Maud Howe Elliott, 1877, by Benjamin Curtis Porter. Newport Art Museum, purchased from the Museum of Fine Arts, Boston, 1993, through the generosity of many donors, particularly R. Campbell James

PLATE 11. Maud, 1880s, by John Elliott. Newport Art Museum, Bequest of Grisella Hall Kerr

PLATE 12. Maud, 1880s, by John Elliott. Newport Art Museum, bequest of Grisella Hall Kerr

PLATE 13
Maud at an unknown exhibition, c. 1905. Photograph by Jesse Tarbox Beals; Newport Art Museum Archives

PLATE 14.
241 Beacon Street, Boston, reception room with portrait of Maud.
Reproduced from Maud Howe Elliott, *Three Generations*

PLATE 15.
Portrait of Uncle Sam Ward, 1884
by John Elliott. Reproduced
from Maud Howe Elliott,
Three Generations

PLATE 16.
Portrait of Maud Howe Elliott, 1939,
by Adele Herter. Courtesy of Society
of Four Arts, Palm Beach, gift of
Mrs. Lorenzo E. Woodhouse

PLATE 17.
Portrait of Maud Howe Elliott, 1894, by José de Villegas. Sold at auction from collection of family, present location unknown

PLATE 18.
Portrait of John Elliott, 1894, by José de Villegas. Sold at auction from collection of family; present location unknown

PLATE 19.
Portrait of Maud Howe Elliott,
1937, by Mabel Norman Cerio.
Newport Art Museum, gift of
Patricia Hall Saunders

PLATE 20.
Portrait of Maud Howe Elliott, 1938, by Durr Freedley (unfinished owing to the artist's death). Newport Art Museum, purchased by the Art Association of Newport, 1938

PLATE 21. *Diana of the Tides* (Study), by John Elliott. Newport Art Museum, purchased by the Art Association of Newport from the Memorial Exhibition, 1925

PLATE 22.
The Ocean Giant, 1909, illustration for *The Great Sea Horse*, 1909, by John Elliott. Newport Art Museum, gift of Ellicott Wright

PLATE 23.
Old Man of the Sea's Ransom,
1909, illustration for *The Great
Sea Horse*, 1909, by John Elliott.
Location unknown

PLATE 24.
The Fairy Admiral, 1909, illustration
for *The Great Sea Horse*, 1909,
by John Elliott. Location unknown

PLATE 25.
Portrait of Julia Ward Howe,
by John Elliott, copied from 1861
daguerreotype. Newport Art
Museum, gift of Rosalys Hall

PLATE 26.
Francis Marion Crawford, 1877, photographer unknown. Reproduced from Maud Howe Elliott, *Three Generations*

PLATE 27.
The Triumph of Time (detail, Maud), 1894–1900, by John Elliott. Photo by author; courtesy of Boston Public Library

PLATE 28.
The Triumph of Time, 1894–1900,
by John Elliott. Photo by author;
courtesy of Boston Public Library

PLATE 29.
Cover illustration for *Phillida*, 1891,
artist unknown

PLATE 30.
Maud at Lilliput, with painting *The Making of the First Musical Instrument* [Pan] by John Elliott. Photograph by Carl Thorp, 1930s; Newport Art Museum Archives

PLATE 31.
Samuel Gridley Howe, by John Elliott, from a photograph by John Adams Whipple. Reproduced from Maud Howe Elliott, *Three Generations*

PLATE 32.
Maud and John on the terrace, Palazzo Rusticucchi, 1894–1900. Courtesy of Newport Historical Society, gift of Rosalys Hall

PLATE 33. Maud's 90th birthday celebration at the Art Association of Newport, 1944. Newport Art Museum Archives

PLATE 34.
John Elliott at age 22, 1881.
Reproduced from Maud Howe
Elliott, *Three Generations*

PLATE 35.
Maud (with Miss Gilbert and Maxim Karolik) speaking on WPRO, Old Colony House, Newport, about the Art Association, 1947. Newport Art Museum Archives

PLATE 36.
The May Dream (Maud),
by John Elliott, 1880. Reproduced
from Maud Howe Elliott,
Three Generations

PLATE 37.
Art Association of Newport Council Members, c. 1928. Harrison Morris (far left), Maud in black. On the grounds of the John N.A. Griswold House, home of the Art Association. Photo by Ernst Studio, Newport; Newport Art Museum Archives

"There is no pleasanter time to meet with one's artist friends than the autumn. I like to go to their studios when they first come back to town and hear about their summer outings. They are refreshed by the vacation, the painting out-of-doors, the communion with nature which is so necessary to their souls. Their studios are full of sketches, studies and notes of color and those who have been industrious have pictures to show you. They want your sympathy and think they want your criticism of their summer's work."[12] In the fall of 1890 Maud visited the studio of George Inness, who by then was painting his late tonalist landscapes. She described one, "a dreamy twilight scene full of mystery and charm. There is a full moon swooning in its own light — there is water in the foreground, a shadowy group of trees in the background, there is mystery, melancholy and poetry everywhere, in this quiet evensong on canvas."[13] Presenting this lecture to a Newport audience, Maud chastised, "Are there any of Inness's pictures in Newport? I really do not know. I hope there are — they should be here, they should be in the house of every American collector of pictures. We have too many third, fourth and fifth-rate foreign pictures everywhere in this country."[14]

Maud and Jack had known Augustus Saint-Gaudens since 1879, when he was working in Rome at the time they were there. He apparently had been very put off by Maud's youthful vanity and affectation, but the two were later thrown together in the American art world and became friends.[15] In her lectures Maud recounted a studio visit around 1890 when Saint-Gaudens was modeling a group commemorating the death of the wife of Secretary of State Hamilton Fish. At first she expressed her doubts about consigning these magnificent statues to a burying ground, but she is relieved then to remember Kerameikos, the beautiful street of funerary sculptures in Athens. Always it was back to the Greek! Saint-Gaudens was also working on the bas relief of Violet Sargent, beautiful younger sister to the famous artist; Sargent was going to paint Saint-Gaudens' wife and son in exchange for the relief, an arrangement that Maud found very practical. At the time of her visit Saint-Gaudens was still at work on his Robert Gould Shaw monument, which he told her was now a labor of love, as costs had risen to such heights that his commission would not cover more than the expenses incurred.

Maud met the famous American art collector Thomas B. Clarke at an auction of La Farge's pictures in the 1880s, where he outbid her on a watercolor. Clarke was exactly the kind of patron that Maud applauded; he bought good American paintings by living artists and influenced his friends to do the same. Her approval of Clarke, whose collection she visited at his unpretentious New York home in the 1880s, also signified Maud's insight as a connoisseur of great American art, as the paintings of which she approved included "a rich autumn landscape by Inness, and a sailing vessel with sailors 'wet with the flying spray'," by Winslow Homer. Her observations on Abbot Thayer's head of a young girl were very perceptive, noting the artist's power to interpret the "mystery" behind the young woman's face. She further admonishes her audience to appreciate the artistry in a good portrait: "What makes a good portrait is not the color of the eyelashes shall be matched to a tint, nor that the highlights in the hair should be exactly as they are in nature: color, outline composition even, are qualities which are subservient to that greatest quality of the portrait painters, *expression*."[16]

Affiliated with the fine arts of painting and sculpture upon which Maud elaborated in her lectures was the new appreciation for beauty and fine craftsmanship in one's everyday surroundings. Since her acquaintance with William Morris on the 1877 visit in England, Maud had been keenly aware of the arts and crafts aesthetic. Julia had allowed her to decorate (at Uncle Sam's expense) their home at 241 Beacon Street. Maud wrote enthusiastically to Laura about the "blue Brusselsmith carpet with a gold brown figurine of architectural acorns over it, the wallpaper a Morris known as Blue Indian . . ."[17] But Maud spoke to her audiences on the American accomplishments, noting the extraordinary progress since William Story's scathing report on America's lackluster contributions to the Paris Exposition of 1878: "In pottery, in iron work, in the manufacture of tiles, we are doing work of no mean quality. In all manner of goldsmiths' and silversmiths' work, our best men are on a par with the best Europeans." Maud reserved her highest accolades for stained glass, a medium that she said had languished since the Middle Ages. But now there was John La Farge, followed closely by Louis Tiffany, creating remarkable windows of originality and magnificence. Maud lamented the fact that so many of them were in private houses and churches, but she encouraged listeners to visit Trinity Church in Boston and Memorial Hall at Harvard, in Cambridge, to view La Farge masterpieces. "This window [at Harvard] should be seen in the morning when the sunlight lights up the figure of that superb young warrior and turns the flag he carries into a living flame of ruby."[18]

Maud disparaged the machine and said that the inherent beauty in an object comes from being handmade. "A work of art *cannot* be machine made."[19] And yet she was not condemning technology; steam, machinery, and electricity made the hardest labor easier. In the arts she thought that great strides had been made with wood engraving, etching, photogravure, and photography. The illustrated periodicals such as *The Century, Harpers,* and *Scribners,* with their superlative wood engravings, were better than anything being done in Europe. The art of etching, inspired by some Englishmen but primarily the American James McNeill Whistler, was now very respected in America. What she did not approve of were fakes: things that pretended to be what they were not. A good example was the chromolithograph, which Maud considered "cheap art," and therefore not respectable. While she admitted that very few could have great art in their homes, all could surround themselves with simplicity and truth. Whatever was admitted "to the sanctuary of the family life should have intrinsic value of its own."[20]

Harmony, simplicity, peaceful surroundings, were especially necessary to middle-class and upper-class Americans in the period between the Philadelphia Centennial of 1876 and the World's Columbian Exposition of 1893, which saw an economic depression, the threat posed by Eastern European immigrants, and violent labor strikes. Indeed, Maud herself, with her frantic pace of life and frequent bouts with neurasthenia, often benefited from being sequestered with beautiful art and music. She recounted one such incidence to her audiences: on a busy weekday in New York City she escaped into the Church of the Ascension, at the corner of Fifth Avenue and Tenth Street. There in all its glory was the recently completed La Farge mural *The Ascension of our Lord* above the main altar, along with sculpted angels by Louis St. Gaudens, the brother of Augustus, as well as several La Farge stained-glass windows. She sat in silence contemplating the art: "I was bathed in its beauty, it soothed my tired nerves better than sleep; it had no spoken prayer to lift my soul — it soared upon the wings of those angels."[21] Art was religion to Maud, and it was precisely this message that she and late nineteenth-century artists were trying to deliver to the burgeoning American masses: that art was uplifting and good for the soul, that it could make us more productive and successful in our daily lives.

While Maud marveled at the art of Christianity and considered its religions to be the source of man's greatest creativity, she was not a true believer. As her mother had written to Uncle Sam, when Maud was twenty-six: "Dear Maud isn't smooth, we might say, on piety. But to the religion of obligation, her little soul is very faithful. She never liked to go to church, was always taken as a child, but when she grew to woman's estate, was allowed to take her own way."[22] Obviously Maud had never found solace in religion as she knew it. Neither her mother's philosophical sermons nor her father's devout Bible readings had made it easier for her to understand the place of religion in her life. Maud informed Laura that *she*, personally, did not believe in another life, but that if she had children she should educate *them* as Catholics, so that they would have a good sense of right and wrong and be less anxious about life.[23] The advent of Protestantism in the new world — "the old bare Puritan meeting house" — had done nothing for art, in fact "the Pilgrims had brought a hatred of art." There was much work to do, Maud intoned, to remedy this situation: "The ministry of art must lend its hand."

Espousing nineteenth-century theories of evolution, Maud saw civilization as a progression from savagery and brute force to a more just, rational nature, guided by creative forces. In art, this translated to "primitive man" creating the first tools, the hammer and hatchet, and centuries later discovering that tools could possess beauty: thus, the origin of decorative yet functional art. Artistic excellence reached its peak with classical Greece and Rome, but was reborn in the Italian Renaissance with the painting geniuses Michelangelo, Raphael, Titian. A new respect for the beauty of the human body, "the most perfect of God's creations," emerged from the Renaissance and was once again brought to the fore in the American Renaissance. She believed that the world at the time contained "races and creeds" at these different stages of development: "our Indians are still busied with bows and arrows."[24] And she attributed the gains made by women artists to the advent of Christianity, which rejects the teachings of the religions of the Orient that "man only is capable of civilization, and have made woman man's slave."[25]

Judeo-Christian women fit into this cycle of civilization as well; in fact they were the civilizers. Maud basically followed Julia Ward Howe's essentialist argument that women softened men's harsh natures; they were nurturing and peace-loving as opposed to destructive and warmongering. As the argument applied to the art world, women had three distinct roles: as inspiration, as educator, and as creator. In her lectures in Chicago, Maud quickly dispensed with the first two fairly obvious and stereotyped roles: woman as the "abstract ideal or the concrete embodiment of Beauty, Purity, of Goodness" and woman as the teacher of children. But, she remonstrated, we live in a democracy, which calls for "higher education fitting [woman] to earn her living by her brain as well as by her hand." Women, as well as men, needed to be "breadwinners," and in addition to occupations as seamstresses, teachers, and domestics, they should be allowed to be lawyers, doctors, clerks, ministers — and artists.

"Because there have been no women who can be mentioned in the same breath with ... Phidias, Raphael, Michelangelo, Van Dyck, some people are under the impression that woman has done nothing of importance in art. It is a tiresome argument! ... And upon such ignorance! ... Woman has never, until the nineteenth century, had an opportunity of developing her intellectual and artistic faculties."[26] Maud proceeded to give copious and well-researched reports of women artists dating back to the anonymous artist-daughters of the Greek and Roman sculptors. She gave lively accounts of the lives of Elisabetta Sirani, Élisabeth Vigée Le Brun, and Angelica Kauffman among others, placing them and their work in the context of their times. Most extraordinarily, for the early 1890s, Maud spoke of American women artists: Elizabeth Boott, Sophia Peabody, Harriet Hosmer, Emma Stebbins; and England's Rosa Bonheur, as well as quoting the art critic and writer Mariana Van Rensselaer about American women etchers.

In her lectures on women in art Maud was likely building on the momentum supplied by the upcoming Woman's Building and exhibition at the World's Columbian Exposition. As President of the Board of Lady Managers, Bertha Honoré Palmer wanted to show work by women from all over the world, especially by women "breadwinners."[27] Palmer contracted Goupil and Company of Paris, who specialized in fine art publications, to give credibility to the catalogue. The book was to contain essays by experts in different fields and she sought to avoid "women on the make," as Julia Ward Howe referred to certain women with more clout than qualifications. Doubtless the hiring of Howe's daughter to compile and edit the volume *Art and Handicraft in the Woman's Building* was a good political move, but it also was indicative of the status that Maud now held in the world of arts and letters. She continued to lecture, had published her fifth novel, and was on the publication committees for aspiring authors such as the Chicago poet Harriet Monroe.

Maud wrote the introductory essay on "The Building and Its Decorations," chapters on "The Library," and "Belgium," as well as the Epilogue. She did not avoid mentioning the controversy regarding those women who chose to exhibit instead alongside the men, arguing that the point of the Woman's Building was to highlight primarily designs and handiwork that afforded a living to the women who produced them. Another purpose was to bring together women from all over the world in harmony and unity. As she wrote, "Who can foretell how potent an influence for the unity of the nations may spring from this meeting of the Slav and the Teuton, the Celt and the Mongol, The Gaul and the Latin, the Greek and the Anglo-Saxon?"[28] She did, however, continue her premise that women's work represented "the feminine side of the human effort." In her analysis of the building's architecture, created by Sophia Hayden, Maud wrote: "In Mr. Henry Van Brunt's appreciative account of Miss Hayden's work, the writer points out that it is essentially feminine in quality, as it should be. If sweetness and light were ever expressed in architecture, we find them in Miss Hayden's building. Every line expresses elegance, grace, harmony."[29]

The color frontispiece of Maud's book shows a modern woman holding a palette, at her feet the many accoutrements of a professional woman's artisanry: textile equipment, inkpot, ceramics, sculpture, books, book covers. Maud along with others recruited the contributors to the volume, many recognized today for importance in their fields: designer Candace Wheeler, illustrator Alice C. Morse, art historian Sarah H.

Hallowell, among them. Of course Julia wrote the chapter on "Associations of Women," and Laura Richards wrote on "Women in Literature."

> My heart,... Can and will you deliver to me on the 24th of April an article not over 2000 on women in literature — American women? It's for this World's Fair book. I have tried everybody I could think of before coming to you! It should be cheery, not bombastic, not personal as far as living authors are concerned. A resume of what woman has done and is doing and best of all, what she can do. There is one more person I will try: Louise Chandler Moulton! I will try to see her tomorrow afternoon and will let you know.[30]

While Maud acknowledged in several instances that the artwork presented was soothing, intended to induce feelings of tranquility and peace, she also critiqued the sculptural figures by Alice Rideout as being more light-hearted than the usual "hackneyed types that serve to represent Virtue, Sacrifice, Charity and the other qualities which sculptors have personified time out of mind, by large, heavy, dull-looking stone women."[31]

Maud walks us through the building, describing murals by the then little-known Mary Cassatt, among others; the exquisite tapestries and textiles and pottery; and to her favorite room, The Library. In Maud's opinion the library, designed by Wheeler, was the most artistic room in the building, especially noteworthy for the ceiling mural done by Wheeler's daughter Dora Keith. Indicating that her sympathies were with the arts and crafts ideal of harmonious surroundings, she wrote, "Among the founders of the new American school of design which has done so much for the education of our people, there is no figure more striking than that of Candace Wheeler."[32] In fact, it is often the people, the artists themselves, who impress Maud. She cites being served tea by a Ceylonese woman, receiving a fresh flower from a Texas woman, and marvels at the qualities of patience, skill, and industry that characterize these women from around the world. So while Maud is celebrating the triumph of art over commerce in the United States, and the particular strength of women's accomplishments everywhere, she is also broadening her outlook as a citizen of the world. And shortly she was to embark on a new adventure, one that would bring her into more contact with the culture and customs of those in other countries.

SEVEN

"The Nineties" have already taken on a romantic glow to all who remember them, and even to those who have only read about them. We were in America when the famous decade began, and it was then Jack had received the order for his *magnum opus*. The imagination of the cultured world had been captivated by the idea of the coming of the new century . . .
The air was full of roseate prophecy.
MAUD HOWE ELLIOTT, *JOHN ELLIOTT*

THE DECADE OF THE NINETIES BEGAN FOR MAUD AND JACK IN Boston, where they inaugurated the new year with Julia. Maud's loyalties continued to be divided between her mother and husband; she had been spending months at a time back in Boston and Newport, leaving Jack in Chicago. The family was used to the idea of Maud as the caretaking daughter and the doting maiden aunt until she surprised them by marrying. Maud reassured Laura, "That you should go and think, or pretend to think that [anybody] could take your place or make me love you any less—it hurts me that this was said. Jack *knows* that I always said I didn't love him better than you or mama, but now there are *three* of you instead of two—and isn't it funny—I think I love both of you better than I did before."[1] Jack did not seem to be jealous of this arrangement; having lost his parents very early and his only brother in a drowning accident,[2] he doted upon Julia and likely found the family's many connections promising for his career. In fact he was painting little Julia Richards's portrait.

But Jack did not like Chicago or his job. Maud wrote to Laura, "J. and

Pretyman are as I may have stated dissolved." Although the Elliotts and Pretymans were to remain friends over the years, the two men could not work together. Jack did enjoy his numerous portrait commissions while in Chicago, much more so than his decorative work. They included an oil portrait of Rose Farwell, the beautiful daughter of the Illinois senator, and a red chalk drawing of Mrs. John Root, the wife of the architect of the Exposition, as well as an ivory miniature of Bertha Palmer. Jack became intrigued with miniature painting and during the next few years made miniatures on ivory of Jenny Pretyman; friend Helen Williams; Maud's cousins Elizabeth, Alida, and Margaret Chanler; his brother Edward "Ned" Elliott; and others. However, Maud wrote to Laura that as far as Jack's commissions, "No money yet paid in and little Maud from the time she left you has earned and paid for all the moving expenses, clothes and so forth of the firm. Hard work? Bet your life — so, pardon bad correspondence. Here's been the day. Getting Jack up! B'fast and other household business (we have a clean little maid now) pick up deeds then do much work as possible."[3]

The summers at Oak Glen still provided a pleasant combination of family, work, and socializing. The month of August 1890 was particularly festive, with Jack, Maud, and friend Helen Gardner attending a party at the Vanderbilts, Maud and Helen going to the Casino, Benjamin Curtis Porter and family visiting. Picnics in the Lawton's Valley area were also popular, and Charles de Kay and his wife attended one. Polo and sailing were avidly pursued, and gatherings at Oak Glen often included croquet; two of the younger guests who were to become important friends in Maud's life were Mabel Norman and Isabel Perkins. Friendships were one benefit of the summers, but social contacts were another. Maud appeared in the society columns: "Mrs. Maud Howe Elliott, daughter of Julia Ward Howe, will be heard each Monday at the drawing rooms of Mrs. Frederick W. Vanderbilt, Mrs. W. C. Whitney, the Misses Mason and Mrs. James P. Kernochan, and she will talk about art, a subject which doubtless will interest and instruct the guests who will be invited to hear her. Mrs. Elliott will do her best to call the attention of her respective audiences from the distractive pleasures of August."[4]

While Chicago had provided a fast-paced life and opportunities for Maud to expand her artistic repertoire, Boston offered a far more genteel and intellectual climate to hone her literary skills. Be they Brahmins or bohemians, the group of writers with whom Maud now surrounded herself was decidedly avant-garde. As Julia wrote in her journal, after the deaths of Longfellow, Emerson, James Russell Lowell, John Greenleaf Whittier, Francis Parkman, and Oliver Wendell Holmes, the old Boston was going away. In its place arose a new generation of literary figures who wanted to make a stir and create a new aesthetic; these young writers were ready to discard the Victorian age. Foremost among them was Ralph Adams Cram, who, like Maud, wrote art criticism for the *Boston Transcript* before becoming a successful architect and man of letters. As Maud recalled, Cram and a young Bernard Berenson came to the Howes' drawing room at 241 Beacon in 1887 to engage her in plans for a new magazine to be called *The XXth Century*.[5] Cram's thoughts were that "romance and poetry and beauty were coming back to a drab century," and this publication would deal "with all the arts, including letters, postulating the unity of art and its basic importance in the scheme of life."[6] Cram proposed Maud be in charge of a section on Boston literature (or cultural activity in general, according to another source).[7] The project was frought with dysfunction from the start; poet Louise Imogene Guiney objected to Berenson's suggestion that Mrs. Jack be involved (they did need financial help), and poet Bliss Carman did not want Maud included.[8] The magazine never appeared, and in a later letter to Maud, Cram wrote, "You may not remember, but you were involved in this golden dream yourself, but the century came before the magazine, and now our only hope is in the 21st century."[9]

Another literary personality who had been involved with the *XXth Century* episode was Harvard professor Barrett Wendell, a family friend of the Howes. Wendell has been credited with a number of innovative approaches to teaching English literature, especially with regard to composition and creative writing. Maud possibly attended some lectures Wendell gave to the public at the Lowell Institute in late 1890, and she engaged in a "literary experiment" with him, of which remains a packet of correspondence called "Barrett Wendell vs. Maud Howe Elliott." Former students of Wendell's later reminisced on his controversial methods of teaching students to think and write creatively and independently. Likely this correspondence with Maud, in which they debated back and forth on the behavior of men and women, was such an exercise:

In the particular scandal to which you refer, it was of course the man's fault. He tired of the beloved object, as soon as it was his own. He is by nature a hunter, the business which stood between him and the woman seemed insurmountable; none but a man of an iron will would have tried to overcome them. He conquered all, and the delight was in the conquering—most difficult of all he conquered the woman herself. At last she surrendered unconditionally. There was her mistake. She spread her soul open for him to read into, as in a book. He thinks he has turned the last page, and returning it to its shelf has taken another book to read. When he learns that the first romance is written in more than one volume, he may return to read it—then pray heaven, she will know enough not to let him read the last page. It is in this way that so many couples who seemed to have finished with each other, begin over again, and live out their lives together happily enough.[10]

Maud was never the scholar that Julia was, but she was increasingly comfortable with the topics of literature, philosophy, religion, history, and certainly familiar with music, theater and art history. In 1890 and 1891 she repeated her Chicago lectures on art and literature in Boston, New York, and Philadelphia. The drawing rooms of upper-class women were popular places for these refined speaking engagements, designed to cultivate and educate the populace. With Maud's reading and research and undoubtedly the tutelage of her mother, she became increasingly respected for her breadth of knowledge as well as her speaking ability. One newspaper noted, "The Century Club did well when it had Mrs. Elliott come to visit and talk to them. She is a cultured lady of an intellectual family, entertaining, interesting, well informed, deeply read. She has something to say and a pleasing way of saying it—rather a rare thing although it does not sound so."[11] An 1895 newspaper story on the Howe women mentioned as always Maud's beauty, her novels, but noted that "her great success has been as a lecturer."[12]

For Maud the lecture circuit was rewarding, but it was grueling and she needed the money. "Went to Brookline and read my first paper at Mrs. R——'s; she gave me $155 for the course. A hard audience to speak to, rather severe and wooden. I think they were pleased." And in New York: "Margaret Chanler sent me $250 for my New York course of talks. Not much money for such great trouble, but will pay for Rosalind's schooling at Miss Biggs."[13] The entire Howe family, excepting engineer Harry Howe, was in dire financial straits. Up in Maine, the Richards' paper mill was in trouble, and six children had to be educated. The boys were going to Harvard and the oldest daughter, Alice, went to Smith College. Maud considered it her duty to help, but she wrote Laura, "God willing when Rose's education is finished I will be responsible for Julia's, but not for Heaven's sake, Northampton."[14] Flossy and David Hall, a lawyer, were perpetually poor; Flossy also wrote and lectured, predominantly on suffrage; she spent every summer keeping house for her mother at Oak Glen, and she and her children were resourceful in finding financial aid for their schooling. The three boys worked and had scholarships to Harvard; daughter Carrie was sent to Paris to study art by Mrs. George Richmond Fearing of Newport.[15]

Maud persevered with different avenues for her writing. In 1890 she wrote a play called *Man Without a Shadow*, commissioned by the popular British actor and producer Richard Mansfield. Based on Adelbert von Chamisso's story, this was intended as a children's fairy tale. As Maud wrote, she forwarded the acts to Mansfield, who sent back his positive comments, and told her he was going to produce it in New York. This never happened, for what reason is unknown. Maud also became involved in her first nonfiction venture, writing about the education of Laura Bridgman, Samuel Gridley Howe's blind pupil. For this project Maud and Flossy were called upon by their widowed brother-in-law, Michael Anagnos,[16] director of the Perkins Institute, and it turned out to be a tedious process of transcribing both their father's letters and Bridgman's diaries. The book was not ready for publication until 1903. Far more interesting to Maud was the emerging magazine industry. "The advance of Art and Letters in our country is going on in an inverse ratio [from other countries]. Literature is assuming a more important aspect than it has ever done before in any era in any country of the world. Individuals and whole classes of people with us are included in the Reading Class, who in the other countries would go thru life without reading six books. The cheap periodicals have such an enormous circulation that the best of them are a flood of good literature."[17] Maud recognized that her articles would reach wide audiences and she began submitting stories for publication to *Lippincott's Magazine, Harper's Bazaar, The Outlook,* and many other magazines.

As for her husband, Jack's "magnum opus" was a ceiling mural painted for the new "palace for the people," the Boston Public Library building designed by the great beaux arts architectural firm McKim, Mead and White. Other commissioned artists were Puvis de Chavannes, John Singer Sargent, and Edwin Austen Abbey, heavy hitters of their day, while John Elliott's renown lay chiefly in being the son-in-law of Julia Ward Howe. The commission came about through the advocacy of several prominent Bostonians and arts patronesses, especially Sarah Choate Sears, the artist and photographer, and her husband, J. Montgomery Sears, said to be the richest man in Boston. Sarah Sears eventually gave one thousand dollars to the project.[18] Maud put her lobbying skills to work, meeting with Harold Williams, a Boston physician who had served as the Secretary of the Examining Committee of the Library; he wrote a letter to the president of the Library's Board, Frederick O. Prince, proposing a commission dependent on raising the funds. Pending the Trustees' and architect's approval of the design, which as yet did not exist, the proposal was given a go-ahead in April, 1892.[19] By June, the lack of a definite contract was thoroughly anxiety-provoking for Maud, and indeed gave an opportunity for "contemptible and vindictive opposition of some certain persons who have schemed to prevent Mr. Elliott from being employed in the matter."[20] Soon after, the Board gave written approval for the design to be executed and designated a room for the mural. Jack had been working out of a series of Boston studios, but now declared that he must be in Rome to create a design.

Maud and Jack, with Julia and niece Alice Richards in tow, sailed for Europe in June 1892. The trip began as a vacation, leaving Julia and Alice, now twenty, to bond and go to museums and churches in London, while Maud and Jack went to the Paris Salons. Maud approved of the paintings and sculpture, but found that Paris was now "dirty and dowdy: like seeing Mrs. Langtry in curl papers, fat and frowsy."[21] Back in England, the foursome attended a bash at the Royal Academy, where Jack apparently was mistaken for the Greek minister, and then visited two venerable English painters, George Frederick Watts and Lawrence Alma-Tadema. Both of these artists were finishing their careers painting in a classically inspired manner, but introducing a contemporary symbolist element, also present in some of Jack's later work. In July the group traveled to the Netherlands and Belgium to renew their passion for Frans Hals, Rembrandt and Rubens, but also to visit the studios of the Hague School artists. A Dutch counterpart to the French Barbizon movement, the Hague School featured landscapes and figurative works painted in a loose brush technique with subdued tones imparting a poetic feeling. The older painters, Jozef Israëls and Paul Gabriël, and the younger ones, Hendrik Mesdag, Anthon Mauve, and Jacob and Willem Maris were all welcoming and forthcoming about their art. Maud observed that the freemasonry among European artists was much greater than in the United States, where she theorized that they needed all their strength to support themselves, never mind each other.

By September Julia was troubled by a persistent case of bronchitis and wanted to go home. Maud decided she was needed by her mother more than by Jack—a scenario that was to repeat itself—and she returned with Julia and Alice to America, packing her husband off to Italy. Jack and his mentor, José de Villegas, who led the Spanish art colony in Rome, commiserated over the design for the designated ceiling in the patent room of the Boston Public Library, which was unfortunately divided by a major supporting beam. Thus began nine months of agonized deliberations on the part of Jack, as to his design, all detailed in letters to Maud, who remained in America, caretaking and breadwinning.

> My darling I have been feeling very seedy all day, my head has not been aching, but I feel as if it was going to burst. At least I have felt so but it is a little better now. Perhaps it is on account of the weather which changed last night with the new moon and it has been raining in torrents all day—most dejecting. I have been working out a scheme which I hope to have sufficiently formed to take [to] Villegas tomorrow or Sunday, but I fear he will jump on it—on the other hand he may not. The drawing I have made is Progress tearing across the sky urging on six or eight (which ever makes the best composition) cream colored horses, one of which has come a cropper over *the beam* with two groups of figures with ropes around it representing Ignorance trying to stop the way. But for all that only one horse has stumbled and most of them have passed the beam. Minerva

leads the way with a torch surrounded with a group of trumpeters and the American Eagle hovers over the head of the figure representing Progress and Fame is crowning it with laurels. You see I am straining my nerves to profit by the obstruction and if I succeed I shall hide a very bad fault in the architecture for which I shall get no credit, for in no Italian structure of the Renaissance that I know of is there a visible beam.[22]

When Maud wrote the biography of her husband in 1930, she included many of Jack's distraught letters during this period. Jack was presented as the struggling artist, suffering for an ideal, trying to create art that would bring comfort and peace, not necessarily make him famous. What emerges instead is a man struggling with depression and by today's standards any number of other disorders. He had tremendous trouble focusing and following through. Four months after his arrival in Rome, he was finally making progress, but never enough: "I have put in a better day's work today than I have for some time. I think I begin to see my way out of the first darkness, but I know from bitter experience that I shall be overwhelmed again and again by dark almost hopeless days before I am through." In February 1893 he was "totally disheartened" with his work and himself: "The worst of all is that I have not only made a pitiful mess of my life, but I have been a drag on your wheel of Fortune too." And a few days later, "I hope I shall not have another bout of the blues. You have no idea how desperate I was." Maud wrote to him about Sargent's designs, and of course he was nervous about having his work compared: "I am sure they will be great, and I grow more and more terrified . . . You cannot begin to know my loneliness and lostness without you in this struggle, which either means I am going to swim or sink." And in March, "You say I am not to give way to depression. I don't give way, it is simply stronger than I am and overcomes me."[23]

In her letters Maud alternately bolstered his self-esteem and nagged him about his fussiness and procrastination. Even when they were together she despaired over his inability to get going in the morning. But apparently he was more lost without her, though he took great solace in his men friends. His constant companion when not working was "Kempie," the same English friend who had been with him when he met Maud. Frederick Shakerley Kemp, the son from a second marriage of

Thomas Read Kemp, a Parliamentarian and land developer, was twenty years older than Jack. As Maud described him, Kemp was "a confirmed bachelor with a fondness for travel and a dislike of traveling alone ... [and] a pretty taste for collecting illuminated missals, coins and quaint bits of rococo."[24] Kemp lived with Jack while he was in Rome without Maud; he was Jack's great comfort, but there is no evidence that he was his lover. "My Kempie is sitting with me, and we have a jolly fire which I insist upon having, and we are as comfortable as it is possible to be without wives which is saying less than you realize."[25] If Jack had homosexual leanings, all indications are that he repressed them; indeed that may be a reason for his feelings of inadequacy.

In June 1893 the design, consisting of two panels, was completed and Jack rolled them up and brought them back to his Mount Vernon Street studio in Boston. Frederick O. Prince, former mayor of Boston and President of the Boston Public Library Trustees, visited, along with two other trustees, Thomas Dwight and Phineus Pierce. Jack received the commission to go ahead with *The Triumph of Time*, "an expression of the universal feeling of a world standing on tiptoe for the coming of the century."[26] All of a sudden Jack had a standing in the world; Mrs. Jack congratulated him; he was invited to visit artist and Howe family friend Sarah Wyman Whitman's studio—"a great success." Even Maud's usually disapproving brother, Harry Howe, was cordial: "H. seems so much nicer to me since my success—not that he was ever otherwise. I have been wondering whether it was really so or only my imagination."[27] Jack dutifully showed his design to the Bostonians who mattered, for there remained funds to be raised. And he was more in tune with himself than in a long time: "The cobwebs are out of my brain, and I have, not the best I might have done, but the best I could. I have been through one of those experiences Margaret Deland speaks of that either raise or lower one, and I firmly trust I am a grade higher for it. Your ownest own, Jack."[28]

Meanwhile, Maud had also reached a higher place. With her devotion to her mother, if not always to her causes, it was only a matter of time until she experienced an awakening of her own social conscience. Her friendship with Margaret Deland was likely also a catalyst for her reform efforts, as Deland wrote novels that dealt with single motherhood, divorce, adultery, and suffrage. Earlier, in Boston, Julia had hosted the Russian revolutionary Sergio Stepniak, and Maud had been eager to join the fight to end Russian oppression by accompanying a delegation to the country. In a role reversal, Julia refused to let her become involved.[29] Both Maud and Jack were friends and supporters of John Boyle O'Reilly, a strong voice for the Irish who had fought and spent years in an Australian prison. She began to attend conferences and club meetings and push for reforms, such as the building of hospitals for the poor and dispossessed, as well as the need for immigration reform. In a series on "Ethical Relations," at the Anniversary for the Advancement of Women, Art Institute of Chicago, Maud advocated for Chinese immigrants, whose plight she had recognized on her California trip in 1881. In her visit to London, Maud found her passionate humanitarian cause, the Salvation Army. Visiting the Army's convict shelter center was a revelation, and after interviewing many of the inhabitants and reading General William Booth's manifesto *In Darkest England,* she developed a lecture titled "With Booth in Darkest London," which she began delivering in 1893. Her goal was to counteract the ignorance about the Salvation Army that existed in the United States and to show it as a force—like art and literature—that furthered civilization. "Winch spoke of the dreadful wickedness of the boys, but that they could grow out of it so quickly when placed in the right atmosphere, proving that the natural direction of human growth is towards higher things."[30]

Maud herself was a force to be reckoned with. She had emerged from her childish whining to become a full-blown, assured presence who usually got her way. A case in point is a story told by Margaret Deland, which paints a vibrant picture:

> She and I were walking along Beacon Street . . . Maud, tall and stately, in a red cloak and a big black hat, looked like Queen Boadicea. I, sheltered in her magnificence of color and presence, must have suggested "respectable New England female." Maud set the pace of strolling slowly along, until, suddenly, we heard behind us the scream of a fire engine, and the pounding of hoofs, and turning, we saw a great red fire engine drawn by three superb horses, thundering down the street. The driver, on the edge of the seat, was leaning forward, slapping his reins on the horses and shouting at them. As we stood there on the corner, Maud, looking like part of the splendor of

the sunset, cried to the galloping horses: "Oh, you gorgeous creatures," and flinging out her arms from under her spreading crimson cloak, she kissed both her hands to them crying out: "I adore you!" The driver must have had a flashing glimpse of the whole combination—the beautiful woman, the snow, the red cloak, the flung kisses and the flaming words, for his left hand jerked and one of the horses stumbled—then the whole avalanche of sound, and color, and glittering brass, and galloping speed, crashed down!

Fortunately all were quickly righted—the driver and the horses—and they proceeded on their way to the fire. Maud, however, went home and called the fire chief, an acquaintance from her youth. When told that the driver would be dismissed she related to him what had happened and said "Therefore, I will not permit him to be discharged." When told that the Captain would take it under advisement, she retorted, "I have advised you. All you need do is to tell me, now, that you won't discharge him. If you do, I'll—I'll turn your old Fire Commission upside—don't make me write a letter to the *Transcript*, confessing what I did—and asking the public to join me in a petition to the Governor to save the driver!" The driver retained his job.[31]

It was a foregone conclusion that Jack would need to return to Rome to make his mural. The Howe family believed that a woman should follow her man, but they didn't understand why Jack could not work in Boston. "I don't in the least believe that a picture cannot be painted in Boston, as well as in Rome,"[32] wrote Laura. But Maud, like her father, had a "vagabond instinct," as she called it,[33] and liked new challenges. For instance, while Rome was their destination, and they set sail in January 1894, Maud persuaded Jack to take a detour and visit Morocco, followed by Seville and Granada. She loved what she considered the exotic lands of the Moors and used these locales for her first published travelogues. Rome was another story. Their first apartment was uninhabitable, it was freezing and the fireplace did not work; they forfeited three months rent and moved temporarily into the Palazzo Santo Croce, a building owned by Marion Crawford. Maud resorted to complaining to Laura: "If I said how I hated Rome, here even to Auntie, they would say I wasn't happy with my husband! I would rather live in Gardiner, Maine, if I could have a warm house." And as far as her social efforts: "Somehow there seems no place for me here. Everything is for men, or rich, smart, society women. The artists have their own good times but they are purely male reunions. J. E. doesn't care to bring me in relation much with his artist life which is undoubtedly bohemian, using the word seriously in the European sense. We, at home, call anything a little picturesque, a little 'bohemian,' but here it means things which are really not respectable."[34]

Fortunately, in the Vatican quarter Jack soon found the perfect studio: two floors in the Palazzo Giraud Torlonia, built in 1503. Vincenzo Moscatelli, who had cleaned brushes for Villegas, came to live on the ground floor and assist Jack, who, now "vitalized and roused," began work on his two mammoth canvases on the cavernous second floor. By July Maud and Jack had moved into an apartment in the Palazzo Rusticucci near the studio, in the Borgo, where they would live six years. Through a courtyard and at the top of three flights of stairs was a suite of large rooms and above them a terrace that overlooked the Square of St. Peter's, with the Roman Campagna, the Sabine, and the Alban hills beyond. Maud wrote,

> The terrace is our poetry, and we have parlous good prose downstairs. The walls are three feet thick, built to keep out both heat and cold; the whole house is paved with red, white and black tiles in geometrical designs. The old green door opens into a vestibule leading to the *anticamera*, which has two big windows. The *salotto* opens from this; it has a splendid *sei cento* carved wood ceiling, and pale green doors with gilt mouldings and handles. The dining-room, square and high, leads from the *salotto;* beyond is a charming room with a fresco of Apollo driving the horses of the sun.[35]

Jack was handy; he put in fireplaces and worked with a plumber to have running water and a means to irrigate the garden he was to install on the terrace. There were servants: Filomena, the Umbrian housemaid and waitress; Pompilia, the "black-browed" Tuscan cook; and Nena, who did errands. Although it was frowned upon, Maud bought her own groceries, taking advantage of a certain latitude allowed to artists.[36]

Maud began to enjoy Rome; having had Roman fever, she welcomed the improvements made in the areas of health and welfare. She began a new enterprise, writing columns about the life of the city, and sending them to syndicated newspapers in the United States: the *Boston*

Transcript, Kansas City Star, New Orleans Times Democrat, Chicago Inter Ocean and *New York World;* eventually the *St. Louis Journal* and *St. Paul Dispatch*. She worked out of an Italian printing office, with a typesetter who didn't speak a word of English![37] This first foray into true journalism allowed Maud to dive head first into the world of Italian politics, social customs, religion and art. In communications with newspaper editors, such as the *Transcript's* E. H. Clement, she sought to avoid newsy items that already were telegraphed and to concentrate more on cultural activities and artists.[38] She made it clear, this was not to be a column about the socially elite; it was to portray stories of all the country's inhabitants. These "Roman Letters," as she titled them, incorporated her personal life and her observations; a typical one was titled "The Feast of Giovanni, "which described a Roman festival.

> The scene in the wide piazza beggars description. Imagine a vast open air fair, with booths and eating houses stretching half a mile, crowded with a dense throng of men, women and children all ringing their bells and most of them carrying huge garlic stalks surmounted by the round, bulbous seed vessel of the plant, which is like enough to the classic thyrsus of the ardent bacchanals to be mistaken for it by the flaring torchlight. I have never but once seen anything that approached the vast concourse of people and that was the World's Fair on Chicago Day. Men and women wore the gay paper and tinsel flowers which were sold by wheedling fellows who assured their customers that these were the only roses worth buying, the roses that do not fade. Only a few days ago I wrote that the Italians were poor, and yet as I looked at the myriads of people in the flower-garlanded drinking booths, decent, sober people taking their suppers of snails and pure wine, laughing, jesting, careless, happy, I felt that no people with such a capacity for fun and frolic can be called poor.[39]

Maud and Jack were surrounded by poverty and beggars, and appeared rich to those they encountered in their everyday lives. This was far from the truth, although they did not lack the amenities of life customary for gentrified Bostonians. To be without servants was unheard of. Marion Crawford lent them furnishings for their apartment. The cost of living seemed to be directly proportional to how well one haggled with the street vendors, but finances always loomed large in Maud's letters home.

She urged Julia to help her get more subscribers for her Roman letters. She contemplated giving lessons in English literature in Rome. Kemp lived in two rooms in their apartment and paid rent; he also helped them out: "Kemp seems inclined—in fact has offered—to back us in the present emergency."[40] Maud's trips home were planned when she needed a way to raise money. In the summer of 1895 she returned to do a series of lucrative lectures in Newport, Lenox, Massachusetts, and Bar Harbor, Maine. She was approached by the very wealthy Commodore and Mrs. George Hamilton Perkins, of Boston and Newport, to take their daughter Isabel on the grand tour. Maud had qualms about earning money that way and sought Laura's advice. She replied: "Accept, by all means, say I. Bowing the knee to Mammon? I should like to know why or how. This would be good honest work. More that that, and I confess to my mind a more important view than any other, it may very likely be the saving of a really fine child, whom her fool parents are doing their best to spoil. Consider the position of this lamb, I pray you. Natural (I fancy), bright, and all her days hitherto spent with absolutely unintellectual people: fortune-hunters swarming around her like bees: no wise person to guide or guard her."[41] There was a reason Laura and Harry Richards brought up their six children in the Maine woods!

By October 1896 Maud was off with her charge, Isabel Weld Perkins, for a yearlong cultural tour. Isabel, at twenty, was an only child and heir to seventeen million dollars, the fortune made by her grandfather, William Fletcher Weld, through his Black Horse Flag fleet of clipper ships and other transportation ventures. Maud wrote that Isabel was the nearest thing to a daughter she ever had, and learned to feel the anxieties that parents have. She also adapted very well to traveling in the lap of luxury, sailing in a new high-speed luxury ocean liner, the White Star Line's *Teutonic*—she wrote "I never again wish to cross on any other."[42] Beginning in London and Paris they stayed in the finest hotels, dined extravagantly (it was at this time that Maud developed a bit of a weight problem), shopped, rode horses, attended theater, opera, museums. No expenses were spared as Maud tried to recreate her own remembered experience at the hands of her mother; they read the Bible and traveled to Egypt and the Holy Land. Back in Rome, Jack was at work, supposedly on his commission, but distracted by household improvements and always, the terrace: "I have not been to the studio today; great things have been done on the terrace however . . ."[43] With the help of Vincenzo, Jack installed a trellis for his roses and filled huge Tuscan flower pots with azaleas, honeysuckle, chrysanthemums, geraniums. He made hanging vines of passion flowers and hired a blacksmith to build an arched pergola. Maud and Isabel joined Jack in Rome in late January 1896.

The flowered terrace, cool on the hottest of days, aglow by moonlight in the evening, was admired far and wide in Rome. As the century drew to a close, American artists, Roman dignitaries, and friends of all persuasions congregated there. Maud and Jack's terrace salon was the place to be, just as her ailing Aunt Louisa's Palazzo Odescalchi had been two decades earlier. Maud, like her mother, loved to surround herself with young people. Ambassador Wayne MacVeagh and his underling, First Secretary Larz Anderson, were frequent guests, and they were introduced to Isabel Perkins, with whom Anderson was immediately smitten.[44] Other regular visitors who were just beginning distinguished careers were John Loudon, secretary of the Dutch Embassy, and Charles Elliot Norton's son Richard, an archaeologist who was killed in the First World War. More seasoned guests included old friend Marie Spartoli Stillman and her husband journalist William Stillman, Rome correspondent to *The Times*, as well as Hall Caine, a popular novelist at work on *The Eternal City*. Henry James was in Rome in 1899, and as Maud wrote to her mother, "We saw him constantly while he was preparing the material for a life he is to write of Mr. Story. He is now old bacheloresque, but so dear, though a wee bit cranky."[45] It was at one of Maud's soirees that James became enamoured of the handsome, blond Norwegian-born sculptor Hendrik Andersen, whose family lived in Boston and Newport. James purchased one of his works and wrote to Maud:

> My fancy pressed on your heels through all the sequel to that lovely *festin de noces* on your terrace—altogether the most beautiful and distinguished little *festin* I ever saw . . . My own adventures are meek and mild and it's a fortnight since I got home . . . the vistas are long and I dream always of the old enchanted Rome. It has just been brought more intimately home to me by the arrival of a charming object I at the very last hour, made bold to purchase (on very modest terms) from our wonderful young friend H.

C. Andersen—the coloured terra-cotta bust of the young Bevilacqua, which struck me, on the whole, more than anything in his studio. It perches now on my chimney-piece and diffuses extraordinary life, expression and charm. It bids fair to be a delightful possession and without you I shouldn't have had it, nor known the touchingly interesting youth. I hope Elliott is fighting more and more on the winning side. I think often of his strain and solitude—that is of yours, too, and I pray for you both. And I am yours, dear Mrs. Elliott, very constantly. H. J.[46]

Maud did thrive on society, and she played hard. She wrote Laura, "Blessed Creature! How you must be wondering what has kept me so long silent. The answer is 'original sin.' I have been fagging so. Two weeks ago I went to Sorrento for the Tasso fetes and staid [sic] a week at Mimoli's villa near the Crawfords. I slept and had early breakfast at Mimo's house and lunched and dined and passed the rest of my time at Villa Crawford. Then came a flight back to Rome, one day here and the next off to Venice where I spent a week with Mrs. Jack at the Palazzo Barbaro, the Daniel Curtis house, which she had hired for a month. I returned home last night and found Helen and Jack well, but so glad to see me that they evidently have not fallen in love with each other."[47] Helen Gardner, no relation to Mrs. Jack, and about as far apart in personality as possible, was a friend from her Boston childhood who evidently had suffered losses in family and love. She visited Maud in Rome for weeks at a time and they learned to ride bicycles together: "Tell Helen I rode six miles, and while I can't yet mount, I can dismount and go down a mild hill. She will know just what progress I have made." Maud kept tabs on Helen, writing to her mother, "Would you like Helen to go to Newport? Her letter would have touched you, by its happiness and her appreciation of being at 241. She is our inexpressive person. You must always remember that. She is true, loyal, a real gentlewoman and never could make any mischief for anybody. She is really attached to us all and has our interests at heart."[48] She was a regular presence in the Howe family until her death from cancer in 1900.

Jack did not fall in love with Helen Gardner and there is no evidence that he was ever drawn to any female but Maud. His "Kempie" continued to keep him company when Maud was away and he had other male companions, specifically one Giacomo Boni, Jack's exact contemporary, who was an Italian archaeologist. In the hindsight of the sexual revolution, Maud's description of their friendship takes on certain nuances: "Boni loved birds, owned a terrace, and like Jack, found his greatest pleasure pottering among his flowers. The two men took to each other from the first and spent happy hours together swapping seeds and stories. Boni was one of the few who knew the knock that opened the studio door."[49] The idea of their being lovers is strengthened by the fact that Boni shared a love for antiquities with Horatio Brown,[50] an English author who had been the biographer and onetime lover of historian John Addington Symonds, the first Victorian to write openly about his homosexuality.

Although Maud was secure in her roles as artist's wife and unofficial cultural attaché, at the same time she found it hard to relinquish control of her mother's well-being at home. Soon after her arrival in Rome Maud had beseeched, "I beg of you, for all our sake, and your own, not to keep up the racket which everyday since I left you have carried on. In six weeks you went once to Washington, three times to New York, once to New Haven . . . I will remind you that you promised me not to take these long journeys in the dead of winter, promised me in so many words and this is the result. I foolishly believed you. Is there nothing worthwhile in life but the platform and the public? . . . I don't want you to hold your hands in your lap, but neither can I endure your constant and exhausting wanderings. It makes me feel that I must give up all ideas of returning here next winter."[51] She prevailed upon her mother, now approaching eighty, to find time for one last visit to Rome and after she and Jack spent the summer and fall of 1897 in Newport, they returned to Rome with Julia. Unfortunately, Julia's last remaining sibling, Louisa Terry, had died three months before, but Julia enjoyed the chance to see Maud happy in her surroundings. She even agreed to sit for two portraits, one with Villegas, who had painted stunning portraits of Maud and Jack in 1894, another with Hendrik Andersen, the neoclassical sculptor. Andersen, who had been taken under Maud's wing in 1897, was an ardent defender of all things classical, a trait that undoubtedly raised his profile in Maud's eyes, although his sculptures were curiously cold and unfeeling. In both of her portraits Julia appeared rather militant, Maud attributing this to the fact that she was quite indignant over Spain's recent sinking of the *Maine*, a prelude to the Spanish American War. Although Louisa was gone, Julia was able to visit with her family, especially beloved Daisy, married to Sam Ward's grandson Wintie Chanler, and now with three small children. With her brother-in-law, Luther Terry, Julia heaped bunches of Jack's roses on Louisa's grave, before departing for America escorted by her nephew, Arthur Terry, and his wife Julia.

In 1900 Julia Ward Howe had ten more years to live and she continued to push herself to the limit, much to the dismay of her children. But these same children, while often feeling the futility of trying to have successful careers in light of their super-parents, also drove themselves relentlessly. Maud's one big frustration with her husband was that he did not have her work ethic. Finishing his Boston Public Library commission almost killed him, she wrote. And he probably would never have finished it but for the intervention of representatives from the Library's Board of Trustees; Morton Prince wrote to Maud: "Tell Jack to hurry up and finish it, and not let himself be seduced into dwelling too long on finishing touches."[52] One can only imagine Maud's reaction when toward the completion of the mural Jack came home and told her he had painted out the figure of Eros which had introduced the procession of the centuries: "the work of years was wiped out in an hour." As the new century dawned, it found Maud and Jack still in Rome, surrounded by a rousing crowd of Catholics in St. Peter's Square celebrating the Pope's Jubilee. They were ironically held captive by a painting called *The Triumph of Time*, intended to be futuristic, while they were very much still part of the nineteenth century.

EIGHT

I remember the early years of the new century as a time of inspiration: the spirit of hope was abroad, the whole world seemed to have received a new impulse; good resolutions blossomed into good works. Men felt their strength to be as the strength of ten, and women that the twentieth century was theirs as no other had ever been.

MAUD HOWE ELLIOTT, *THREE GENERATIONS*

THE TRIUMPH OF TIME WAS TRIUMPHANTLY INSTALLED IN THE Boston Public Library in late 1900 and opened with a private reception on March 17, 1901. Boston's elite were in attendance: Mrs. Jack, Charles Eliot Norton, the Barrett Wendells, the Morton Princes, the Montgomery Searses, the David Kimballs, the Larz Andersons, Judge and Mrs. Oliver Wendell Holmes ... Colonel Thomas Wentworth Higginson wrote, "Yesterday, Sunday, Mary and I walked across to the public library and saw by invitation the beautiful decoration of a ceiling painted in Rome by Maud Howe's husband ... The scheme is to typify the passage of the centuries by means of horses and figures. The whole picture is of light pearly tints that are nowhere departed from, the intention being plainly to produce an effect of a dreamy cloudland."[1] The ceiling, resplendent with its Greek classicism, met the expectations of gentrified Bostonians and received some attention by conservative art critics. Higginson found it a spiritual experience, not withstanding the "human beings in black coats and furred pelisses, humming around" at the reception. Most intriguing and undoubtedly noticed by some of those guests is that the first of the bare-breasted, winged female "Hours" leading the winged horses was undeniably Maud, as can be seen from a drawing that Jack had made of her earlier in their marriage. Maud's best friend, Isabel Perkins Anderson, can be viewed "just above and to the left on entering," corroborated by Maud herself.[2] Another model was Lady Katherine Thynne, a London beauty who was spending the winter in Rome when Jack painted her.[3] And Father Time was apparently modeled on Samuel Gridley Howe.

The completion of *The Triumph of Time* marked the end of one era and the beginning of a new one both in terms of the new century and the changed circumstances of Maud and Jack. Although they were to spend much of the next ten years traveling, they now laid down roots in New England. Their Roman home had been so well renovated that the landlord refused to renew their lease and rented it to the Pope's sisters! Jack had been evicted from his studio (possibly a plot to make him finish his opus), for the walls were so cracked that the roof was in danger of falling in. For Maud, who felt redeemed in the eyes of her family and friends, the occasion marked a need to reconnect with them. Laura had written "I note as always, all you say of Jack, the man-babe; the good and gentle and loving, and beloved, who yet cannot fill that great heart because he is not big enough; so that it cries out, and wants its own people too, and mother and sister and girl-nieces and friends; yet loving him no less wholly and tenderly for wanting the rest."[4] Maud settled right back into her role as Julia's caretaker; she also enjoyed being with her nieces and nephews and did not spare childrearing advice. Both Alice and Rosalind Richards were attractive young women who had no desire for society, much to Maud's disbelief. Laura assured her that Alice preferred people like "Katherine Loring, Sarah Jewett and Mrs. Whitman's afternoons—everything pleasant I can find out of the dancing way."[5] Laura became very annoyed when Maud procrastinated about sending the visiting Rosalind, age twenty-five, home from Rome: "By this time you will know that in spite of all, the child's heart turns so strongly toward her own home and her own mammy and pappy, that it is best to let her go. I know that child better than you do; she wants to come home now, that is what she wants. You see, she went for three months at the utmost and now she has stayed six. You think of this as a dreary little hole, in winter I mean, but you see, it doesn't seem so to them; they love the cold and the snow, and the snuffy people, and every bit of it, yes, they do."⁶ As for Flossy's children, Maud was close to Carrie, who had been studying art in Europe; she disapproved of the second son Harry's lack of motivation and advised tech school, not Harvard, for him (he performed admirably at Harvard and received a Ph.D. from Columbia University in literature).

Being back at home also was a boon for Maud's literary aspirations, as she was now able to confer with magazine editors personally, whereas she had often relied upon Laura and Julia to act as her agents. Maud's experiences living in Rome and her expanded Roman Letters provided the material for most of her early magazine articles. A series appeared in *Lippincott's Monthly Magazine*, where the editor was her friend Harrison Morris, the former director of the Pennsylvania Academy of the Fine Arts and Rhode Island summer resident. Published in 1903–04, these combined travel, people, and personal anecdote: "Roman Holiday," "Presentation to Leo XIII," "Royal Interview with Italy's Queen," "From Italy to Pittsburgh," "Father Kneipp and His Cure," "In the Abruzzi Mountains," "Ischia," "Rome at Easter." "Roman Codgers and Solitaries," an entertaining look at some of the city's more eccentric personalities, appeared in *The Outlook*, and "The Evil Eye and Witches' Night in Rome" in *The Century*. Maud had such success with these stories of her colorful life in Italy that she gathered them into two successive books, *Roma Beata* and *Two in Italy*, published by Little, Brown in 1903 and 1904. She capitalized in other ways on her knowledge of Italy, giving an address on "Hawthorne in Italy" at the author's centennial in Concord, Massachusetts, in 1904.

The first decade of the twentieth century was the most prolific for Maud's magazine stories and nonfiction articles. Jack had presented Maud with a Remington typewriter for their sixteenth wedding anniversary, which facilitated her writing. She wanted to be taken seriously and despite Laura's admonishment to use her married name,⁷ Maud wrote most of her work under "Maud Howe." She did not always have an easy time. "*Harper's* and *Atlantic* have returned my article on the unemployed rich of America. I shall send it today to *Collier's Weekly*. If *Colliers* returns article, send *McClures*. *McClures* declines. *Outlook* declines. Send to *North American Review*."⁸ A handwritten apparently unpublished manuscript,

"The Unemployed Rich in America," criticizing the idle rich, remains. *The Outlook,* a "weekly magazine of news and opinions," whose guest editor was Theodore Roosevelt, published "Who Will Be the Next Pope?," a serious look at papal politics. An unpublished manuscript titled "A Challenge Answered: Atheism or Christ?" remains. She carried over the theme of labor unrest in the mining industry, which she had explored in *Mammon,* in a story called "The Strike," in which striking mill workers come into conflict with the labor committee. Then she proceeded to lampoon labor politics in an apparently unpublished manuscript called "The Furniture Strike," in which pieces of furniture come to life and plan to go on strike.

Queen Margherita of Italy had been a supporter of the arts, had visited Jack's studio to view his mural, and had told Maud how much she enjoyed America's illustrated periodicals. The reach of these magazines was not lost on Maud, and she began to target women with her writing. *Harper's Bazaar* was particularly receptive to her articles and published a series of what might today be considered light-hearted self-help articles. "Whom Shall We Entertain?" does justice to today's women's magazines with their helpful but economical hints. Maud gave examples of simple "blue teas" given at Oak Glen by her mother and the use of friends' creativity for party décor, in her philosophy of entertaining. And she expressed a strong belief that she practiced herself: "Do not make the mistake of asking people of the same age to meet each other. People of our own age know very much what we know. Their minds have been formed by the same currents of thought, the same world events that have affected ours. I can always learn more from one of a generation older, or a generation younger than myself."[9] In "Sun and Air as Physicians," Maud admonished her public on the health benefits of healthy outdoor exercise.[10] "What Is a Lady?" gives tongue-in-cheek advice on how to be a successful rich man's wife. "Nerves," a subject on which Maud seemed especially qualified to write, advised ways to combat neurasthenia by way of the three "s's": silence, solitude, and sleep. "We hear altogether too much lamentation about our 'nerves'—We ought rather to thank God that we belong to the most nervous, restless, all-pervading race the world has seen since the days of Julius Caesar."[11]

With her networking abilities, recognition of her audience, and plain old bravado, Maud brought a superb marketing acumen to her career, and she did the same thing for her husband's, which she still considered of paramount importance. She warned her mother, "Beware what you say on the subject of Jack. My only future is with him and his work. He must do what he feels best, without thought of me. This sounds brutal ... My own ambitions having been thwarted, all of me is in his."[12] She wrote to Charles Hamilton Aide, a British society writer and artist who had organized a benefit exhibition for relief from the recent Boer War, in which Jack had exhibited several red chalk portrait drawings of the dead war heroes. He answered, "So although I hope to see you back in England, I can't honestly hold out much hope in this direction. If congenial work presents itself in the U.S. Jack better not reject it. Portraits in chalk, these I feel sure he will get, but this I fear is work he doesn't like."[13] Portraits and potboilers: these they needed to earn a living, and consequently, in the summer of 1903 Maud and Jack joined the artists' colony in Cornish, New Hampshire, hoping to find a suitable spot in which to be productive. Cornish had been a Utopian haven for American Renaissance and aesthetic movement artists since its initial colonist, St. Gaudens, arrived in 1885, but by 1900 it also featured notable modernists, writers, and politicians. Maud wrote to Laura, "We are working away on our hilltop, I have finished another page for *Lippincott's*, that will make five. At last Jack has found a place where he can work. He is doing a great many things, most of which, I hope, he will turn into pot boilers."[14]

In the shadow of Mount Ascutney, surrounded by terrain that evoked the Italian landscape, Maud and Jack were sublimely happy. "We don't see people much for we are grindstoning ..., but they are all kind, willing and anxious to be friendly. Newport has given us such a horror of summer society—not the dear Papetertie, and our few cronies—but the big dreadful vulgar Newport, that to be among people of one's own sort, and have them all observe as a sacred commandment that nobody goes to any house in the afternoon, the rule being to work all morning ...'[15] Two of their sponsors were Lucia Fairchild Fuller, of the Boston and Newport Fairchilds, and her husband, Henry Fuller, the painter son of Maud's artist savior, George Fuller. Lucia, by 1900, was known as a miniature painter; she had done a mural in the Woman's Building at the Columbian Exposition, which Maud had critically admired in her book,[16] and

Henry painted classical and allegorical works. Maud read Laura's recently published *Hurdy Gurdy* tales to the Fuller children, who could not get enough. Frances Lyons Houston, a portrait painter originally from Boston who had studied in Paris, was also a sponsor and landowner in Cornish. Through her influence Jack bought twenty acres of land on Home Hill in Plainfield, with a view of Mount Ascutney and a small cottage he named *Farthest North*. Just as he had in Rome, Jack enlisted help to renovate the house and plant a garden; his assistant was Henry Vincent Hubbard, later to become an important beaux-arts landscape architect. Maud and her artist husband had finally made it: "I have been to supper with St. Gaudens and feel that I am now a member in regular standing of the artists' colony of which the St. Gaudenses are the leaders."[17]

Jack found the god Pan in the woods of Cornish, New Hampshire. From his upbringing in the glens of Scotland, he had been enamored of the Greek legend of Pan, his pipes, his music, his nymphs, his shepherds and pastures. He wrote to Maud who was away at Oak Glen,

> This morning the birds started their early morning tuning up—a song, a sparrow, a woodpecker, and a song bird common to these parts, but I cannot name him by his song; robins digging for worms in the grass. It was misty and the trees were wonderful with huge webs of spiders all jeweled with dew, and the grass covered with fairy tents of gossamer, as if all their cohorts were camping there—but they have struck their tents and departed. At last the sun is out, and the robins are trying their pipes. —I would give a good deal to hear the solitary thrush. It is the wildest and most inspiring song I know. I am sure it is the tune Pan played upon his pipes—the little reed call, of the Italian shepherds on the mountainside, so like it.[18]

Jack's delight, especially when Maud was not in residence, was to paint the life of Pan. *The Infancy of Pan* and *The Childhood of Pan* are two compositions that surely embody the definition of kitsch. In another two paintings Jack tells the story of Syrinx, the water-nymph of Arcadia, who was transformed into a reed when she resisted the advances of Pan. Pan fashions his flute from this reed, thus creating an opportunity for Jack to create a large painting titled *The Making of the First Musical Instrument*. Pan was often celebrated for his sexual prowess, and Jack indeed portrayed the large, long silver birch tree trunk that the nude Pan straddles as unmistakably phallic. This painting hung over the mantel in Maud's living room in her final years.

As was too often the case, Maud worked while Jack dallied. Her correspondence from that summer also shows that she was struggling to obtain a new decorative commission for Jack. In May, she had written Laura, "I think in NY we put in good work; it is too soon yet to speak of results but I feel the time was profitably spent. We could ill afford to give the time to come to Washington but it was imperative. I don't go into details, which you will understand, all is uncertain yet."[19] Then, "Dearest, The maelstrom begins when I go to Washington. You see I must go and fight with wild beasts. I shall not stop fighting til I get the commission for Jack. If Washington fails it will be NY."[20] Julia's journal notes that Maud left Jack at Cornish to go to New York in October of 1903 and later Julia was "much depressed at waking, mostly about Maud's affairs."[21] During the following winter Maud and Jack followed their prospects to the artists' hub of Washington Square in New York City. Jack did not like New York any more than he had liked Chicago. "New York is as hellish as ever, but I almost doubt whether we ought not to come here. The people — I mean the people in the street — all chew gum, and they look like a lot of fish in a glass globe, opening and shutting their mouths ceaselessly."[22]

But as in Rome, Jack found his friends, a group of illustrators and writers, some little known today, who contributed to the literary life of the city. The group included humorist and artist Oliver Herford — "the American Oscar Wilde"; illustrator Charles Dana Gibson; artist Albert Pinkham Ryder; political satirist Finley Peter Dunne; and John Ames Mitchell, an artist and collaborator with Laura Richards, who published some of Jack's verses in his new enterprise, *Life Magazine*. Jack rebelled against the fine arts community, however; he refused to submit his work to the standard exhibition venues, claiming that his pictures could not be appreciated when placed next to the work of others! Maud was aghast: "The price paid for this stand was a heavy one; for it meant comparative obscurity, while men of less talent achieved wide reputation." Jack was finally prevailed upon by one Thomas Alibone Janvier, a writer who chronicled the bohemian ways of Washington Square, to hold a solo exhibition — location now unknown. He showed work from Cornish: *Mt. Ascutney by the Hunter's Moon, The Melting of the Mists;* a series of studies for imagined mural paintings, and portraits in both red chalk and silverpoint, the last two mediums fancied by Jack as an homage to the Italian Renaissance masters.

Maud darted back and forth between New York, Washington, D.C., Boston, Gardiner, Maine, Cornish, New Hampshire, and Oak Glen. In 1903 *Dr. Howe and His Famous Pupil, Laura Bridgman,* compiled by Maud and Flossy, was finally published. Maud prevailed upon Julia to use her contacts to get reviews and she sent copies to everyone she and her mother had known. At this time there arose in the family a certain resentment of Maud for taking advantage of Julia, now in her late eighties. In what was to become a pattern, Laura was placed in the middle between Harry Howe's disdain of Maud's maneuverings and Maud's belligerence and defense of her methods. Maud wrote, "I see that save for a possible brief visit I shall not intrude my fat carcass at 241 Beacon St. this winter. So being I trust it is not too late for two slim and lovely young carcasses to take my place, which according to our brother Harry has been so disastrously occupied. If I am what he says and implies, why the best thing that could happen to me and especially for my family, would be for me to disappear as speedily and silently as possible. Best of it might be into the next world if not to some very remote and distant part of this. I have been made ill by the letter. I cannot yet bring myself to speak of it, only I shall not answer it, I return it to you, without further comment."[23]

In fact, Maud and Jack profited from Jack's numerous depictions of Julia Ward Howe. As he did for his portraits of deceased war heroes, he copied old photographs of his mother-in-law—and some of Samuel Gridley Howe—into oil, red chalk, or silverpoint. Jack saw nothing wrong with this: "I had so hoped to do another portrait of Mama this summer which I think would pay as well as anything, looking at it in a business light."[24] When Jack did a portrait from life, as he did when he created a wonderful oil portrait of Julia in old age, or the late painting of Uncle Sam Ward, his true talents shone. But the paintings he copied—from an 1861 photograph by J. J. Hawes; from a full-figure photograph of Julia in a hoop skirt, also 1861; as well as the strange portrait of a young Samuel Gridley Howe called *The Chevalier,* apparently partially copied from a portrait by Jane Stuart; as well as the blatant copy in silverpoint of Chev from a photograph by John Adams Whipple, were not even "pot boilers." They were shameless imposters. The fact that Maud saw no ethical dilemma is odd in that she advocated for original works of art and disapproved of chromolithographs.

Two more summers at the Cornish art colony had indelible influences on both Maud and Jack's future endeavors. For Maud the theatrical productions in the tradition of *tableaux vivantes* and the games of charades were memorable: "The spectacles of modern pageantry do not compare in beauty to the rustic fetes the Cornish artists made to please themselves."[25] In 1905, to commemorate the twentieth anniversary of St. Gaudens' arrival at the colony, the artists held the "Masque of 'Ours': The Gods and the Golden Bowl," a fete in the tradition of late Renaissance Florentine theatricals, replete with a cast of costumed Greek gods and goddesses. With beautiful women clad in flowing, diaphanous garments, garlands of flowers in their hair, and heroic men including the god Pan "horned, hoofed and gilded, a living replica of an archaic Greek statue," the pageant was over the top. Maud portrayed Pomona, goddess of fruitful abundance, and Jack, "as of old, attended to [her] costume ... The crowning glory of the evening was the sibyl of the golden bowl, who slowly rose from behind the altar in a cloud of smoke and fire that transfigured the temple and cast an opalescent light on the pines ..."[26] The prologue was written by Percy MacKaye, a poet and later good friend of Maud, and Louis Evan Shipman, with musical accompaniment by visiting members of the Boston Symphony Orchestra. Future pageants organized by Maud for the Art Association of Newport harked back to this "Masque." For Jack, the spell of the sylvan countryside with its silver birches, the "deep plum-colored bloom" over the mountain and undeniably the presence of Maxfield Parrish were all to affect his next two big projects. In 1909, *The Great Sea Horse,* a book of fairy tales written by Isabel Anderson, with twenty-four fanciful illustrations by Jack, was published by Little, Brown. And in 1910, the twenty-five-foot-wide, very plum-colored, mystical mural *Diana of the Tides* was installed in the new American Museum at the Smithsonian Institution.

Diana of the Tides was the commission for which Maud had battled. Her diary notes that in May 1905 Maud met with Elliott Woods, architect of the U.S. Capitol Building, who said that the next time Thomas Hastings, of the beaux-arts firm Carrere and Hastings, was in town he would discuss the prospect of her husband doing a mural in the addition to the capitol that he was designing. Undoubtedly Maud used any influence she had with President Theodore Roosevelt, an admirer of the Howe family, and politicians on down. The mural was deemed more appropriate for the new American Museum. Samuel Pierpont Langley, third Secretary of the Smithsonian Institution from 1887 to his death in 1906, and an old well-connected Bostonian, was a booster of the project, as Maud notes at the opening that they were sorry that he had not lived to see it installed, as he had been so interested in the project.[27] Jack received the commission in 1905, and Maud encouraged him to work on it in New York, to no avail. Maud then wrote and invited herself and Jack to work at the home of Villegas, now the director of the Prado Museum in Madrid, and court painter to the young King Alfonso, and they left for Spain in December 1905. Maud's frustration with her husband is evident in a letter she wrote when she was traveling in Tangiers,

> Well, dear, I hope you are solving your problem. You know how terrible it is when you can't or don't make up your mind till the last minute. That dreadful departure from Boston we shall never either of us forget. We must not repeat the experiment in Villegas' house. I hope they'll keep us til after the King's fetes, probably running along til June 7 but after that—perhaps even before, it's up and away—and I must know where. I cannot again be forced to do what you forced me to do last December. This time, dear, you must have your own way, and I am torn for you. You find it so difficult to know what that "way" is. Perhaps my sympathy and anxiety is all wasted though and you may have already laid out your plans and I shall only have to help you carry them out ... You now must consider only yourself and your work. There are objects to everything in life, but there are also good things to most. Don't wabble, I isn't cross, this may sound so![28]

Rome once again proved to be the solution, and the summer of 1906 found them installed in another apartment and studio, surrounded by Jack's old cronies, the painters Enrico Coleman, Aristide Sartorio, and Antonio Mancini, the latter being one of Mrs. Jack's stable of artists. In fact Jack thought that Bernard Berenson—who was at the top of a long list of people he disliked—was Mancini's agent. Maud and Isabella

Stewart Gardner had grown apart, and when Berenson mentioned in a letter to her that he had run into the Elliotts in Rome, she responded. "I am glad to hear from you that Maud Elliott is still handsome. What a miserable existence she leads. If that poor dead weight of a husband would only . . . It is a sad sight to see a woman on the make. . . ."[29] Mrs. Jack did buy a portrait of Dante (another subject that Jack depicted over and over), and Maud commented, "The skies will fall next!"[30] After the initial crisis of where to paint *Diana of the Tides*, its creation was devoid of the anguish that went into *The Triumph of Time*. Jack had his subject: Diana, the moon goddess, presiding from a seashell over the incoming tide, with horses in the form of waves. His inspiration had occurred a few years previous in 1902, when he and Maud had visited Greece. For Jack, "The hours spent on the Acropolis at Athens studying the frieze of the Parthenon were just like a post graduate course to those months of study in his youth among the Greek marbles of the British Museum. The Phidian steeds haunted his imagination and galloped ever through his dreams. In his *Diana of the Tides* they appear as he saw them in the surf breaking on a sandy shore."[31]

Unlike Gardner, Isabel Anderson proved a loyal friend and generous benefactor to the Elliotts in the years after her introduction and marriage to Larz Anderson. The Andersons gifted *Diana of the Tides* to the Smithsonian Institution. In 1906 they joined Maud in Spain and took her off to Morocco and Seville, to distract her from Jack's dilemma. And Isabel commissioned Jack to illustrate her delightful book of fairy tales, *The Great Sea Horse,* to be published by Little, Brown. "These drawings were a new departure for Jack, and gave utterance to the everlasting child within him . . . he was so much at home in fairyland that the task of creating pictures of elves, mermaids, sprites of wood, sea and air, was a pure delight."[32] Jack had found his métier. Unlike his kitschy paintings of cherubs from an earlier time, these whimsical pictures in the vein of Sir Arthur Rackham showed the influence of the Cornish art colony, and with their vibrant pastel shades of lavender, sea greens, blues and yellows, the influence of Maxfield Parrish. Magical horses and mermaids found a context in a book of fairytales, as they had not in architectural murals. When in Spain, Jack had grown friendly with visiting illustrator Charles Dana Gibson, who now wrote effusively about how much he admired the pictures.³³ Henry James corresponded, "John E's book dazzles and delights me, and makes me want to pat him on the back . . . I envy him for his being able to live in this ugly age, as it so aggressively and importunately is . . . in communion with such adorable visions."³⁴ The drawings were shown at the Copley Gallery, Boston, the Knoedler Gallery in New York, and Fischer Galleries in Washington, D.C., and all were sold.³⁵

By 1908 Maud's love affair with Europe was coming to a close, as she felt needed by her mother in her "eleventh hour." Both she and Jack had returned home for the summers of 1907 and 1908, and every time Maud left again, Julia's diary recorded her despair: "I have prayed that if I am not to see her again in this life, I may not know it, but may have the hope of a happy meeting to cheer and uphold me . . . Maud is like a radiant, beautiful sun. She makes summer wherever she is."³⁶ With the political uprisings in Europe and the fear of being cut off from her family forever, the expatriate life was growing old for Maud, and Jack finally agreed. But before she settled back home for good, Maud wanted to have some last forays into writing and publishing her personal impressions of the places she had visited and the people she had met. *Sun and in Shadow in Spain* went much further than her Rome books had, with almost fifty illustrations including many of the country's great paintings. She had wanted to write one more book on Italy, but not necessarily the one she was obliged to do: *Sicily in Shadow and Sun: The Earthquake and the American Relief Work*. Soon after the disastrous earthquake in December 1908 that killed 200,000 in Sicily, Jack enlisted in a relief brigade under Commander Reginald Rowan Belknap, whom Maud knew from the Naval War College in Newport. Jack proved an invaluable relief worker and architect for the rebuilding of an American village to house survivors. In a telling comment, he said "I would rather have this invitation than an order to paint the biggest decoration in the world." He canceled his plans for exhibiting *Diana of the Tides* in Paris, London, and Madrid, and almost lost his book contract for *The Great Sea Horse*, because of his attention to the disaster relief. For his efforts Jack received numerous citations and medals, both from the Italian government and the Red Cross. Maud returned to the United States in May 1909, and Jack followed in September. They were there for the duration.

As the century entered its second decade, an interesting little story of

Maud's, published ten years earlier, was prophetic. "Ralph Darrow's Tryst" told of four friends on the eve of the new century, making plans to meet again in twenty years and see if they were to accomplish the great things they planned. Ralph Darrow, an architect, had the most grandiose scheme, to see through construction of his visionary designs for a new park system, a public library, an art museum, and a school of design. Darrow and his friends Basil and Philip veritably ignored Darrow's little sister, who sat meekly in attendance, bolstering their egos. That night Darrow is so sleepless that he takes an overdose of Mildred's sleeping potion and expires in his chair by the fire.[37] Twenty years later to the night, Mildred sits in the same room wondering if Basil and Philip will keep their assignation. They arrive and are amazed to discover that Mildred has masterminded the construction of her brother's buildings and is now widely respected as a friend and benefactor of the arts. "Who could have believed the little sister would do such large things?" Philip and Basil ask.[38]

NINE

Of these home fires that must be kept burning lest another Dark Age settle upon the world, the one that is in the gravest danger of neglect is the sacred flame of art. In all times of depression the artists are the first people to suffer ... As prices of food go higher, other men get an increase of wages, but the artist gets no wages at all, for as art is commonly looked upon as a luxury, it is the first thing to go. This is a grave danger and must be gravely met and prepared for.

MAUD HOWE ELLIOTT, "KEEP THE HOME FIRES BURNING"

THE DEATH OF JULIA WARD HOWE IN OCTOBER 1910 ALTERED THE Howe family dynamics and circumstances to a great extent. Once the division of the estate was attended to, the preservation of their mother's legacy proved far more acrimonious. 241 Beacon Street was sold. Maud and Jack acquired a renewable two years' lease on Oak Glen, leading to hard feelings by Flossy, now widowed and poorer than ever, who pictured Maud dead, and Jack Elliott, whom she had never liked, living on there indefinitely.[1] Brother Harry emerged as the real villain in the ensuing arguments, as he had had enough of Jack using Julia for profit. "This morning came a letter from brother Harry in which he expresses himself as distressed about the Fanueil Hall portrait and said that he spoke for himself and his sisters in saying that the family did not wish to back Jack's having the order for mama's portrait, but for any other portrait would do as well ... I feel that I have been stabbed in the back by my brother and sister."[2] Harry had to defend this decision to Laura: "My explanation is a dislike of Elliott's work, and my feeling that you, Tom [Flossy], and I should join in telling Maud kindly that in our judgment she should make it clear . . . that the family wishes the committee [Boston Art Commission] to feel that its choice of an artist is wholly unhampered."[3] Harry was also the most assertive in his wish to have Laura write "The Life" of their mother—with no collaboration from Maud, and it went without saying, none from Flossy, whom he deemed totally incompetent. Harry, an academic, felt that Laura's previous work, *The Journals and Letters of Samuel Gridley Howe,* set the standard, and that Laura alone was qualified to write the biography. He was willing to pay for a secretary for the project, only if she worked under Laura's direction in Gardiner.

At the age of fifty-five, Maud still maintained her reputation in the family as impulsive, demanding, and temperamental. In Harry's mind this disqualified her from the serious undertaking of writing a biography. In truth, the year following her mother's death plunged Maud into mood swings and depression. "The worst day since October 17. A dagger, poisoned, was driven into my heart—et tu Brute!" she recorded in her diary.[4] She found it difficult to deal with the mountain of sympathy letters, the tributes, the ceremonies. Harry wrote to Laura,

> Here is Maud speaking in public, according to the newspapers, yet according to Rosalind unable to envisage the future. Why, if she is that, she ought to be in a sanitarium. Really, Laura, I feel much troubled about her. She seems to me absurdly fat, and suggesting dropsical tendency . . . the sort of intensity in which she lives is terrible. I always come home about sick after being with her, and what must it be for her, whose poor body can never escape the turbulent peaceless soul to which it is attached? . . . Let us hope that she may pull herself together; but that she can keep this way for a good long term of life seems too much to expect.[5]

Harry—who incidentally died twenty-six years before Maud—really did not get his sister.

Oak Glen beckoned to Maud and Jack as a place of solace and rejuvenation, and they moved there in July of 1911. Laura and Maud worked out a collaborative plan for "The Life," to be indeed written by Laura at Gardiner, with substantial input by Maud. As Harry had pointed out to Maud, "It is true that you have a vast fund of knowledge which Laura lacks; and that you and mama were most close . . . those facts, as far as they go, are certainly important, and should be allowed weight."[6] On the other hand, Harry was concerned that Maud, being so strident, might not let Laura edit her contributions. Harry suggested to Laura that Maud and Flossy create their own "distinct" projects, as a diversion. Maud wrote an article about her mother's work habits, calling it "The Eleventh Hour in the Life of Julia Ward Howe," named after a sermon by her mother; this she published in 1911 and turned into a successful lecture that she delivered all over New England. Flossy, who was to carry on her mother's suffrage work most ardently, and who felt that the subject was being sorely neglected by Laura, published *Julia Ward Howe and the Woman Suffrage Movement* in 1913.

The fact remains that Maud made significant contributions to "The Life." Her diaries show that although the process tormented her, she read the old letters, she compiled her recollections of the Santo Domingo trip and the London trip, she worked intermittently on episodes during 1912, 1913, and 1914, and she met with Laura on a regular basis to go over the material. Laura's daughter Betty Wiggins later asserted that Maud blackmailed Laura to include her name on the title page, by threatening to withhold the notes she had compiled on her mother's last summer.[7] Indeed, the recollections wrap up the book, with Maud's characteristic prose telling the story of her mother's final days and words. But Maud and Laura worked well together—it was Flossy about whom Laura remonstrated—and lovingly corresponded for seventy years, much of the time advising each other on their writing, so it is difficult to envision "blackmail" as an operative word in their relationship. In fact, Laura acknowledged Maud's writing in several letters:

> I want to impress upon you once more that this last chapter of yours is a great-step over your other ones; I mean Skipper and Rosalind both agree with me and say more power to your elbow. Now here is your very long one, the European. Are you ready to cut that down, go over it at the pace you have now struck? It will have to be brought into relation with the rest: I will do it if you prefer.[8]

Nevertheless the two-volume book itself is hardly creative prose; it is a compilation of Julia's journal entries and letters, strung together chronologically with recollections by and of "our mother." The one thing the four siblings did agree on was sanitizing their family life, never mentioning marital discord, family dysfunction, or "a strain of insanity" proffered by Laura, but vetoed by Harry. *Julia Ward Howe, 1819–1910*, by Laura E. Richards and Maud Howe Elliott, assisted by Florence Howe Hall, was published by Houghton Mifflin Company in 1915 and won the first Pulitzer Prize for biography in 1917. Columbia University "awarded the annual prize of $1,000 established by the will of the late Joseph Pulitzer, to be given for 'the best American biography teaching patriotic and unselfish service to the people.'"[9]

Maud emerged from her doldrums in 1912 and began to regain some momentum. In the month of January alone, between stays at Oak Glen, she went to New York to visit an old suffrage friend of Julia's, to Washington, D.C., to view *Diana of the Tides* in its new location in Mineral Hall, and back to New York to the office of the *Outlook*, where former President Teddy Roosevelt wanted to show her an article on suffrage, filled with tributes to her mother. In Newport, Maud began to cultivate the intelligentsia who might be interested in Jack's pictures, and in doing so made some lasting friends. Roderick Terry, a clergyman and bibliophile, was president of both the Newport Historical Society and the Redwood Library and Athenaeum. His wife Linda was an artist as well as the daughter of Henry Marquand, former president of the Metropolitan Museum of Art. Maud had attended their wedding many years earlier, and they now lived in her father's home, Linden Gate, designed by Richard Morris Hunt; they commissioned a panel painting by Jack.[10] Harrison S. Morris and his wife Anna were cultivated Philadelphians of importance in the world of art and literature who summered at Horsehead, a Jamestown estate built by her father, philanthropist Joseph Wharton. Mary M. Emery (Mrs. Thomas), the widow of an Ohio manufacturing magnate, lived at the Mariemont estate in Middletown; she acquired a portrait of Julia by Jack that she bequeathed to the Cincinnati Woman's Club.

Maud's sister Flossy considered herself the heir to her mother's club activities and participated in the Federation of Women's Clubs, in which Julia had been a leader: "The women of America had outgrown the old, narrow, often selfish life of utter absorption in the affairs of the individual home. They now longed for wider culture, for the broadening of their ideas by association with other women, for opportunities to improve not only their own, but all homes."[11] Maud had never before stayed in one place long enough to be a devotee of women's clubs, even though Julia had founded one in her honor—the Saturday Morning Club, in 1871, in an attempt to introduce Maud to cultured females of her own age. In turn, as the Town and Country Club was dying a natural death in the early 1900s, as a "restorative" for the dejected Julia, Maud founded the Papeterie, an informal group that exchanged paperback novels. "The 'delicious fooling' that marked the first year of the Town and Country Club was the animating spirit of the Papeterie . . . A valueless book was a P.B.—pot boiler; a worthy but dull work was an M.A.S.—might amuse somebody."[12] Over the years the presentations became more thought-provoking. "A good walk and in the afternoon to the Normans where the Papeterie met and we had a very good lecture on Emerson and the transcendental movement in New England by Mr. Jones." And "In spite of rain, to town in the Pumpelly's auto with Daisy Waring . . . took us to Mrs. Josephs' for the Papeterie Club. Mr. Peasley read a noble paper on Dante . . . Daisy Waring and Miss Betten slept profoundly and Daisy afterwards discussed the paper as though she had followed every word!" And "We went with the Braytons in the afternoon to Mrs. Sturtevant's where we had a fine Papeterie meeting! With music of a good amateur quality, orchestra of the boys from St. Georges School, Mrs. Howard sang very well and Miss Herter, a handsome young painter, played the violin."[13]

In truth, Maud found women's clubs a bit stifling and much preferred meetings in which the sexes freely mingled. On a visit to Washington, D.C., in 1910, she realized that "today the world is run by committees."[14] Committees had agendas and platforms, they enacted legislation and reforms, they raised awareness.

> Went into the General Assembly before the House hearing. The appearance and speaking of the men compare favorably with any legislative body I know. Two very fine young men of socialistic sympathies spoke in favor of bills increasing employers' responsibilities towards men injured or to the survivors of men killed . . . The opposition was presented by "the gentleman from Little Compton," Mr Burchard . . . He spoke for Capital and

when the votes were taken, the vote for the socialistic measures was light, the voices high and hopeful . . . then came the heavy masterful "Nos" of the opposition, the Capitalists votes hard, cruel, with no resonance but a sound of resentment. Very interesting day.[15]

In committees Maud would use her considerable persuasive powers for causes that mattered to her. In a comment not intended as a compliment, brother Harry had said that Maud could make a male say anything. Harrison Morris wrote of his appointment as commissioner of the 1911 International Art Exposition in Rome, "Mrs. Elliott was in Washington that season, and as was natural, she was meeting all the dignitaries of the Government. Mr. Taft was President; Mr. Knox was Secretary of State, and with these she used her persuasive knowledge of the qualifications that an art commissioner to Italy should possess. She and I had been much thrown together in the cause of art, and she was good enough to think I might do, and might accept."[16]

The cause of art once again presented an opportunity for Maud to step forward and lead. On March 20, 1912, she presented a lecture to Newport's Current Topics Club, a discussion club on current events begun by Jeannette Swasey in 1892. The topic, "An Artist's Life in Rome," related to an article she had recently published on "American Artists in Rome,"[17] but now she wanted to present "three glimpses of Rome: the ancient, the Renaissance, the modern."[18] There was to be a small exhibition held in conjunction with the lecture at the YMCA on Mary Street, and Maud was on the phone rounding up pictures. Jack's portrait of Uncle Sam Ward, a pastel from *The Great Sea Horse*, and some of Linda Terry's watercolors were included, as were paintings by the prominent American artists William Sergeant Kendall, Albert Sterner, and Samuel Colman, all of whom summered in Newport. The young Helena and Louisa Sturtevant, professionally trained in Boston and Paris, came from a staunch old Newport family and were very enthusiastic about the endeavor. The work of installing the exhibition fell to Maud, however, who was irritated that the Terrys held a luncheon for her to meet some Navy people in the middle of her work: "This was very odd and showed how little the Terrys understand working life. I had fagged all the morning to hang the show . . . I wanted to be at my freshest . . . and they had invited people to meet us!" The fact that all this artistic talent existed in Newport was a revelation to the community, and several citizens banded together to form the Art Association of Newport, with eight founding artist members, of whom Jack was one.

The Art Association was far from the only endeavor with which Maud was involved in this pivotal year of 1912. Julia had been very cheered by her youngest daughter's gradual embrace of suffrage, and Maud took up the banner, literally, when she and Flossy marched with the Massachusetts delegation in a suffrage parade in New York City in May. Maud had given a suffrage talk at the Oliphant Club in Newport and in June attended a meeting for the Newport Suffrage League, where she spoke along with society's grand dame—and suffragist—Alva Belmont, whom Jack described as condescending. "Maybe!" wrote Maud. The other women in the League were put off by Belmont's haughty behavior, and Maud wrote, "It will be best to have her work independently of us another summer. She reminds me of Mrs. Jack Gardner. Not easy—hardly possible—to work with."[19] Maud became president of the Newport County Woman Suffrage League and under this mantle she brought her unique blend of reminiscence and forceful argument to audiences in southern New England. While she, like her mother, argued that the mother's vote is essential for the well-being of their children and as a moral initiative, she also made impassioned pleas for far different reasons: women needed the vote to counteract the vote of ignorant men, to appoint other women to responsible positions, to allow progress. Likely thinking of her own situation, was it fair, she asked, that an alien man who has only been in the country a few years could gain the right to vote when she could not? Voting was a woman's right! In her newfound political voice, Maud urged her League to "concern itself in future more directly in influencing the different legislators in the community in every possible way. Education, persuasion, example—all these have their effect in molding the minds of men and women. I ask every one of you here present to endeavor directly, as well as indirectly, to influence the men holding political and legislative offices, for, in the end, it is from them that we must receive the great invitation to share the duties and responsibilities of the voters of this state."[20]

In a suffrage speech Maud explained her earlier change of heart by saying that there were two forces in the world: conservatism, which holds all the beautiful lessons of the past, and progress, which gives us the vision of the future. She decided she would rather be with those who go ahead than with those who act as a brake on the wheels of progress.[21] Like some other Americans, Maud's belief in progress was directly aligned with her admiration for Teddy Roosevelt, "the champion of human progress."[22] She felt that the hope for America to succeed as a strong nation lay with Roosevelt again becoming president; that William Howard Taft, the president in 1912, was the "mouthpiece of the rich class, while Roosevelt [was] the tribune of the people."[23] In fact in February 1912 she (among others) told him so, and Roosevelt announced he would accept the Republican nomination if offered. Maud jumped to his defense when detractors said bad things; one was her own minister, the Reverend William Safford Jones of Channing Memorial Church, another was her Art Association colleague William Burgess, a Newport summer resident who taught political science at Columbia University. Burgess called Roosevelt's followers "rabble," an insult Maud took personally. She wrote a letter of protest to the newspapers after a U.S. senator criticized Roosevelt. Roosevelt lost the nomination to Taft at the Republican convention, but soon he rallied support through the Progressive or "Bull Moose" party, with a platform that called for stiff regulation of industry and protection of the middle and working classes. Maud was asked to form the women's branch of the Rhode Island Progressive Committee, which she did with her usual gusto.

Maud was a born politician; after one of her speeches a colleague said, "If you were a man you would be a senator. No reason you shouldn't be one if you are a suffragist!"[24] This political savvy was sorely needed in her work for the Progressive cause and for the Art Association. She had to be careful not to talk about Roosevelt to her suffrage audiences as "there is a division in that camp." She converted some of her Art Association colleagues to Progressives, hosting gatherings at her home: "In the afternoon Dresser, Harrison Morris, Dr. Dinan, Mr. Griswold, Biesel and the Sturtevants came and talked over the Progressive Party." Daniel Leroy Dresser, brother-in-law of John Nicholas Brown, was president of the Newport Progressive League and not one of Maud's favorites: "Dresser is slower than cold molasses ... distrust his very leisurely nature. Slow and stupid, good and right-minded, but I fear ineffectual."[25] Artist Charles

Biesel, an Art Association founder, and his wife became loyal Progressives. For her committee she approached wealthy women such as Ethel Rhinelander (Mrs. Leroy) King and Sara Whiting (Mrs. George) Rives; they each gave five dollars to the cause—King on condition her name was kept out of the newspapers as her sons were opposed! While fundraising was integral to both organizations and Maud did her share of managing fairs and rummage sales, the excitement was in choosing candidates, forming a platform: "I brought in two planks: the infant mortality and the domestic education of homemakers." She traveled often up to the Providence Progressive League[26] and around Rhode Island, sharing the podium with such prominent social reformers as Jacob Riis, Jane Addams, and Frances Kellor. "Spoke in the afternoon on social conditions, spoke chiefly of suffrage and the need of studying politics by the women. Riis very good. In the evening in a larger hall spoke on the political situation and I related how I had become a Progressive."[27] She sat in motorcades carrying signs that read "Protect the laborer," "Let the people rule," visited textile mills, and sat for hours in smoke-filled meeting rooms. She thrived on it. On November 5, 1912, Woodrow Wilson defeated Taft and Roosevelt to become president. Maud's allegiance to her new party, however, was not to wane.

The Art Association of Newport had only slightly less politics than the Progressive campaign. An open letter to the community outlined plans for incorporation and a constitution and invited interested citizens to participate. Maud's diary records, "Home to find the ballot for the Art Association little to my liking, poor Jack almost distracted over it.... To see the Sturtevants about the Art Association ballot. They too are not pleased. Find too much politics but where can we go to escape politics? Are they not necessary for all human relations?" She recognized that in order to work toward a common goal, one needed to put up with "all sorts of people." The charter was granted in June 1912, followed by the first annual meeting. Sergeant Kendall was elected president, with Maud as secretary, Biesel as treasurer, and six members making up the council: Jack, the two Sturtevants, Albert Sterner, Reverend John B. Diman, Harford W. H. Powel, and Jeannette Swasey. The object of the Association was to be "the cultivation and promotion of artistic endeavor and interest in the arts." The Charter was amended in 1915 to broaden the definition of arts to include "education by literature, music and science, aiding in the cultivation of the arts of design; advancing study and research in art, literature, music and science; establishing, collecting, maintaining and preserving a museum ... conducting exhibitions, lectures and classes for instruction in the various branches of art, literature, music and science."

With the same zeal and foresight that guided her efforts in the areas of human rights and suffrage, Maud co-founded and guided this new organization that promoted the arts as a civilizing influence. "Our strength lies in the fact that we are a truly representative association, including people of every age and every sort of income, that we welcome with equal cordiality all sorts and conditions of men, women and children, asking only one thing, that they come to us in the same spirit of devotion to the cultivation of artistic endeavor that inspired our founders."[28] Over half of the 142 charter members were women. In its first twenty-five years, the Council consistently had three or often four women on it. Maud recruited the great benefactors of the institution: Gertrude Vanderbilt Whitney, Mary Emery, Natalie Bayard Brown, Anna Falconnet Hunter, Ellen and Ida Mason, Edith Wetmore, Mabel Norman Cerio, and Elizabeth Swinburne. She enlisted her friend Harrison Morris to become president in 1916, and with his contacts in the art world they enticed important modern American artists, including members of The Eight, or Ashcan School, and The Ten, American impressionists, to exhibit in the annual exhibitions. Maud herself inaugurated the lecture series, held at the Art Association's first home, the old William Morris Hunt studio, where John La Farge and Henry and William James had received instruction. She spoke on the "Art Traditions of Newport," and "Some Pioneers of American Art," and began to conduct research that later culminated in a number of exhibitions celebrating the importance of artists and architects who worked in Newport.[29]

This frenetic activity of 1912 was a prelude to the coming years of activism. The Art Association provided creative outlets for talents Maud had been nurturing for decades. She recognized the importance of art education on a formal level and indeed, said that it was the most valuable work the Art Association could accomplish. After a few false starts by men — her husband and Albert Sterner — Helena Sturtevant became the director of the school and established an academic program of study, based on classical models. Maud and Sturtevant were very conscious of creating opportunities for students of limited means to take courses. When the United States joined the First World War, Maud led efforts to relate the Art Association activities to war work. She called forth speakers in the lecture series who related their work for the Red Cross, their military expertise, their political prognoses. She spearheaded entertainments and classes for officers and enlisted men of the Navy, Army, and Marines stationed in Newport. The entertainments offered at the Art Association drew upon Maud's past theatrical adventures and particularly her experiences at the Cornish Art Colony that were inspired by her friend, the dramatist Percy MacKaye. Maud introduced the pageantry of costumed artist balls, staged a production of Shakespeare's *Twelfth Night*, and in 1922 a very lavish "Viking Pageant." She lectured on art, literature, and the stage and was not shy about advocating for political and other reform. She worked with esteemed businessmen of the day, especially Marsden Perry, to acquire the John N. A. Griswold House as the Art Association headquarters in 1915.[30] In the 1920s she and Morris recognized that in order to be sustainable, the Art Association needed an endowment fund, a mission of which Maud ably took charge. Maud's family was bewildered by this flurry of very meaningful activity, although Harry in his usual caustic—and erroneous—opinion noted, "I am grieved that dear old Modge fritters her time away, yields to self-indulgence with her old committees, for that is what it is. She has a decided talent which she is too indolent to use, preferring the excitement of administration for which she has no talent."[31] Fortunately Maud never did listen to Harry.

The Progressive cause was in full force again in October 1916, when Maud joined "The Golden Special," a barnstorming cross-country campaign train of women speaking on behalf of the Republican presidential candidate Charles Evans Hughes—who had been endorsed by Roosevelt. Frances Kellor, an immigrant rights activist who had served under Hughes when he was governor of New York, cajoled Maud into this venture. Other prominent Progressive-era women on the trip were Mary Antin, a writer and immigrant Jew from Poland, Dr. Katherine Bemont Davis, a New York State prison reformer, and journalist Rheta Childe Dorr, who when asked why she was for Hughes, answered, "because he does not consider women as a ladies' auxiliary of the human race, but as people and part of the race." Maud's speaking ability was such that she usually went first, as she had studied up on the local conditions and of course reflected on her noble parents. When she realized that people were more interested in hearing about Julia Ward Howe than her own message on labor and capital, she manipulated her mother to her advantage. Her most popular story was that Julia and Hughes both received honorary doctorates from Brown University and how much her mother admired him. The train barnstormed through New York, Ohio, Illinois, Minnesota, Michigan, North Dakota, Wyoming, Montana, Washington State, and onward through California and Arizona before returning through the more southern states. She later addressed the Art Association on her visits to art galleries and museums in the far west, stressing the importance of developing art associations across the country.

Staying home and taking care of her man did not seem to be an overriding concern at this point in Maud's life; in fact her activism was likely necessary to escape Jack's continuing lethargy and lack of ambition. On their wedding anniversary in 1918, she wrote, "Thirty one years ago today, we took up life together 'for better for worse.' For me it has been one increased betterment in all the things that count, save one, Production. I haven't produced enough, nor have you! Well, let's go in for the 11th hour with all our mights and means!"[32] In her diary she lamented Jack's dislike of their involvement at the Art Association, his feeling that they could not cope with living at Oak Glen, that he did not want to consult with Maud's artist niece Carrie Birckhead about selling work. Living in the United States he felt "over-shadowed" by the Howes. He did not want to show her his work, he no longer seemed to want her advice. What he apparently did want was for her to continue to act as his agent: in one letter to Maud when she was in Washington, D.C., he advised, "Mind you get invited to some of the functions. What's the good of staying with Ministers and such, I should like to know. What's the good of being who you are if you [can't use it to advantage?] Do you take my meaning?"[33] She wrote that "his two biggest works I helped him to: *The Triumph of Time* and the *Diana*." But now she was at a loss and decided, very astutely, "I wish I could help my husband more, but something stronger than I must do that — himself!"[34]

Maud and Jack continued to come together in their relief work. As in the case of the Messina earthquake, Jack rose to the occasion when people were in need. In 1913 he organized an art exhibition for the Massachusetts Red Cross to raise funds for victims of the Balkan-Turkish War. He tried to enlist when war broke out in Europe in 1914, but he was too old. He offered his Newport studio as the surgical dressing unit, and was active in the Italian War Relief Committee. Maud was quick to affirm the importance of art in wartime: camouflage, war posters, among other needed talents. Creating memorials was close to her heart; Jack began to make drawings from photographs of the sons of their friends who died in the war. Beginning with Victor Chapman and Norman Prince, Jack produced twelve portraits that were sold to benefit the Blinded Soldiers' Relief Fund and reproduced in a portfolio funded by Gertrude Vanderbilt Whitney. The portraits were commended by many and shown in an exhibition at Knoedler's in New York. For her war work, Maud kept the "home fires burning," a phrase she used in her annual reports at the Art Association and in an article she published in 1917.

In 1918 Maud and Jack had had enough of living out in the wilds of Portsmouth, Rhode Island, and arranged to rent a house on the Terry estate on Rhode Island Avenue in Newport—a few blocks from the Art Association. The maintenance of Oak Glen had proved daunting, there had been litigation over the use of the Howe land for the Norman Waterworks, traveling into Newport on the trolleys was tiresome, and Jack naturally found himself lonely most of the time. On January 19, 1919, they closed up Oak Glen and "moved our goods and chattels to the little Terry bungalow. Jack called it the Butler Asylum. I shall call it Lilliput." Lilliput was to become the center of Maud's last years, a warm, cozy house where she held "afternoons" for her guests. She especially delighted in the backyard with a goldfish pond, and a beauteous garden—her own "green parlour."

TEN

> For you the storied seasons have rolled, a stately stream,
> Of rich and magic enterprise, inspired glow and gleam.
> Of travel and of romance, achievement and of dream.
> Till now within this gray-roofed town you hold a torch on high.
> And all who see that flame shall know what name to call it by,
> For Art is written in the light—nor shall it wane and die.
> Dear leader, so to you we bring our garland bright with praise.
> For all you are and all you do, the wisdom of your ways;
> And may the long light follow you down many generous days.
> EDITH BALLINGER PRICE, 1924

IN 1925 MAUD AND JACK WERE ON THEIR WAY HOME FROM A winter visit to St. Augustine, Florida, when Jack became seriously ill in Charleston, South Carolina. He had "angina" followed by pneumonia and died there in May at the age of sixty-six. Maud had lost her brother Harry, sister Flossy, and niece Alice in 1922; Belle Gardner in 1924; and now came this devastating blow, necessitating a complete rethinking of her life's purpose. She cloaked herself in black and wore her husband's and her medals on her chest, as shown in a Bachrach photograph from 1928. As Maud later recalled, she went to a therapist, Dr. Joseph Pratt of Boston: "It was just after my Jack's death when life seemed over for me. He taught me to walk alone! Never in the twenty years has he prescribed any drug. His advice and the books he sent me or made me buy gradually lifted me from black despair to active life again."[1] In 1923 Maud had published an anecdotal autobiography called *Three Generations,* and now she began work on her husband's biography, *John Elliott, the Story of an Artist.* Without Jack there to discourage her, she renewed her efforts to place his work in public and private collections, writing letters to all her old contacts. The Art Association held a memorial exhibition in 1925.[2] One reviewer noted that in spite of Jack's connections through the Howe family, he essentially "lived in a world of his own, a world of poetry which he tried to express in paint."[3]

With her biography of Jack, Maud began the last phase of her writing career, in which she both documented and disguised her family history. In *The John Elliot,* published by Houghton Mifflin in 1930, Jack was transformed from an indolent, irritable artist into a brilliant visionary, too exalted to even sign his work or try to promote it. His tedious execution of the Boston Public Library Commission, which drove Maud so crazy she couldn't live with him, is presented as a struggle for an ideal, a legacy for the ages. According to Maud, Jack's destiny was to convey through his art the beauty that he, among few, was privileged to see. As for the Art Association, which he once said was "gobbling up our lives," he originated the design and implementation of adding the Griswold House stable onto the house, transforming it into a gallery and exhibition hall (working with Maud's nephew, architect Samuel Prescott Hall); he taught a few courses before deciding teaching was not for him, he went to Council meetings — but he certainly was not and had never been, as she wrote, "the leading spirit, the lengthening shadow" of the institution.

Maud wrote innocently about her husband's penchant for making her costumes, fussing over her appearance in public, decorating for parties and arranging flowers — all activities that one hundred and fifty years later some would certainly find suggestive of homosexuality. Laura once wrote — perhaps equally naively — "As to Peter Wiggins — his name is Carl, by the way — I really don't know what Jack would do if he saw him; carry him off bodily, I fancy — no, he couldn't — but manage somehow to paint him . . . A splendid young Hercules."[4] The liberal and tolerant Howe family likely would be among the vanguard in supporting gay rights today, but in the nineteenth century there were no such options, no mention of homosexuality. The most intriguing indication of Jack's sexual orientation was his friendship with Giacomo Boni, the Italian archaeologist who shared Jack's love of gardening, birds—and Dante, on whom he wrote a treatise. As mentioned previously, Boni was closely associated with Horatio Brown, who was connected to Victorian gay society. Another strong hint was the set of photographs of Sicilian nude boys photographed by Wilhelm von Gloeden, found in boxes from Maud and John's estate that came down to her niece, Frances Minturn Howard. Von Gloeden was a German photographer who worked in Italy; he often posed his young models in classical Greek costumes and poses. His openly gay lifestyle was tolerated in Sicily, where he also photographed damage from the Messina earthquake, at the same time Jack was there in 1909.[5] Then there is Jack's very homoerotic painting of Pan, which reportedly went to a gay bar after Maud's death. Whatever his sexual preferences, Jack adored Maud; he had pursued her with ardor, and their marriage appeared to be mutually satisfying.

By 1926 Maud was recovered enough to launch a new crusade. She went to Greece to return Lord Byron's helmet, which had been in the Howe family since her father had brought it back to the United States in 1830. The poet, who had taken up the cause of Greek independence, had died there in 1824, shortly before the arrival of Samuel Gridley Howe. Byron's effects, including sword and helmet, were sold at auction, and "The Chevalier," after six years of fighting alongside the Greek soldiers and tending to their wounds, acquired the helmet. All his children recalled that the helmet was displayed at the end of the hallway at Green Peace and in other homes as a symbol of freedom for oppressed peoples. Harry inherited the heirloom, and after the death of his widow in 1926, Maud made plans for an expedition to return it and renew her faith in Greek ideals. She visited the Ethnological Museum where she determined the helmet should join the other mementoes of the Greek fight, which included photographs and drawings of her parents as well as the Byron objects. With proper pomp and circumstance, Maud was feted by the officials and dignitaries, attending a performance of Greek dance at the Theatre of Dionysus on Midsummer's Eve by a dancer who told Maud that she "had been declared the superior of Isadora Duncan, Ruth St. Denis and Rachel."[6] Maud presented the helmet—which she had carried in a hatbox all across Europe—at a ceremony embellished by her usual stirring oratory. "Noticing that there were many young people among the guests who looked like students from many different countries, I adjured them to kindle their torch at Athena's flame, and quoted the poet's immortal lines,

> Awake, not Greece—she is awake,
> Awake my spirit![7]

The month in Greece and the next month's travel to France, Belgium, the Netherlands, and England served to reintroduce Maud to activism and travel. After leaving Athens she spent several weeks touring Greek refugee camps and meeting with relief groups. She went to France in hopes of having the French Heroes Lafayette Memorial Fund acquire Jack's memorial portraits of the heroes who died in the Lafayette Escadrille, for the Château Chavagniac Military Museum. She went to Belgium to present Jack's portrait of Edith Clavell to the Royal Museum of Beaux Arts.[8] Seeing England without Jack was cathartic: "This is the first time I have been able to enjoy anything of beauty, thankful to have the sense of beauty without the heart. Jack seemed with me all the time. He knew the country well. How pleased he would be to have me see it."[9] This trip, her first to Europe since before the First World War, broadened her perspectives on world diplomacy, lessened her opposition to the League of Nations, and increased her belief in the importance of the United States. America was now respected, and she noted that in her youth she was treated hospitably because of her parents; now she was received kindly because she was an American. But she continued her old refrain: "It is the artists and the poets who make the real treaties that bind us together in spite of armies, navies, politicians and bankers."[10]

In 1892 Maud had said that "a great art can only spring from a great religious connection. Religion, or the human ideal, is the tree from which at different periods of the world's history the fair blossoming of Art has sprung."[11] She had only slightly changed her tune thirty years later. She opened a speech to the American Federation of Arts, in which she was an active member, with: "If civilization is to survive—and this is a matter about which I feel grave doubt—it must be through the instrumentality of the two chief civilizing influences, religion and art." The analogy to religion was reinforced by her use of the word "missionary"— those with museum expertise should go forth and preach their gospel of art with missionary zeal. She advocated for museum studies, wherein "men and women striving to build up the smaller foundations might be received for a brief term as students and initiated into the mysteries of running a museum properly. How collections are made, how classified, how cared for . . ."[12]

In both her Art Association annual reports and her lectures Maud was prescient in establishing a model for American museums as educational institutions—a model that exists today. Using the Art Association of Newport as an example, she cited two exhibitions in which the young people of Newport learned not only the importance of their city's heritage of finely crafted furniture, but also the importance of preserving it. She told of the lectures at the Art Association, such as one on Hungarian peasant costumes delivered by an expert from the Brooklyn Museum, in which the local needlewomen and the workers of Aquidneck Industries crowded the galleries. During this postwar period, America's museums were acquiring European art at a great pace, and Maud urged these large museums to share the wealth; she advocated for loans to smaller institutions of work that might otherwise sit in storage. She also encouraged gifts and legacies to museums, with no strings attached. In her advocacy of artists, Maud's rhetoric also rings true a hundred years later.

In Newport, Maud reinvigorated her efforts at the Art Association and in other community endeavors. She conceived of the Association's lectures as a continuance of the Town and Country Club, and called upon her Boston and New York friends—and relatives—to come and speak on diverse topics. Among these were Laura Richards, niece and artist Laura Chanler, nephew Henry Marion Hall, Margaret Deland, Ralph Adams Cram, Joseph Lindon Smith, art historians from the major metropolitan museums, famous archaeologists and architects, diplomats and artists she had known in Europe. She wrote, "The Lyceum, for so long the leading cultural feature of our small town life, has gone . . . It still exists in Newport, where famous speakers from all over the world share their experiences with their listeners at the Art Association. Here, too, concerts and festivals are held; perhaps it is the Masque written by a young genius, or a ball given by the art students."[13] Many affluent yet civic-minded citizens such as Natalie Bayard Brown, Ida and Ellen

Mason, Senator George Wetmore and his daughters Maude and Edith Wetmore, volunteered their efforts at the Art Association, just as Maud worked for other causes in town, such as beautification and preservation. In 1914 she had petitioned the Mayor of Newport to preserve the historic Brick Marketplace. "This beautiful building has been too long neglected and abused. It should be preserved and restored to its original use and beauty."[14] She served on a committee to create a Newport flag, which was finalized a few years later. With the Great Depression, Maud led efforts at the Art Association to raise funds for maintenance projects around the buildings and encouraged members to hire workers for their own household projects — and have their portraits painted by local artists!

"Maud befriended every man of consequence in the U.S. Navy," according to family lore passed down by the Richards branch of the family. Niece Laura (Betty) Wiggins told the following story:

> When Admiral Nimitz once visited Newport during the Second World War, he said there was only one person there he wanted to meet. That was Maud Howe Elliott. At the appointed hour, cocktails were readied, Rosa the maid opened the door and Laura Wiggins received the Nimitz entourage. Maud as usual was waiting to stage a grand entrance. The young subalterns rigidly lined up ... When Maud finally did come down "properly naked in a cocktail dress," she paused at the landing on the staircase, the butler brought a cocktail tray to her and then passed cocktails to the others. Maud lifted the glass and offered the toast: "as they say in the Navy, 'down the hatch'!" Tension broke, and the Maud Howe Elliott hospitality prevailed.[15]

While this story is likely rooted in truth, it is doubtful that in the 1940s, the ninety-year-old Maud would have been "properly naked in a cocktail dress." Nevertheless, the naval presence at the Art Association was always very visible, with social events and lectures by many military personnel, especially from the Naval War College. Captain Reginald Belknap, a Newporter who had led the relief missions during the Messina earthquake, spoke on the "Mine Laying Barrage of the North Sea" in 1919. Maud's personal favorite was Admiral William S. Sims, who had been attending suffrage meetings since 1911 and was commonly seen riding his bicycle about Newport. In 1922, he was one of four lecturers from the military, speaking on "The First Line of Defense." Sims's wife Anna headed the Miantonomi Park Memorial Commission, of which Maud was a member, to build a granite war memorial to Newport's dead; Maud led the dedication ceremonies on August 29, 1929. She later summed up her appreciative feelings about our naval men in a paper that was published as part of the U.S. Naval Institute Proceedings, "The Navy at Newport."

By 1930 Maud was growing tired of long, cold New England winters. On her 1925 trip to St. Augustine, the intention had been to explore possible winter escapes for health reasons. Florida now loomed as another great adventure, "booming" as it was with communities, resorts and winter visitors. In St. Augustine she had socialized with bibliophile John Ketterlinus and his wife Elizabeth, the daughter of Standard Oil mogul William Warden. Warden had been a partner of Henry Flagler, the robber baron of the South, with his railroad and hotel enterprises. The newspapers told her that "during December 1500 motors passed through Jacksonville going south, carrying between 4000 and 5000 people to the winter playground." These were the middle classes who stayed in tourist camps. Her chief concern was the lack of young people: "I miss above all, youth! Middle age and age everywhere. We have a little game we play in the streets: every young person (under 28) we meet counts five cents. We often come home from a prowl with a record of ten or fifteen cents only."[16] Another deterrent were the snakes and alligators, which terrified her. But Laura wrote from Maine that they were having a brutal winter, thirty-five degrees below zero. Palm Beach was recommended by her friends, and in 1930, as with most things, Maud once again became a pioneer — a snowbird.

Maud went to Palm Beach by way of Panama, Jamaica, and Havana, Cuba. She would rather visit Panama than Paris, she wrote exuberantly in her little memoir "What I Saw and Heard in Panama," printed to benefit the Greek War Relief. And ever since her 1972 expedition to Santo Domingo with her parents, she had felt the allure of the Caribbean. During her time in Panama Maud experienced a New Years Day revolution, being welcomed by a president who was arrested that same night! She witnessed the entire episode, crouched behind closed shutters and an iron balcony. "The noise of firing kept increasing. A repeating rifle under my balcony spat out shots with a curious burring sound. The figures in the square ran from corner to corner . . ."[17] But revolutions in

Panama, she found, were fairly common, and she continued her visit, meeting with diplomats, taking Spanish lessons, participating in the local festivals and shopping in the marketplace. In March 1931 she continued on to Jamaica, an island that surpassed her greatest expectations of beauty. She was invited to stay in the luxurious home of Eugene Finzi and his Boston wife. "Mr. Finzi's money, and it appears almost everybody's, is made in rum. Of this I highly approve. Good old Jamaican in moderate quantities I believe is good for humans, especially the elderly." She didn't object to the food either. "I wish I could see papaya, mangoes, plantains, chyotes, lots of other tropical fruits and vegetables become the fashion."[18]

Maud left Jamaica and arrived in Cuba which she had not visited since 1872. "I drove about town trying to find the old Havana [but] the wide avenues, the eighteen million dollar white marble capitol, the rows of modern business buildings, the milling crowds — all might have been New York."[19] On her way to Key West, "the journey across the Flagler Railway will always remain in my memory as one of the most remarkable day's travel I have ever made. From the window of the Pullman car it looked as if the train were crossing the water entirely without support. The bridge was invisible, and I had the strange sensation of being borne across a broad stretch of blue sea on a magic carpet." This was 1931 and in lower Florida, the housing boom was over. Maud drove from Miami to Palm Beach, a route that seemed eerie to her, noting, "Everywhere the same desolation — wide streets, handsome signs, telephone and telegraph wires and no homes, no shops, nothing but sand and scrub palmetto. Here and there a little group of houses, a club, a hotel, but the greater part — just dead waste."[20] She did prefer Palm Beach over anyplace else, and was to return almost every winter — with excursions to Greece again in 1930 to oversee the installation of a statue dedicated to her father, to California and the Southwest in 1932, and to Capri to visit her friend Mabel Norman Cerio in 1937.

Unlike many of the senior set, Maud was not just seeking sun and relaxation on her winter sojourns. In fact she had complained about St. Augustine, "I have yet to meet any person, man or woman, actively at work here. Of course they must exist, but I haven't found them yet. Time is passed, rather than used, here."[21] Like the model of ancient Rome in which men were active in service to their last days, Maud had little use for "retirement." When she set out for California in 1932, it was with a sense of adventure and desire to see how the country had changed since her 1916 "Golden Special." She visited the Naval Base Coronado near San Diego, where her good friends from Newport, Admiral Harry and Emily Yarnell, were currently stationed. Emily had been assistant secretary at the Art Association and her sister Ruth Thomas, an artist, was one of Maud's closest associates in her last years. Harry, later to be commander in chief of the Asiatic Fleet, at the time was pioneering air carrier tactics, and invited Maud to fly with him, but she did not like the loud noise of the engines. Sometime, she thought, when they make them quieter. Maud found a grim line of warships in Long Beach, quite a contrast to the social nature of the Navy in Newport. With the Yarnells she went to Hollywood, chatting with Wallace Beery and fellow actors at a restaurant. In San Francisco she met with her Mailliard cousins and went to Chinatown.

Maud's next destination was the H & R ranch near Taos, New Mexico, owned by Marie Garland, an heiress, a writer, and a fixture in the Taos art colony. Garland often rented rooms to artists, and had in fact hosted her friend Georgia O'Keeffe the previous year.[22] Maud approved of her guest quarters: "The house is built around a patio with a pond, goldfish, flowers not yet in bloom and strings of Mexican pottery, red peppers and yellow corns. The big living room is a royal apartment. It has a gigantic carved roof beam, filled with fine old New England furniture Marie had collected at Cape Cod through the years. Rugs, both of Navajo and Canadian hooked variety. A grand piano, a noble fireplace, bookcases set flat into the walls. I am reminded of Belle Gardner's entourage. Taste, imagination, money and hard work created this oasis in the desert."[23] Leaving New Mexico, she returned to Newport by train, by herself, chatting with passengers and porters, as was her custom.

The pattern of Maud's life during her eighties was formed. She went to Palm Beach in the winter, where she swam, socialized, wrote and co-founded a new arts organization. Swimming had always been Maud's favorite form of exercise, whether skinnydipping and exuberantly flinging herself into the waters of Narragansett Bay off Newport, the Mediterranean Sea, or, as an older woman, making a daily pilgrimage to Third Beach near Newport. But Palm Beach did not faze her: "Swam this morning.

A woman about 35, stark naked, walked about the Solarium, one of the most beautiful bodies I ever saw, which she doubtless knew. The women, mostly naked, lie on inclined boards so they get the sun on their backs. Today, hardened by the sight of so many people of all types and ages nearly naked I discarded my outer bathing dress, loose and to the knees and went boldly to my bath in my Annette Kellerman—Nobody knew or cared how I looked!" Maud was certainly a very liberated Victorian![24]

Maud carried her torch for the arts to Palm Beach, where she co-founded the Society of the Four Arts. She was appointed Honorary President, and was the inspiration behind the opening of the institution's library in 1940. Classical murals by Albert Herter—who wrote appreciatively of her persuasive abilities—decorated the portico to the new building and a resplendent portrait of Maud by Adele Herter was installed in a place of honor in the library. The library was the focal point of Palm Beach's civic and cultural activities, including poetry readings and other literary happenings organized by Maud. In her own writing, at this stage of her life Maud wanted to reminisce and capture her family for posterity.[25] In 1934 *My Cousin, F. Marion Crawford* was published by Macmillan, followed by *Uncle Sam Ward and His Circle* in 1938. Both books were filled with anecdotal family history, valuable for her inclusion of letters, recollections of events and people, but glossing over unsavory or sensational aspects of their lives—which existed in abundance for both of them! Maud and Laura continued to write daily, and advise each other on the need to cover up anything unseemly. Laura burned letters periodically, as did her daughter Rosalind, who inherited the family papers.

Laura visited during the summer in Newport and was a regular guest at the Art Association, where Maud continued to reign supreme, alongside her colleague Harrison Morris—although he wrote in one letter that it was she who ruled. One of the young male artists at the time, Francis Gyra, remembered how Maud sat regally in her peacock rattan chair, attired in a lace mantilla, receiving guests at her home, Lilliput. No one ever could take her husband's place, but she developed a close friendship with the artist Durr Freedley, who had come to Newport to paint the murals in the chapel at the Seaman's Institute, and then became involved at the Art Association, where he organized the 1936 Tercentenary. Freedley, who was apparently openly gay in 1930s Newport, lived across the street from her there. He wrote to her when she was away, "I hope you are well and warm and happy. I miss you terribly but perhaps will meet in Palm Beach the end of March. I am holding the thought." Maud arranged for an exhibition of his work at the Society of the Four Arts. Tragically, Freedley died in a car accident in 1938; he left a dramatic but unfinished portrait of an elegant, elderly Maud. The great-nieces who visited in her later years recall a kind but slightly intimidating woman who was lionized by all.[26] In 1940 Maud received an honorary doctor of letters from Brown University. Her friend Herbert Pell wrote from his post as minister of Portugal, "I have just seen in the paper that you have received a degree of doctor of letters. There is no one who deserves it more. You have fought a difficult fight to keep education alive in Newport, and you certainly deserve anything you get."[27]

Maud slowed down, but the Second World War galvanized her into action once more. In 1941 she wrote an article called "Civilization Will Survive" for the *Christian Science Monitor,* stating that while she wished she could be a pacifist, she truly believed that war was an inevitable malaise, that peace often breeds softness and skepticism, while war toughens us and "begets patriotism and heroes . . . it would seem that in the divine plan peace and war both serve alternately to help mankind in its long, hard climb out of darkness into light."[28] She cited the many wars through which she had lived, beginning with the Civil War. She wrote letters to the young men who went to war, keeping up an active correspondence with Francis Gyra: "People here are faithful to your interests, and all the many gatherings of men and women, girls and boys, that take place in my house, have one reason for being—that they are for Our Boys."[29] At the war's end Maud was appointed chairwoman of the Books and Authors War Bond Rally, in which Lillian Hellman, Bennett Cerf, Robert Henriques, and Carl Van Doren (and their autographed manuscripts) were recruited for a fundraiser. The event was held on June 6, 1945, at the Opera House. Maud wrote that she hoped to open the show with a brief Hellenic dance of Greek maidens: "Greece, the mother of all democracies, and the Greek people who in the beginning of the war made such a stand, make this seem fitting."[30] As a tribute to Maud, *The Battle Hymn of the Republic* was sung by the Swanhurst Chorus of the Art Association.[31] She later received a citation from the government for this event.

In 1944 *This Was My Newport* was published by A. Marshall Jones and the Mythology Company, in Cambridge, Massachusetts. Writing the book and getting it published had been a long and arduous task, as her usual mainstream publishers saw it as only of local interest. The book was compiled from earlier papers and lectures delivered at the Art Association and from articles she had published for the *Bulletin of the Newport Historical Society,* as well as fresh reminiscences. Her assistant in this project was Edith Ballinger Price, who also illustrated the title page. Endlessly fascinating and informative, filled with a who's who of Newport history, personal reminiscences of some of the country's most illustrious literary, artistic, political, military and social personalities, *This Was My Newport* remains Maud's most well-known book, aside from "The Life." She promoted it avidly, as usual, writing to Jones that she would go on WJAR in Providence to speak about it — Maud was a big radio fan. There were errors; as Price wrote in a letter to the publisher, "It was impossible for me to check on everything, and Mrs. Elliott was either sure that her memories were correct, or else had not the foggiest idea of where to look for verification. I hope that the circle of critics will set down the inaccuracies to the advanced age of the author, and as Mrs. Elliott says, 'People do LOVE to write to the author about mistakes.'"[32]

In 1943 Laura Richards died, surrounded by her husband and children, and left Maud feeling quite bereft. But she had always called the Art Association her child, and in 1944 — she was now Secretary Emerita — the institution celebrated Maud's ninetieth birthday, appropriately, with a pageant. "Wearing a white gown and white lace mantilla," Maud was escorted to a throne by Navy officers to the strains of a march composed for the occasion. The participants dressed as characters from *This Was My Newport* and enacted *tableaux vivants*. Newport's Greek citizens who were members of the local chapter of Aetna, named for Maud, participated in the festivities. There was Greek dancing, singing by the Swanhurst Chorus, and music by the Rogers High School Band. A birthday cake with ninety candles was provided by the Navy. An illuminated parchment scroll signed by every organization and institution in the city of Newport was presented to her.[33] Maud was now resigned to remaining in Newport and suffering through the cold winters and their attendant physical ailments. She was attended by Dr. José Ramos, a Newport native of Portuguese descent. As she wrote in her diary, "His visits are the highlights of these tiresome bed days. He got his medical education in France and Switzerland and is a young man of promise. He is a good linguist, speaks good French and I believe Italian, Spanish and Portuguese as well. He brings quite a European flavor to my bedroom."[34] Her last visit to the Art Association, for a lecture on Russia, was in January 1948. In March her two nieces, Frances Howard and Julia Shaw, were summoned to Lilliput, where Maud died on March 20. Her memorial service was held at Channing Memorial Church in Newport, and she was buried in Mount Auburn Cemetery in Cambridge, Massachusetts.

The officers and council of the Art Association passed a resolution:

> No formal resolution can express our sense of loss in the passing of Maud Howe Elliott. Her identification with the Art Association of Newport was so complete over the years—it was so much a part of herself—that it is impossible to think of the Association without thinking of her: her vision of what it could mean to the community, her unceasing devotion which attended every phase of its growth. It was her child; and her loving care guided and nurtured it from infancy to maturity. We feel that we speak not only for our entire membership, but for the community as well, when we express our undying obligation to this outstanding leader for the legacy she has left to us all, and to many yet unborn.[35]

In her autobiography Maud Howe Elliott wrote that if she was to be remembered at all, she hoped "it would be as one of the founders of the Progressive Party."[36] One hundred years after she founded both the women's branch of the Rhode Island Progressives and the Art Association of Newport, she is seldom remembered outside of Newport. Myths and revisionist history tend to transform those who were heralded in earlier times; in the greater historical literature Maud has been relegated to the role of flighty daughter, society woman, and proper Victorian. In truth she was her parents' daughter; she emulated them both in her own unique manner. "To learn, to teach, to serve, to enjoy" was the credo by which Julia Ward Howe conducted her life; Maud was not far behind. Like her father, Samuel Gridley Howe—and the horses that they both loved—Maud was always ready to lead the charge for her causes. In fact, Julia wrote, "She is like her father, full of chivalry and of power to carry out her generous impulses."[37] Maud's rhetoric might have been "Victorian," as some critics noted in the twentieth century, but her core values, her aspirations for "civilization," her embrace of changing times, her respect for strong leadership, are all very relevant in the twenty-first century. Like the artists for whom she carried the torch, Maud Howe Elliott should be remembered and recognized today.

NOTES

ABBREVIATIONS

MHE Maud Howe Elliott
JE John Elliott
JWH Julia Ward Howe
SGH Samuel Gridley Howe
LER Laura Elizabeth Richards
SW Sam Ward

PREFACE

1. Maud Howe Elliott, unpublished handwritten notes of lectures on art delivered in Chicago, c1889, John Hay Library, Maud Howe Elliott Papers, Box 2, F.5:7.
2. Maxim Karolik "Maud Howe Elliott Seen as Symbol: Maxim Karolik Tells of Her Interest in Art Association, Newport's Cultural Life," *Newport Daily News,* March 24, 1948, 9.
3. Maud Howe Elliott, *Three Generations* (Boston: Little, Brown, 1923), 4.
4. Art Association of Newport, *Annual Report*, 1921, Newport Art Museum Archives.
5. Elliott, unpublished handwritten notes of lectures on art delivered in Chicago, 1889, John Hay Library, Maud Howe Elliott Papers, Box 2, F.5:7.

ONE

1. Florence Howe Hall, *Memories Grave and Gay* (New York: Harper & Brothers, 1918), 32.

2. JWH to Annie Ward Mailliard, February 7, 1854, Houghton Library, Howe Family Papers (554).

3. Ibid.

4. JWH to Louisa Ward Crawford, July 23, 1854, continued on November 4, 1854, Houghton Library, Howe Family Papers (385).

5. Maud Howe Elliott, Diaries, May 1, 1912, John Hay Library, Maud Howe Elliott Papers.

6. Hall, *Memories Grave and Gay*, 32.

7. *American Magazine of Useful and Entertaining Knowledge* 3: 4, 130.

8. Maud Howe Elliott, *Three Generations* (Boston: Little, Brown, 1923), 6.

9. Elliott, *Three Generations*, 10.

10. Laura E. Richards, *Samuel Gridley Howe* (New York and London: D. Appleton-Century, 1935), 186.

11. Elliott, *Three Generations*, 15.

12. Henry Wadsworth Longfellow, Journal, October 19, 1845, quoted in Gary Williams, *Hungry Heart: The Literary Emergence of Julia Ward Howe* (Amherst: University of Massachusetts Press, 1999), 78.

13. Richards, *Samuel Gridley Howe*, 188.

14. Ibid., 180.

15. Hall, *Memories Grave and Gay*, 13.

16. Elliott, *Three Generations*, 30.

17. Howe, *Reminiscences*, 238–39.

18. Ibid., 239.

19. Maud Howe Elliott, *This Was My Newport* (Cambridge, MA: Mythology Company, 1944), 59.

20. Richards, *Samuel Gridley Howe*, 181.

21. Nathan H. Dole to MHE, 1923, John Hay Library, Maud Howe Elliott Papers, Box 1, F.1:22.

22. Elliott, *Three Generations*, 21.

23. Laura E. Richards, *Stepping Westward* (New York: D. Appleton, 1931), 74.

24. Elliott, *Three Generations*, 33.

25. Maud Howe Elliott, *Memories of the Civil War, 1861–1864 (Privately printed to benefit the Newport chapter of the Red Cross, 1943)*, [3].

26. Hall, *Memories Grave and Gay*, 142.

27. Laura E. Richards and Maud Howe Elliott, *Julia Ward Howe, 1819–1910* (Boston and New York: Houghton Mifflin, 1915), vol. 1, 205; and Elliott, *This Was My Newport*, 91.

28. Elliott, *Three Generations*, 41.

29. Ibid.

30. Ibid.

31. Richards and Elliott, *Julia Ward Howe*, 41–42.

32. Louis Legrand Noble, *The Life and Works of Thomas Cole* (Cambridge, MA: Harvard University Press, 1964), 203.

33. Howard S. Merritt, *Thomas Cole* (Rochester, NY: Memorial Art Gallery of University of Rochester, 1969), 36.

34. Elliott, *Three Generations*, 63.

TWO

Epigraph: Julia Ward Howe, Journals, November 9, 1867, Houghton Library, Howe Family Papers.

1. MHE to LER, January 3, 1867, *The Yellow House Papers: the Laura E. Richards Collection,* Gardiner Library Association and Maine Historical Society, Coll. 2085, Record Group 15A, F.1.

2. MHE to JWH, February 15, 1867, *The Yellow House Papers*, Coll. 2085, Record Group 15A, F.1.

3. Hall, *Memories Grave and Gay*, 98.

4. Julia Ward Howe, *From the Oak to the Olive* (Boston: Lee and Shepard, 1868), 296.

5. Howe, *From the Oak to the Olive,* 45.

6. Julia Ward Howe, Journals, May 22–23, 1867, Houghton Library, Howe Family Papers.

7. Ibid., April 26, 1867.

8. Ibid., September 18, 1867.

9. Elliott, *Three Generations*, 119.

10. Howe, *From the Oak to the Olive,* 296–97: "It would be most important for us to form at least one gallery of art in which American artists might study something better than themselves. The presence of twenty first-rate pictures in one of our great cities would save a great deal of going abroad and help to form a sincere and intelligent standard of aesthetic judgment. Such pictures should, of course, be constantly open to the public, as no private collection can well be. We should have a Titian, a Rubens, an Andrea, a Paul Veronese and so on. But these pictures should be of historical authenticity. The most responsible artists of this country should be empowered to negotiate for them, and the money might be afforded from the heavy gains of late years with far more honor and profit than the superfluous splendors with which the fortunate of this period bedizen their houses and their persons."

11. Richards and Elliott, *Julia Ward Howe*, vol. 1, 296.

12. Howe, *Reminiscences,* 321.

13. SGH to LER, Boylston St., 1868. *The Yellow House Papers*, Coll. 2085, Record Group 20.

14. SGH to LER, February 21, 1870. *The Yellow House Papers*, Coll. 2085, Record Group 20.

15. Julia Ward Howe, Journals, January 8, 1868, Houghton Library, Howe Family Papers.

16. Ibid., January 5–8, 1868.

17. SGH to LER, March 3, 1869. *The Yellow House Papers*, Coll. 2085, Record Group 20.

18. Ibid., March 5, 1869.

19. Elliott, *Three Generations*, 62.

20. SGH to LER, April 10, 1871, *The Yellow House Papers*, Coll. 2085, Record Group 20.

21. Elliott, *Three Generations*, 94.

22. SGH to LER, April 10, 1872, *The Yellow House Papers*, Coll. 2085, Record Group 20.

23. Lucy Derby Fuller, "The Humor of Edward Askew Sothern," *The Century*, June 1902, 199.

24. Howe, *Reminiscences*, 72.

25. Elliott, *Three Generations*, 131.

26. Louise Hall Tharp, *Three Saints and a Sinner: Julia Ward Howe, Louisa, Annie and Sam Ward* (Boston: Little Brown, 1956), 47.

27. Eliza Cope Harrison and Rosemary F. Carroll, "Newport's Summer Colony, 1830–1860," *Newport History: Bulletin of the Newport Historical Society* 74: 253, Fall 2005, 15. This home was built by John Gilliatt, a merchant invested in Newport real estate, who sold it to Samuel Ward. Elliott, *This Was My Newport,* 53. It was torn down a hundred years later to enlarge the grounds of the Redwood Library. Elliott, *Uncle Sam Ward and His Circle* (New York: Macmillan, 1938), 206–7. The house was no longer owned by the Howe family, as unfortunately, after Samuel Ward Sr.'s death, his brother John, a banker, sold much of the family's valuable real estate, including the Newport home.

28. Elliott, *Three Generations*, 69.

29. Ibid., 116.

30. Ibid.

31. Richard, *Stepping Westward*, 163.

32. SGH to LER, September 21, 1874, *The Yellow House Papers*, Coll. 2085, Record Group 20.

33. SGH to LER, September 11, 1875, *The Yellow House Papers*, Coll. 2085, Record Group 20.

34. Howe, Journals, April 10, 1873, Houghton Library, Howe Family Papers.

35. Donna M. Lucey, *Archie and Amélie: Love and Madness in the Gilded Age* (New York: Harmony Books, 2006), 52.

36. Elliott, *This Was My Newport,* 147.

37. Elliott, *Three Generations*, 13.

38. Richards and Elliott, *Julia Ward Howe*, vol. 1, 356.

39. LER to JWH, August 1872, *The Yellow House Papers*, Coll. 2085, Record Group 14. "Papa has given orders that we should have no more meat from the Institute. I suppose he has some good reason but he might have taken the trouble to tell us as it would have saved some inconvenience and much mortification. He said nothing about it to us, but merely told Peter not to let us have anything. I wish you would ask him for an estimate of what the Newport house cost. You see, he has not paid Harry anything for it and the money would be so convenient now as we have so many bills to pay." (Samuel Gridley Howe was very penurious when it came to his family, not so with his outside causes.)

40. Howe, Journals, February 14–15, 1874.

41. JWH to MHE, October 7, 1867, *The Yellow House Papers*, Coll. 2085, Record Group 16, F.7.

42. Ibid., June 11, 1872, *The Yellow House Papers*, Coll. 2085, Record Group 16, F.7

43. MHE to JWH, June 10, 1876, *The Yellow House Papers*, Coll. 2085, Record Group 15A, F.1.

THREE

Epigraph: MHE to LER, *The Yellow House Papers: the Laura E. Richards Collection,* Gardiner Library Association and Maine Historical Society, Coll. 2085, Record Group 15A, F.1

1. According to Maud's great-niece, the late Posey Wiggins and other Richards family members. However, as Louise Hall Tharp points out in *Three Saints and a Sinner,* beautiful American girls in search of European husbands usually had fortunes.

2. JWH to MHE, 1877, *The Yellow House Papers*, Coll. 2085, Record Group 16, F.7.

3. Richards and Elliott, *Julia Ward Howe*, vol. 2, 4.

4. Elliott, *Three Generations,* 139.

5. Richards and Elliott, *Julia Ward Howe*, vol. 2, 9.

6. Elliott, *Three Generations,* 140.

7. Ibid., 147.

8. Tharp, *Three Saints and a Sinner,* 322.

9. Christopher Newall, *The Grosvenor Gallery Exhibitions: Change and Continuity in the Victorian Art World* (Cambridge: Cambridge University Press, 1995), 17.

10. Maud Howe Elliott, "Artists I Have Known," *North American Review*, 1939–1940: 248; also, Maud Howe Elliott Papers, John Hay Library, Box 2, F. 5:3, 6.

11. Ibid.

12. Ibid.

13. Art Association of Newport, Annual report, 1925. Newport Art Museum Archives.

14. Richards and Elliott, *Julia Ward Howe*, vol. 2, 23.

15. JWH to Julia Romana Agnanos, *The Yellow House Papers*, Coll. 2085, Record Group 15A, F.1.

16. Elliott, *Three Generations*, 159.

17. Caroline Carson, *The Roman Years of a South Carolina Artist: Caroline Carson's Letters Home, 1872–1892*, ed. William H. and Jane H. Pease (Columbia: University of South Carolina Press, 2003), xxviii.

18. Elliott, *Three Generations*, 163.

19. Richards and Elliott, *Julia Ward Howe*, vol. 2, 31.

20. MHE to LER, 1878, *The Yellow House Papers*, Coll. 2085, Record Group 15A, F.1.

21. Elliott, *Three Generations*, 163.

22. Maud Howe Elliott, *John Elliott, the Story of an Artist* (Boston: Houghton Mifflin, 1930), 12.

23. Maud Howe Elliott, unpublished handwritten notes of lectures on art delivered in Chicago, 1890, John Hay Library, Maud Howe Elliott Papers, Box 2, F.5:9, 23.

24. MHE to LER, September 1878, *The Yellow House Papers*, Coll. 2085, Record Group 15A, F.1.

25. Ibid., August 12, 1878.

26. Ibid., May 1878.

27. Ibid.

28. Ibid.

29. Elliott, *Three Generations*, 190.

30. MHE to LER, May 1878, *The Yellow House Papers*, Coll. 2085, Record Group 15A, F.1.

31. Elliott, *John Elliott*, 16.

32. Elliott, *Three Generations*, 146.

FOUR

Epigraph: MHE to SW, September 7, 1883, quoted in Elliott, *This Was My Newport*, 99.

1. Alice Maud Richards, Rosalind Richards, Henry Howe Richards, and Julia Ward Richards; Samuel Prescott Hall, Caroline Minturn Hall, and Henry Marion Hall. There were to be four more grandchildren: Maud Richards (who lived less than two years), John Richards, and Laura Elizabeth Richards; and John Howe Hall. Neither Henry Marion Howe and his wife Fanny Gay Howe, nor Julia Romana Howe and her husband Michael Agnanos had children.

2. LER to MHE, 1877, *The Yellow House Papers*, Coll. 2085, Record Group 14, F.1.

3. Confirmed by librarian Elizabeth Prince, from records at the School of the Museum of Fine Arts, Boston, July 2009.

4. Elliott, *Three Generations*, 194.

5. Elliott, *Uncle Sam Ward and His Circle*, 646.

6. Howe, Journals, April 17, 1880, Houghton Library, Howe Family Papers.

7. Elliott, Diaries, April 21, 1885, John Hay Library, Maud Howe Elliott Papers.

8. Howe, Journals, January 1, 1881, Houghton Library, Howe Family Papers.

9. Elliott, *Uncle Sam Ward and His Circle*, 577; Elliott, *This Was My Newport*, 162–63; Kathryn Allamong Jacob, *King of the Lobby* (Baltimore: Johns Hopkins University Press, 2010), 137–38. Sam had fallen on financial hard times and his benefactor was John R. Keene, who had amassed a fortune as a stock speculator and thoroughbred horse breeder. In the California gold rush days of the early 1850s Sam had come to the aid of Keene when he was a sick young English youth; later in New York City Sam mentored Keene in his efforts to acquire culture and social standing. Sam also introduced Keene and his family to Newport, where they summered in a house on Bellevue Avenue.

10. Elliott, *Uncle Sam Ward and His Circle*, 577.

11. Elliott, *Three Generations*, 197. Georg Henschel, later conductor of the Boston Symphony Orchestra, felt that Crawford did not have a true enough "ear" to succeed as a singer.

12. Elliott, *Three Generations*, 196.

13. Ibid.

14. "The Culture of Neurasthenia in Nineteenth Century America," *American Art Review* 16: 6 (December 2004), 48.

15. JWH to SW, June 19, 1881, *The Yellow House Papers*, Coll. 2085, Record Group 18, F.1.

16. MHE to LER [March 1881], *The Yellow House Papers*, Coll. 2085, Record Group 15A, F.2.

17. LER to MHE, April 8, 1881, *The Yellow House Papers*, Coll. 2085, Record Group 12, F.1.

18. Unpublished manuscript, "Afternoon Tea," February 1939, John Hay Library, Maud Howe Elliott Papers, Box 1, F.4:6.

19. MHE to SW, June [1881], *The Yellow House Papers*, Coll. 2085, Record Group, RG 15A, F.3.

20. JWH to MHE, July, 1881 *The Yellow House Papers*, Coll. 2085, Record Group 15A, F.3.

21. Margaret Chanler, *Roman Spring* (Boston: Little, Brown, 1934), 104–10.

22. MHE to SW, July 1, 1881, *The Yellow House Papers*, Coll. 2085, Record Group 15A, F.3.

23. LER to SW, July 14, 1881, *The Yellow House Papers*, Coll. 2085, Record Group 12, F.1.

24. JWH to MHE, August 14, 1881, *The Yellow House Papers*, Coll. 2085, Record Group 16, F.1.

25. Elliott, *Uncle Sam Ward and His Circle*, 616.

26. Elliott, *John Elliott*, 6.

27. John Pilkington, Jr., *Francis Marion Crawford* (New York: Twayne Publishers, 1964). Jeannette Gilder, sister of famed editor Richard Watson Gilder, was an editor and writer who along with another brother, Joseph B. Gilder, in 1881 established *The Critic: A Fortnightly Review of Literature, Science, Fine Arts, Music, and Drama*.

28. Whitelaw Reid to MHE, June 26, 1883, John Hay Library, Maud Howe Elliott Papers, Box 1, F.3:2.

29. Elliott, *Uncle Sam Ward and His Circle*, 632.

30. Elliott, *My Cousin, F. Marion Crawford* (New York: Macmillan, 1934), 127; Pilkington, *Francis Marion Crawford*, 49–52. At dinner in New York Sam Ward encouraged Marion Crawford to write about Mr. Jacobs, the diamond merchant in Simla, India; also in attendance was George Brett, an editor from Macmillan, which was to publish the book, who also claimed credit for urging Crawford to write his stories down.

31. Elliott, *Three Generations*, 378.

32. Louise Hall Tharp, *Mrs. Jack: a Biography of Isabella Stewart Gardner* (Boston: Little, Brown, 1965), 47.

33. SW to JWH, March 23, 1882; quoted in Pilkington, *Francis Marion Crawford*, 47.

34. *Mr. Isaacs* was followed in May 1884 by *Doctor Claudius*, also published by Macmillan.

35. Clipping from *New York Tribune*, undated, c. 1883.

36. LER to MHE, August [1883] *The Yellow House Papers*, Coll. 2085, Record Group 14.

37. Maud Howe Elliott, *A Newport Aquarelle* (Boston: Roberts Brothers, 1893), 121–22.

38. Ibid.

39. Tharp, *Three Saints and a Sinner*, 331.

40. Elliott, *Uncle Sam Ward and His Circle*, 619; *My Cousin*, 126.

41. Elliott, *Uncle Sam Ward and His Circle*, 694.

42. Howe, Journals, January 29, 1882, Houghton Library, Howe Family Papers.

43. Elliott, *Uncle Sam Ward and His Circle*, 607.

44. Adamowski, a Polish-born composer and first conductor of the Boston Symphony Orchestra, was a frequent visitor at Oak Glen, where he performed for parties. *Lord Buncombe's Daughter* was never performed.

45. Elliott, *Uncle Sam Ward and His Circle*, 629.

46. Alan Chong and Noriko Murai, *Journeys East: Isabella Stewart Gardner and Asia* (Boston: Isabella Stewart Gardner Museum, 2009), 15; Francis Marion Crawford to Louisa Crawford Terry, April 3, 1883, Houghton Library, Howe Family Papers.

47. JWH to MHE, April 7, 8, 1883, *The Yellow House Papers*, Coll. 2085, Record Group 16.

48. Elliott, *My Cousin*, 157.

49. Douglass Shand-Tucci, *The Art of Scandal: The Life and Times of Isabella Stewart Gardner* (New York: Harper Collins, 1997), 51.

50. Tharp, *Mrs. Jack*, 82.

51. Ibid.

52. Chong and Murai, *Journeys East*, 284, 360; Morris Carter, *Isabella Stewart Gardner and Fenway Court* (London: William Heinmann, 1926), 84. Letters are from transcripts, originally published in Carter's book without mentioning that the addressee was Maud Howe; in fact, although Morris writes about Julia Ward Howe and Marion Crawford, he totally neglects Maud.

53. Chong and Murai, *Journeys East*, 329. Crawford had written two more successful novels while still living in the United States: *Dr. Claudius* and *A Roman Singer*. *To Leeward*, written after his return to Rome, contained characters based on himself and Isabella Stewart Gardner who have a doomed love affair.

54. Carter, *Isabella Stewart Gardner*, 84. This is from a letter not included in Chong and Murai's *Journeys East*; Morris does not mention that the letter was to Maud Howe.

55. Howe, Journals, August 19, 1884, Houghton Library, Howe Family Papers.

56. *The Critic*, June 21, 1884, no. 25, 290–91.

57. Maud Howe, *The San Rosario Ranch* (Boston: Roberts Brothers, 1884), 50–51.

58. Ibid., 104.

59. Ibid., 74.

60. Ibid., 112.

61. Ibid., 177.

62. MHE to SW, November 28, 1883, *The Yellow House Papers*, Coll. 2085, Record Group 15A, F.3.

63. MHE to LER, March 1884, *The Yellow House Papers*, Coll. 2085, Record Group 15A, F.1.

64. LER to MHE, June 1, 1886, *The Yellow House Papers*, Coll. 2085, Record Group 12.

65. "World's Exposition: Ladies' Day—Interesting Exercises in the Woman's Department," *Daily Picayune*, 31 May 1885, cited in Miki Pfeffer, *Exhibiting Women: Sectional Confrontation and Reconciliation in the Woman's Department at the World's Exposition, New Orleans: A Thesis* (University of New Orleans, May 2006), 54.

66. MHE to LER, December 1886, *The Yellow House Papers*, Coll. 2085, Record Group 15A, F.2.

67. Showing an old and uncharacteristically introspective Sam Ward, the portrait was reportedly stolen from a descendant's home in 2007; in Jacob, *King of the Lobby*, 167.

68. SW to JE, March 3, 1884, quoted in Elliott, *John Elliott,* 25.

69. John Lowell Gardner, Jr., to George Gardner, Massachusetts Historical Society, Gardner Family Papers, Personal Papers, Series I, F.2.

70. Howe, *A Newport Aquarelle,* 145.

FIVE

Epigraph: Maud Howe Elliott, unpublished handwritten notes for lectures on art, John Hay Library, Maud Howe Elliott Papers, Box 2, F.5:9, 56.

1. John Lowell Gardner to George Gardner, February 11, 1887. Massachusetts Historical Society, Gardner Family Papers, F.4.

2. Howe, Journals, February 7, 1887, Houghton Library, Howe Family Papers.

3. "Hymen" refers to the god of marriage ceremonies in Greek mythology.

4. *The Yellow House Papers,* Coll. 2085, Record Group 15A, F.2.

5. Elliott, *My Cousin,* 260–61.

6. Elliott, *Three Generations,* 195.

7. MHE to LER, *The Yellow House Papers,* Coll. 2085, Record Group 15A, F.2.

8. Lloyd Goodrich, *Albert P. Ryder* (New York: George Braziller, 1959), 113.

9. Elliott, Unpublished handwritten notes for lectures on art. John Hay Library, Maud Howe Elliott Papers, Box 2, F.5:9, 69.

10. Charles de Kay, "Three American Painters," *New York Times,* December 12, 1890.

11. Quote from review and letter, Grace Channing Stetson to EBK, May 23, 1912, in Charles Walter Stetson, *Endure: the Diaries of Charles Walter Stetson,* ed. Mary Armfield Hill (Philadelphia: Temple University Press, 1985), 48.

12. Howe, Journals, May 7, 1884, Houghton Library, Howe Family Papers.

13. Elliott, Unpublished handwritten notes for lectures on art, John Hay Library, Maud Howe Elliott Papers, Box 2, F.5:9.

14. "Art Notes," *Boston Evening Transcript,* December 13, 1883.

15. Elliott, Unpublished handwritten notes for lectures on art, John Hay Library, Maud Howe Elliott Papers, Box 2, F.5:9, 75.

16. Elliott, "Artists I Have Known," 245.

17. Jack Gardner was so upset by the controversy sparked by the portrait that he withdrew it from St. Botolph's and it was not shown publicly during his lifetime. Tharp, *Mrs. Jack,* 134.

18. Howe, Journals, February 10, 1888, Houghton Library, Howe Family Papers.

19. Ives Gammell, *Dennis Miller Bunker* (New York: Howard, McCann, 1953), 19.

20. Maud Howe, "The Flower o' May," *Godey's Magazine,* 1887, 5.115: 449–55.

21. Ibid.

22. Maud Howe, *Atalanta in the South* (Boston: Roberts Brothers, 1886), 32.

23. Elliott, Unpublished handwritten notes for lectures on art, John Hay Library, Maud Howe Elliott Papers, Box 2, F.5:9.

24. Howe, *The San Rosario Ranch*, 266.

25. Ibid., 58.

26. Elliott, *John Elliott*, 41.

27. "Phil Owens: A Life Sketch" in *America: A Journal for Americans* (Chicago: Slason, Thompson & Co: 1889).

28. *Mammon* (a nineteenth-century term for money) was serialized in *Lippincott's Monthly Magazine* in 1888 and published as *Honor* (St. Paul, MN: Price-McGill Company, 1893).

29. Howe, *Honor*, 199.

30. Ernest Rhys to MHE, November 1, 1888, John Hay Library, Maud Howe Elliott Papers, Box 1:3, F.4.

31. Maud Howe, *Phillida* (New York: John W. Lovell & Co., 1891), 178.

32. Ibid., 176.

33. Ibid., 183.

34. Ernest Rhys to MHE, November 1, 1888, John Hay Library, Maud Howe Elliott Papers, Box 1, F.3:4.

35. Elliott, *Three Generations*, 202.

36. Ibid.

37. Howe, Journals, August 14, 1889, Houghton Library, Howe Family Papers.

SIX

Epigraph: Maud Howe Elliott, unpublished handwritten notes for lectures on art, John Hay Library, Maud Howe Elliott Papers, Box 2, F.5:7.

1. Rossiter Johnson, ed. *A History of the World's Columbian Exposition* (New York: D. Appleton, 1897), vol. 1, 295.

2. Elliott, *John Elliott*, 36.

3. MHE to LER, April 3, 1888, *The Yellow House Papers*, Coll. 2085, Record Group 15A, F.2.

4. MHE to LER, May 1889. *The Yellow House Papers*, Coll. 2085, Record Group 15A, F2.

5. Howe, Journals, April 11, 1889, Houghton Library, Howe Family Papers.

6. *Chicago Tribune,* July 28, 1889.

7. Two lectures on literature accompanied this series, held at the homes of Mrs. Charles Schwartz, Mrs. O. R. Keith, and Mrs. Charles P. Kellogg, and facilitated by Frances (Mrs. John J.) Glessner, the wife of a farm machinery magnate and Maud's friend. Information on these lectures has been provided from the diary of Glessner courtesy of John Waters.

8. Elliott, Diaries, February 4, 1890, John Hay Library, Maud Howe Elliott

Papers; she mentions Frank Lent's "Success in Art," in Arlo Bates, *Various Phases of American Art*.

9. Elliott, Diaries, January 1890, John Hay Library, Maud Howe Elliott Papers.

10. Elliott, Unpublished handwritten notes for lectures on art, John Hay Library, Maud Howe Elliott Papers, Box 2, F.5:7, 35.

11. Ibid.

12. Elliott, Unpublished handwritten notes for lectures on art, John Hay Library, Maud Howe Elliott Papers, Box 2, F.5:9, 71.

13. Ibid.

14. Ibid.

15. Louise Hall Tharp, *Saint Gaudens and the Gilded Era* (Boston: Little, Brown, 1969), 119.

16. Elliott, Unpublished handwritten notes for lectures on art, John Hay Library, Maud Howe Elliott Papers, Box 2, F.5:9, 65.

17. MHE to LER, October 23, 1881, *The Yellow House Papers*, Coll. 2085, Record Group, 15A, F.2.

18. Elliott, Unpublished handwritten notes for lectures on art, John Hay Library, Maud Howe Elliott Papers, Box 2, F.5:7, 15.

19. Ibid.

20. Elliott, Unpublished handwritten notes for lectures on art, John Hay Library, Maud Howe Elliott Papers, Box 2, F.5:9, 33.

21. Ibid.

22. JWH to SW, May 3, 1881, *The Yellow House Papers*, Coll. 2085, Record Group 18, F.1.

23. MHE to LER, undated, c. 1880, *The Yellow House Papers*, Coll. 2085, Record Group 15A, F.2.

24. Elliott, Diaries, January 3, 1885, John Hay Library, Maud Howe Elliott Papers.

25. Maud Howe Elliott, ed. *Art and Handicraft in the Woman's Building at the World's Columbian Exposition* (Paris and New York: Goupil and Co., 1893), 44.

26. Elliott, Unpublished handwritten notes for lectures on art, John Hay Library, Maud Howe Elliott Papers, Box 2, F.5:6.

27. Maud Howe Elliott, ed. *Art and Handicraft in the Woman's Building at the World's Columbian Exposition* (Paris and New York: Goupil and Co., 1893), 13.

28. Ibid., 48.

29. Ibid., 28.

30. MHE to LER, April 17, 1892, *The Yellow House Papers*, Coll. 2085, Record Group 15A, F.4.

31. Elliott, *Art and Craft in the Woman's Building*, 30.

32. Ibid., 40.

SEVEN

Epigraph: Maud Howe Elliott, *John Elliott*, 92.

1. MHE to LER, [January 1887], *The Yellow House Papers*, Coll. 2085, Record Group 15A, F.2.
2. Elliott, *Three Generations,* 229; Edward "Ned" Elliott was ironically, a sailor, who drowned in June 1891 in a boating accident in Colorado.
3. MHE to LER, April 3, 1889, *The Yellow House Papers*, Coll. 2085, Record Group 15A, F.2.
4. *New York Times,* August 2, 1891.
5. Elliott, *John Elliott,* 92.
6. Ralph Adams Cram, *My Life in Architecture* (Boston: Little, Brown, 1936), 54.
7. Stephen Maxfield Parrish, *Currents of the Nineties in Boston and London: Fred Holland Day, Louise Imogene Guiney, and Their Circle* (New York: Garland, 1987), 85.
8. Louise Guiney to Ralph Adams Cram, June 22, 1887. Quoted in Parrish, *Currents of the Nineties*, 86.
9. Ralph Adams Cram to MHE, December 14, 1915, Newport Art Museum Archives.
10. MHE to Barrett Wendell, June 19, 1890, John Hay Library, Maud Howe Elliott Papers, Box 4, F.13:6.
11. *St. Paul Dispatch,* February 21, 1891
12. "They Are Clever," in *Chicago Daily,* May 11, 1895, 16.
13. Elliott, Diaries, January 13, 14, 25, 1892, John Hay Library, Maud Howe Elliott Papers.
14. MHE to LER, October 6, [1890], *The Yellow House Papers*, Coll. 2085, Record Group 15A, F.2.
15. Hall, *Memories Grave and Gay*, 255.
16. Julia Romana Anagnos had died of typhoid in March of 1886.
17. Elliott, Diaries, January 27, 1890, John Hay Library, Maud Howe Elliott Papers.
18. MHE to LER, November 1893, *The Yellow House Papers*, Coll. 2085, Record Group 15A, F.3.
19. Elliott, *John Elliott,* 43, 107, 115, also Boston Public Library, Annual Report, 1901.
20. Elliott, Diaries, June 22–23, 1892, John Hay Library, Maud Howe Elliott Papers.
21. MHE to LER, [June] 1892, *The Yellow House Papers*, Coll. 2085, Record Group 15A F.3.
22. JE to MHE, October 21, 1892, John Hay Library, Maud Howe Elliott Papers, Box 1. F.1:27, reproduced in Elliott, *John Elliott,* 52.
23. Elliott, *John Elliott,* 64–74.

24. Ibid., 6.
25. Ibid., 58.
26. Ibid., 92.
27. JE to MHE, November 1893, quoted in Elliott, *John Elliott*, 89.
28. Ibid., 91.
29. Elliott, *Three Generations*, 226.
30. Elliott, *Three Generations*, 245.
31. Margaret Deland, *Golden Yesterdays* (New York: Harper & Brothers, 1940), 292–94.
32. Quoted in Valerie Ziegler, *Diva Julia: the Public Romance and Private Agony of Julia Ward Howe* (Harrisburg, PA: Trinity Press International, 2003), 46n, 202. Houghton Library, Howe Family Papers.
33. Maud Howe, *Roma Beata: Letters from the Eternal City* (Boston: Little, Brown, 1904), 31.
34. MHE to LER, February 1894, *The Yellow House Papers*, Coll. 2085, Record Group 15A, F.3.
35. Howe, *Roma Beata*, 12.
36. Ibid., 17.
37. MHE TO LER, January 27, 1894, *The Yellow House Papers*, Coll. 2085, Record Group 15A, F.3.
38. MHE to JWH, April 7, 1894, *The Yellow House Papers*, Coll. 2085, Record Group 15A, F.3.
39. MHE: "Roman Letter: The Feast of Giovanni," July 21, 1894. John Hay Library, Maud Howe Elliott Papers, Box 3.
40. MHE to JWH, *The Yellow House Papers*, Coll. 2085, Record Group 15A, F.4.
41. LER to MHE, August 21, 1895, *The Yellow House Papers*, Coll. 2085, Record Group 14, F.4.
42. Elliott, Diaries, October 4, 1895, John Hay Library, Maud Howe Elliott Papers.
43. Elliott, *John Elliott*, 104.
44. Larz Anderson and Isabel Perkins were married the next year and lived acclaimed lives—he as a diplomat, she as a philanthropist and author.
45. Elliott, *Three Generations*, 294.
46. Henry James to MHE, July 20, 1899, *The Yellow House Papers*, Coll. 2085, Record Group 31I.
47. MHE to LER, May 10, 1895, *The Yellow House Papers*, Coll. 2085, Record Group 15A, F.3.
48. MHE to JWH, *The Yellow House Papers*, Coll. 2085, Record Group 15A, F.3.
49. Elliott, *John Elliott*, 116.
50. Sandro Consolato, "Giacomo Boni, l'archeologo-vate della Terza Roma," in Gianfranco De Turris, *Esoterismo e Fascismo* (Rome: Edizioni Mediterranee, 2006), as cited in Wikipedia.

51. MHE to JWH, July 11, 894, *The Yellow House Papers*, Coll. 2085, Record Group 15A, F.3.
52. Elliott, *John Elliott*, 129.

EIGHT

Epigraph: Maud Howe Elliott, *Three Generations*, 314.
1. Elliott, *John Elliott*, 132.
2. Elliott, *This Was My Newport*, 243.
3. A handout called *The Triumph of Time* is available at the Boston Public Library, which describes the composition: "The twelve female figures represent the Hours and the one male figure, Time. The Christian Centuries are typified by twenty horses arranged in five rows, of four each. In each row the two center horses are side by side, and between these and the outer horses are two winged female figures representing The Hours. On either side of the car in which is the figure of Time are the Hours of Life and Death. The design—viewed from the doorway of the adjoining room at the front of the Research Library building—begins near the lefthand corner and describes a semi-circle, with a downward sweep over an effect of clouds, back to the left again, to a point about two-thirds across the canvas, and culminates in a disk, the sun, before which are the leading horse and the figure typifying the Twentieth Century. In the nearer right-hand corner is a crescent moon with a full disk faintly showing." Nowhere does the description mention the artist. Initially designed for the Patent Room, there was some controversy when the room, with its adult theme, became used as the Children's teaching room.
4. LER to MHE, 1899, *The Yellow House Papers*, Coll. 2085, Record Group 12.
5. LER to MHE, December 4, 1895, *The Yellow House Papers*, Coll. 2085, Record Group 12.
6. LER to MHE, December 18, 1899, *The Yellow House Papers*, Coll. 2085, Record Group 12.
7. LER to MHE, *The Yellow House Papers*, Coll. 2085, Record Group 14.
8. MHE to LER, April 8, 1903, *The Yellow House Papers*, Coll. 2085, Record Group 15A, F.4.
9. Maud Howe, "Whom Should We Entertain?" *Harper's Bazaar* 40 (March 1906), 38–41.
10. Maud Howe, "Sun and Air as Physicians," *Harper's Bazaar* 43 (August 1909), 801–3.
11. Maud Howe, "Nerves," *Harper's Bazaar*, 42 (November 1908), 1136–38.
12. MHE to JWH, Munich, August 1894, *The Yellow House Papers*, Coll. 2085, Record Group 15A, F.4.
13. Charles Hamilton Aide to MHE, [1901], John Hay Library, Maud Howe Elliott Papers, Box 1, F.4.

14. MHE to LER, *The Yellow House Papers*, Coll. 2085, Record Group 15A, F.4.

15. Ibid.

16. Elliott, *Art and Craft in the Woman's Building,* 33. After commending the formal qualities of the painting, which depicts "The Women of Plymouth," at their household chores, Maud makes a controversial statement that the painting hints that higher education for women is a failure unless it makes better wives and mothers. This is not a sentiment that Maud was adamant about and actually contradicts much of her later rhetoric.

17. MHE to LER, July 6, 1903, *The Yellow House Papers*, Coll. 2085, Record Group 15A, F.4.

18. JE to MHE, October, 1903, reprinted in Elliott, *John Elliott,* 137.

19. MHE to LER, May 7, 1903, *The Yellow House Papers*, Coll. 2085, Record Group 15A, F.4.

20. MHE to LER, August 26, 1903, *The Yellow House Papers*, Coll. 2085, Record Group 15A, F.4.

21. Howe, Journals, October 28, 1903, Houghton Library, Howe Family Papers.

22. Elliott, *John Elliott,* 147.

23. MHE to LER, August 26, 1903, *The Yellow House Papers*, Coll. 2085, Record Group 15A, F.4.

24. JE to MHE, 1910, John Hay Library, Maud Howe Elliott Papers, Box 1, F.1:27.

25. Elliott, *John Elliott,* 144.

26. Ibid., 145.

27. Elliott, *Three Generations,* 322.

28. MHE to JE, April 24, 1906, John Hay Library, Maud Howe Elliott Papers, Box 1, F.1:30.

29. Isabella Stewart Gardner to Bernard Berenson, May 25, 1900, quoted in Bernard Berenson *The Letters of Bernard Berenson and Isabella Steward Gardner, 1887-1924* (Boston: Northeastern University Press, 1987), 218.

30. MHE to LER, *The Yellow House Papers*, Coll. 2085, Record Group 15A, F.3.

31. Elliott, *John Elliott,* 167.

32. Ibid., 219.

33. Charles Dana Gibson to MHE, Dec. 18, 1909, John Hay Library, Maud Howe Elliott Papers, Box 1, F.1:38.

34. Henry James to MHE, quoted in Elliott, *John Elliott,* 226.

35. Elliott, *John Elliott,* 228. In 1926 a calendar edition was printed.

36. Howe, Journals, October 9, 1907, Houghton Library, Howe Family Papers.

37. Maud likely lifted the method of this untimely demise from the death of their friend John Boyle O'Reilly, who in 1890 overdosed on his wife's sleeping potion, which contained chloral hydrate, and died.

38. Maud Howe, "Ralph Darrow's Tryst," *New England Magazine* (April 1899) 20: 177–83.

NINE

Epigraph: Maud Howe Elliott, "Keep the Home Fires Burning," reprinted from *The Chronicle*, October, 1917, 1.

1. Henry Marion Howe to LER, February 5, 1911, *The Yellow House Papers*, Coll. 2085, Record Group 32.
2. Elliott, Diaries, January 6, 1911, John Hay Library, Maud Howe Elliott Papers.
3. Henry Marion Howe to LER, December 31, 1901, *The Yellow House Papers*, Coll. 2085, Record Group 32.
4. Elliott, Diaries, January 6, 1911, John Hay Library, Maud Howe Elliott Papers.
5. Henry Marion Howe to LER, n.d. [1910], *The Yellow House Papers*, Coll. 2085, Record Group 32.
6. Henry Marion Howe to MHE, November 22, 1910, *The Yellow House Papers*, Coll. 2085, Record Group 32.
7. As told to archivist Danny D. Smith by Laura (Betty) E. Wiggins, related in the guide to *The Yellow House Papers: The Laura E. Richards Collection; An Inventory and Historical Analysis* (Gardiner, ME: Gardiner Library Association and Colby College, 1988–1991), 24.
8. LER to MHE, April 24, 1913, *The Yellow House Papers*, Coll. 2085, Record Group 14.
9. Columbia University to MHE, June 6, 1917, *The Yellow House Papers*, Coll. 2085, Record Group 31I, F.8.
10. Linden Gate suffered extensive fire damage in 1963 and was demolished in the 1970s.
11. Hall, *Memories Grave and Gay*, 258.
12. Elliott, *This Was My Newport*, 113.
13. Elliott, Diaries, February, March, April 1912, John Hay Library, Maud Howe Elliott Papers.
14. Elliott, *This Was My Newport*, 337.
15. Elliott, Diaries, April 25, 1912, John Hay Library, Maud Howe Elliott Papers.
16. Harrison S. Morris, *Confessions in Art* (New York: Sears Publishing, 1930), 240–41.
17. Maud Howe, "American Artists in Rome," *Art and Progress* 1: 9 (July 1910) 247–52.
18. Elliott, Diaries, March 17, 1912, John Hay Library, Maud Howe Elliott Papers.
19. Ibid., August 27, 1912.
20. Maud Howe Elliott, "Address at Annual Meeting of Newport County Women's Suffrage League," in *Newport Daily News* (?), [c1914].
21. Maud Howe Elliott, "Mrs. Jencks and Mrs. Elliott on Suffrage," *Taunton Gazette* [undated clipping, c.1916], Newport Art Museum Archives.

22. Elliott, *Three Generations*, 343.
23. Ibid., 351.
24. Elliott, Diaries, January 1, 1916, John Hay Library, Maud Howe Elliott papers.
25. Ibid., August 24, 1912.
26. Ibid., August 20, 1912.
27. Ibid., September 2, 1912.
28. Maud Howe Elliott, "Secretary's Report," Art Association of Newport, Annual Report, 1921. Newport Art Museum Archives.
29. The Newport Art Museum Archives contain scrapbooks and correspondence that document these talks and exhibitions. See also: Nancy Whipple Grinnell, "Carrying the Torch in Newport: The Arts Advocacy of Maud Howe Elliott," *Newport History* 74 (Spring 2005), 252.
30. The Art Association of Newport purchased the Griswold residence, Richard Morris Hunt's earliest commission in Newport, for $40,000; the group took occupancy in 1916 and adapted parts of the building as an exhibition space and school. Restored in 2005, the Griswold House is a National Historic Landmark, a project of Save America's Treasures, and celebrates its sesquicentennial in 2014.
31. Henry Marion Howe to LER, October 30, 1916, *The Yellow House Papers*, Coll. 2085, Record Group 32.
32. MHE to JE, February 7, 1918, John Hay Library, Maud Howe Elliott Papers, Box 1, F.1:30.
33. JE to MHE, January 23, 1912, John Hay Library, Maud Howe Elliott Papers, Box 1, F.1:27.
34. Elliott, Diaries, May 31, 1912, John Hay Library, Maud Howe Elliott Papers.

TEN

Epigraph: Edith Ballinger Price, poem read at Maud Howe Elliott's seventieth birthday at the Art Association, November 9, 1924, Newport Art Museum Archives.
1. Elliott, Diaries, January 1, 1943, John Hay Library, Maud Howe Elliott Papers.
2. For this exhibition, 159 works were rounded up, with lenders including Sarah Choate Sears, Isabel and Larz Anderson, Harrison Morris, Margaret Deland, Alice Brayton, Natalie Dresser Brown, and various family members. Glass slides exist to document the exhibition in the Newport Art Museum Archives.
3. Charles M. Stow, "John Elliott, an Exhibition in Memoriam of a Versatile Artist," *Boston Evening Transcript*, August 22, 1925, 8.
4. LER to MHE, July 30, 1906, *The Yellow House Papers*, Coll. 2085, Record Group 14.

5. Boxes from the estate of the Elliotts, containing photographs by Van Gloeden and his cousin Guglielmo Plüschow, who also photographed male nudes in Italy, were purchased by Federico Santi and John Gacher, proprietors of Newport's The Drawing Room, in 1996.

6. Elliott, "Afternoon Tea." Unpublished manuscript, John Hay Library, Maud Howe Elliott Papers, Box 1, F.4:2, 18.

7. Maud Howe Elliott, *Lord Byron's Helmet* (Boston: Houghton Mifflin, 1927), 75. For her efforts Maud was awarded the Order of the Golden Cross of the Redeemer.

8. Norman Prince and Vincent Chapman died in the Lafayette Escadrille. The portraits went to the National Museum at the Smithsonian instead.

9. Elliott, "Afternoon Tea," 36.

10. Ibid., 40.

11. Elliott, Unpublished handwritten notes for lectures on art, John Hay Library, Maud Howe Elliott Papers, Box 2, F.5:7.

12. Maud Howe Elliott, "How the Greater Art Foundations Can Help the Lesser," a paper read at the Thirteenth Annual Convention of the American Federation of Arts, Washington, D.C., May 1922, *American Magazine of Art*.

13. Elliott, *This Was My Newport*, 127.

14. MHE to The Mayor of Newport, May 17, 1914, Newport Art Museum Archives.

15. This story was related to Danny Smith, Archivist for the *Yellow House Papers* by Laura Elizabeth Wiggins in 1980. While it captures the grand dame that Maud became in later years, a few of the details do not correlate. During World War Two Maud was turning ninety and she definitely would not have appeared "properly naked in a cocktail dress."

16. Elliott, "Afternoon Tea." Unpublished manuscript, John Hay Library, Maud Howe Elliott Papers, Box 1, F.4:2, 12.

17. Elliott, "What I Saw and Heard in Panama, A.D. 1930–1931." Privately printed, 4.

18. Elliott, "Afternoon Tea," F.4:4.

19. Ibid., F.4:3.

20. Ibid., F.4:2, 50–62.

21. Ibid., 25.

22. Interestingly, Maud was to meet O'Keeffe in 1937 when the artist and her sister, Anita Young, who summered in Newport, visited her at Lilliput. Maud noted, "A very interesting, vital sort of woman. Plain with little social distinction but more interesting than her sister Mrs. Young. Have not much knowledge of her work but she is one of the few very successful woman painters of the day," in Elliott, Diaries, March 30, 1937, John Hay Library, Maud Howe Elliott Papers.

23. Elliott, "Afternoon Tea," F.4:2, 2.

24. Ibid., F.4:4.

25. In 1943 Maud printed "Memories of the Civil War" to benefit the Newport Chapter of the Red Cross. She also left behind several unpublished manuscripts that she had hoped would be published. These were compiled in the late 1930s. Her "Memories of 80 Years," "Afternoon Tea," and "Golden Special" all describe people, travel, and events of her long life. Handwritten and typed copies reside at the John Hay Library, Brown University.

26. The author has spoken with the late Posey Wiggins, granddaughter of Laura Richards, and Maud Fluchere and the late Griselda Kerr, granddaughters of Florence Hall, about their memories of Great Aunt Maud.

27. Herbert Pell to MHE, July 8, 1940, John Hay Library, Maud Howe Elliott Papers, Box 1, F.1:2.

28. Maud Howe Elliott, "Civilization Will Survive," *Christian Science Monitor*, March 22, 1941.

29. MHE to Francis Gyra, March 5, 1945, Newport Art Museum Archives.

30. Ibid.

31. "Books and Authors Rally Plan Grows," *Newport Herald*, June 6, 1945.

32. Edith Ballinger Price to A. Marshall Jones, October 3, 1944, Newport Art Museum Archives.

33. "Newport's Famous Daughter Honored on Her 90th Birthday," *Providence Journal*, November 10, 1944, Newport Art Museum Archives.

34. Elliott, Diaries, January 1, 1944, John Hay Library, Maud Howe Elliott Papers.

35. Resolution passed May 11, 1948, Annual Report, Art Association of Newport, Newport Art Museum Archives.

36. Howe, *Three Generations*, 345.

37. Howe, Journals, August 4, 1907, Houghton Library, Howe Family Papers.

BIBLIOGRAPHY

PRINCIPAL ARCHIVAL SOURCES

Howe Family Papers, Houghton Library, Harvard University
Maud Howe Elliott Papers, John Hay Library, Brown University
Newport Art Museum Archives
Schlesinger Library, Radcliffe Institute, Harvard University
Yellow House Papers, Laura E. Richards Collection, Gardiner Library Association, Gardiner, Maine
Yellow House Papers, Laura E. Richards Collection, Gardiner Library Association and Maine Historical Society, Coll. 2085

SOURCES

Anderson, Isabel. *The Great Sea Horse*. Boston: Little, Brown and Company, 1909.

Anderson, Larz. *Larz Anderson: Letters and Journals of a Diplomat*. Ed. Isabel Anderson. New York: Fleming H. Revell Company, 1940.

Berenson, Bernard. *The Letters of Bernard Berenson and Isabella Stewart Gardner*. Ed. Rollin van Hadley. Boston: Northeastern University Press, 1987.

The Brooklyn Museum. *The American Renaissance, 1876–1917*. With essay "The Great Civilization," by Richard Guy Wilson. New York: Pantheon Books, 1979.

Broun, Elizabeth. *Albert Pinkham Ryder*. Washington, D.C.: Smithsonian Institution Press, 1989.

Burns, Sarah. *Inventing the Modern Artist: Art and Culture in Gilded Age America*. New Haven and London: Yale University Press, 1996.

Carter, Morris. *Isabella Stewart Gardner and Fenway Court*. London: W. Weineman, 1926.

Chanler, Margaret Terry (Mrs. Winthrop), *Roman Spring*. Boston: Little, Brown, 1934.

Chong, Alan, Noriko Murai and others. *Journeys East: Isabella Stewart Gardner in Asia*. Boston: Isabella Stewart Gardner Museum, 2009.

A Circle of Friends: Art Colonies of Cornish and Dublin. A cooperative exhibition project of the University Art Galleries, University of New Hampshire, and the Thorne-Sagendorph Art Galleries, Keene State College, 1985.

Clifford, Deborah Pickman. *Mine Eyes Have Seen the Glory: A Biography of Julia Ward Howe*. Boston: Little, Brown, 1978, 1979.

Colby, Virginia Reed, and James B. Atkinson. *Footprints of the Past: Images of Cornish, New Hampshire and the Cornish Colony*. Concord, N.H.: New Hampshire Historical Society, 1996.

Cram, Ralph Adams. *My Life in Architecture*. Boston: Little, Brown, 1936.

Deland, Margaret. *Golden Yesterdays*. New York: Harper and Bros., 1940, 1941.

Edel, Leon. *Henry James: The Treacherous Years*. Philadelphia: Lippincott, 1969.

Elliott, Maud Howe. *Art and Handicraft in the Woman's Building at the World's Columbian Exposition, Chicago 1893*. Paris and New York: Goupil & Company, 1893.

———. *The Eleventh Hour in the Life of Julia Ward Howe*. Boston: Little, Brown, 1911.

———. *John Elliott: The Story of an Artist*. Boston and New York: Houghton Mifflin Co.; Riverside Press, Cambridge, 1930.

———. *Lord Byron's Helmet*. Boston and New York: Houghton Mifflin Company, Riverside Press, 1927.

———. *Memories of the Civil War, 1861–1864*. Privately printed to benefit the Newport Chapter of Red Cross. [1943, 8p.].

———. *My Cousin, F. Marion Crawford*. New York: Macmillan Company, 1934.

———. *This Was My Newport*. Cambridge, MA: Mythology Company-A. Marshall Jones, 1944.

———. *Three Generations*. Boston: Little, Brown and Company 1923.

———. *Uncle Sam Ward and His Circle*. New York: Macmillan Company, 1938.

Gammell, Ives. *Dennis Miller Bunker*. New York: Howard McCann, 1953.

Goodrich, Lloyd. *Albert P. Ryder*. New York: George Braziller, 1959.

Grinnell, Nancy Whipple. "Carrying the Torch in Newport: The Arts Advocacy of Maud Howe Elliott," *Newport History: Journal of the Newport Historical Society* 74: 252, Spring 2005.

———. "Remembering the Ladies: Women and the Art Association of Newport." Newport, R.I.: Newport Art Museum, 2011.

———. "From Pennsylvania to Paradise: William Trost Richards, Harrison Morris, and the Art Association of Newport." Newport, R.I.: Newport Art Museum, 2012.

Hall, Florence Howe. *Julia Ward Howe and the Woman Suffrage Movement*. Boston: Dana Estes & Company, 1913.

———. *Memories Grave and Gay*. New York and London: Harper & Brothers, 1918.

Harris, Neil. *The Artist in American Society: The Formative Years, 1790–1860*. New York: George Braziller, 1966.

Harrison, Eliza Cope, and Rosemary F. Carroll. "Newport's Summer Colony, 1830–1860," *Newport History: Bulletin of the Newport Historical Society* 74: 253, Fall 2005.

The Hawthorne Centenary at the Wayside, Concord, Massachusetts, July 4–7, 1904. Boston and New York: Houghton, Mifflin and Company; Riverside Press, 1905.

Hicks, Thomas. *Eulogy on Thomas Crawford*. New York: Privately printed for subscribers, 1865.

Howe, Julia Ward. *From the Oak to the Olive; a Plain Record of a Pleasant Journey*. Boston: Lee & Shepard, 1868.

———. *Reminiscences, 1819-1899*. Boston and New York: Houghton Mifflin Company, Riverside Press, 1899.

[Howe, Maud.] *A Newport Aquarelle*. Boston: Roberts Brothers, 1893.

Howe, Maud. *Atalanta in the South*. Boston: Roberts Brothers, 1886.

———. *Mammon,* a novel. Serialized in *Lippincott's Monthly Magazine*, August 1888, 42, 145–271. Reprinted as *Honor.* St. Paul: Price-McGill Company, 1893.

———. *Phillida*. New York: John W. Lovell Company, 1891.

———. *Roma Beata*. Boston: Little, Brown, 1909.

———. *Sicily in Shadow and in Sun: the Earthquake and the American Relief Work*. With illustrations by John Elliott. Boston: Little, Brown, 1910.

———. *Sun and Shadow in Spain*. Boston: Little, Brown, 1908.

———. *Two in Italy*. Boston: Little, Brown, 1905.

Howe, Maud and Florence Howe Hall. *The Story of Laura Bridgman, Doctor Howe's Famous Pupil and What He Taught Her*. Boston: Little, Brown, 1903.

Jacob, Kathryn Allamong. *King of the Lobby: The Life and Times of Sam Ward, Man-About Washington in the Gilded Age*. Baltimore: Johns Hopkins University Press, 2010.

Johnson, Rossiter, ed. *A History of the World's Columbian Exposition*. New York: Appleton, 1897.

Lowe, David Garrard. *Stanford White's New York*. New York: Doubleday, 1992.

Lucey, Donna M. *Archie and Amélie: Love and Madness in the Gilded Age*. New York: Harmony Books, 2006.

Merritt, Howard S. *Thomas Cole.* Rochester, N.Y.: Memorial Art Gallery of University of Rochester, 1969.

Monroe, Harriet. *A Poet's Life: Seventy Years in a Changing World.* New York: Macmillan, 1938.

Morris, Harrison S. *Confessions in Art*. New York: Sears Publishing Company, 1930.

Newall, Christopher. *The Grosvenor Gallery Exhibitions: Change and Continuity in the Victorian Art World.* Cambridge: Cambridge University Press, 1995.

Noble, Louis Legand. *The Life and Works of Thomas Cole*. Cambridge, Mass.: Harvard University Press, 1964.

O'Connor, Richard. *The Golden Summers: An Antic History of Newport*. New York: G. P. Putnam's Sons, 1974.

Parrish, Stephen Maxfield. *Currents of the Nineties in Boston and London: Fred Holland Day, Louise Imogene Guiney, and Their Circle. A Thesis, Harvard University, 1954*. Reprinted. New York: Garland, 1987.

Pease, William H., and Jane H. Pease. *The Roman Years of a South Carolina Artist: Caroline Carson's Letters Home, 1872–1892*. Columbia, S.C.: University of South Carolina Press, 2003.

Peck, Amelia, and Carol Irish. *Candace Wheeler: The Art and Enterprise of American Design, 1875–1900*. New York: Metropolitan Museum of Art, 2001.

Pfeffer, Miki. *Exhibiting Women: Sectional Confrontation and Resolution in the Women's Department at the World's Exposition, New Orleans. A Thesis*. New Orleans: University of New Orleans, 2006.

Pilkington, John, Jr. *Francis Marion Crawford*. New York: Twayne Publishers, 1964.

Pyne, Kathleen. *Art and the Higher Life: Painting and Evolutionary Thought in Late Nineteen-Century America*. Austin: University of Texas Press, 1996.

Richards, Laura E. *Letters and Journals of Samuel Gridley Howe: the Servant of Humanity*. 2v. Boston: Dana Estes & Company, 1906.

———. *Samuel Gridley Howe*. New York and London: D. Appleton-Century Company, 1935

———. *Stepping Westward*. New York: London: D. Appleton and Company, 1931.

———. *When I Was Your Age*. Boston: Estes & Lauriat, 1894.

Richards, Laura E., and Maud Howe Elliott, with assistance from Florence Howe Hall. *Julia Ward Howe, 1819–1910*. 2 vols. Boston and New York: Houghton Mifflin and Company, 1916.

Shand-Tucci, Douglass. *The Art of Scandal: The Life and Times of Isabella Stewart Gardner*. New York: Harper Collins, 1997.

———. *Boston Bohemia, 1881–1900: Ralph Adams Cram: Life and Architecture*, 1995.

Shannon, Martha A. *Boston Days of William Morris Hunt*. Boston: Marshall Jones, 1923.

Soria, Regina. *Elihu Vedder: Amercia's Visionary Artist in Rome (1836–1923)*. Rutherford, Madison, Teaneck, N.J.: Fairleigh Dickinson University Press, 1970.

Stebbins, Theodore E., Jr. *The Lure of Italy: American Artists and the Italian Experience.1760–1904*. Boston: Museum of Fine Arts and Harry Abrams, 1992.

Stetson, Charles Walter. *Endure: the Diaries of Charles Walter Stetson*. Ed. Mary Armfield Hill. Philadelphia: Temple University Press, 1985.

Tharp, Louise Hall. *Mrs. Jack: A Biography of Isabella Stewart Gardner*. Boston: Little, Brown, 1965.

———. *Saint Gaudens and the Gilded Era*. Boston: Little, Brown, 1969.

———. *Three Saints and a Sinner: Julia Ward Howe, Louisa, Annie, and Sam Ward*. Boston: Little, Brown, 1956.

Toibin, Colm. *The Master*. New York: Scribners, 2004.
Trent, James W., Jr. *The Manliest Man: Samuel G. Howe and the Contours of Nineteenth Century American Reform*. Amherst: University of Massachusetts Press, 2012.
Wadsworth, Sarah, and Wayne A. Wiegand. *Right Here I See My Own Books. The Woman's Building and the World's Columbian Exposition*. Amherst: University of Massachusetts Press, 2012.
Waters, John. "William Pretyman, Designer." *Nineteenth Century*, Spring 2012.
Weimann, Jeanne Madeline. *The Fair Women*. Chicago: Academy Chicago, 1981.
Whitehill, Walter Muir. *Boston Public Library: A Centennial History*. Cambridge, Mass.: Harvard University Press, 1956.
Williams, Gary S. *Hungry Heart: The Literary Emergence of Julia Ward Howe*. Amherst: University of Massachusetts Press, 1999.
Ziegler, Valarie H. *Diva Julia: The Public Romance and Private Agony of Julia Ward Howe*. Harrisburg, London, New York: Trinity Press International, 2003.

INDEX

Numbers in *italics* refer to plates.

Adamowski, Timothy, 54, 150n44
Addams, Jane, 123
Agassiz, Alexander, 53
Aide, Charles Hamilton, 106
Alger, William Rounseville, 8
Alma-Tadema, Lawrence, Sir, 89
Allston, Washington, x, 36
American Federation of Arts (AFA), 131
American Renaissance, 75–76, 80
Anagnos, Julia Romana, 3, 16, 19, 20, 33, 53; photograph with siblings, *pl. 4*
Anagnos, Michael, 88
Andersen, Hendrik, 98–99, 100
Anderson, Isabel Perkins, 85, 97–98, 102, 103, 112; *The Great Sea Horse*, 110
Anderson, Larz, 98, 102, 112
Andrew, John Albion, 9
Antin, Mary, 125
Appleton, Thomas Gold, 6, 48
Art Association of Newport, ix, xiii, 120–21, 122, 123–25, 129, 132–33, 137, 160n30; mentioned in caption of photograph showing Maud Howe Elliott speaking on WPRO Radio, *pl. 35*; photograph showing Council, *pl. 37*; photograph taken on 90th birthday of Maud Howe Elliott, *pl. 33*
Astor, Emily, 23, 25

Bacon, Gorham, 24
Bailey, George (house), 23
Beacon Street, Boston: residence, 45, 48, 61, 78, 115; photograph of reception room, *pl. 14*
Beals, Jesse Tarbox, photograph of Maud Howe Elliott at an exhibition, *pl. 13*
Belknap, Reginald Rowan, Captain, 113, 133
Belmont, Alva Vanderbilt (Mrs. Oliver Hazard Perry), 121
Berenson, Bernard, 86, 111–12
Biesel, Charles, 122–23
Birckhead, Caroline Minturn Hall ("Carrie"), 61, 88, 104
Bisland, Elizabeth, 59
Blind, Karl, 47
The Boatswain's Whistle, 10
Boer War, 106
Bonheur, Rosa, 81
Boni, Giocomo, 99–100, 130
Booth, Edwin, 10–11
Booth, William, General, 93

Boott, Elizabeth, 81
Boston Art Club, 64
Boston Athenaeum, 12
Boston Music Hall, 11
Boston Public Library, 89, 92, 102–3
Boston Symphony Orchestra, 150n44
Boston Theater, 10
Boston Transcript, ix, 54, 65, 96
Brett, George, 150n30
Bridgman, Laura, 5, 88
Brooke, Stopford, 30
Brooks, Charles, Reverend, 18
Brown, Horatio, 100, 130
Browning, Robert, xi
Brown, John, 8
Brown, John Nicholas, 122
Brown, Natalie Bayard, 122, 124, 132
Brown University, Providence, Rhode Island, 138
Bunker, Dennis Miller, 66
Burgess, William, Professor, 122
Burlington House, London, 41
Burne-Jones, Edward, Sir, xi, 31
Burnham, Daniel H., 73
Byron, Lord (George Gordon), xiii, 130–31

Cable, George Washington, 59
Caine, Hall, 98
Carman, Bliss, 86
Cassatt, Mary, 83
Cerio, Mabel Norman, 85, 124, 135; portrait of Maud Howe Elliott, *pl. 19*
The Chanler (house), Newport, Rhode Island, 25
Chanler, John Winthrop, 25
Chanler, Laura, 132
Chanler, Margaret "Daisy" Terry, 33, 42, 46, 101
Chanler, Margaret Livingston, 85, 87
Chanler, Margaret "Maddie" Ward, 23, 25
Chanler, Winthrop, 101
Channing Memorial Church, Newport, Rhode Island, 122, 140
Chapman, Victor, 127
Chicago, World's Columbian Exposition, ix, 73, 81–83, 158n16
Civil War, 8–9
Clarke, James Freeman, 6, 61
Clarke, Thomas B., 77–78
Clavell, Edith, 131
Clemens, Samuel. *See* Mark Twain
Clement, E. H., 96
Cliff Lawn (house), Newport, Rhode Island, 25
Coleman, Enrico, 111
Cole, Thomas, *The Voyage of Life,* 13–14
Colman, Samuel, 120
Conway, Moncure, 30
Copley, John Singleton, x
Cornish Art Colony, New Hampshire, 106–8; "Masque of 'Ours': The Gods and the Golden Bowl," 110
Costa, Giovanni, 34
Cram, Ralph Adams, 86, 132
Crane, Walter, 31
Crawford, Francis Marion, xiii, 33–34, 35, 44–45, 48, 49–50, 52–55, 62, 70, 96, 150n30; photograph of, *pl. 26*
Crawford, Louisa Ward. *See* Terry, Louisa Ward
Crawford, Thomas G., 11–12; *Beethoven,* 12; *Orpheus and Cerberus,* 12
Crowninshield, Frederick, 43
Current Topics Club, Newport, Rhode Island, 120
Curtis, Daniel (house), Rome, 99
Curtis, George William, 6
Cushman, Charlotte, 11
Cushman, George Hewitt, 27
Cutler, Sarah, 23

Davis, George, General, 73
Davis, Katherine Bemont, Dr., 125
de Kay, Charles, 63, 64, 69, 85
de Kay, Janet Drake, 63
de Kay, Helena. *See* Gilder, Helena de Kay
Deland, Margaret, 71–72, 92–94, 132
Derby, Lucy, 22, 64–65, 72
Diman, John B., Reverend, 123
Dole, Nathan, 8
Dominican Republic. *See* Santo Domingo
Doré, Gustave, 33
Dorr, Mary (Mrs. Charles H.), 24, 36
Dorr, Rheta Childe, 125
Dresser, Daniel Leroy, 122
Dunne, Finley Peter, 108
Dunraven, Lord. *See* Wyndham-Quin, Windham
Dwight, John Sullivan, 11, 62
Dwight, Thomas, 92

Elliott, Edward, 85
Elliott, John, xii, 35, 36, 37, 40–41, 47, 59–60, 69, 74–75, 84–85, 123, 124, 126; *The Chevalier*, 109; Cornish Art Colony, New Hampshire, 106–8, 110; death, 128; depression, 91–92; *Diana of the Tides* (mural, Smithsonian Institution), 110–12, 113, 118; *Diana of the Tides* (study for mural), *pl. 21*; *The Great Sea Horse*, 110, 113; *The Great Sea Horse* illustrations, *pls. 22–24*; homosexuality, 99–100, 129–30; Lafayette Escadrille (portraits), 131; *The Making of the First Musical Instrument*, 107–8, and in photograph by Carl Thorp, *pl. 30*; *The May Dream* (ideal portrait of Maud Howe Elliott), 69, *pl. 36*; New York City, 108–9; photograph at age 22, *pl. 34*; photograph with Maud Howe Elliott, *pl. 32*; portrait by José de Villegas, *pl. 18*; portrait of Edith Clavell, 131; portrait of Julia Ward Howe, *pl. 25*; portrait of Sam Ward, 60, 120; portraits of Maud Howe Elliott, *pls. 11, 12*; relief work, 113, 127; silverpoint drawing after photograph by John Adams Whipple, *pl. 31*; *The Triumph of Time* (Boston Public Library), 89–93, 102–3, 157n3, *pls. 27* (detail showing Maud Howe Elliott) and *28*
Elliott, Maud Howe, 26–28, 42–44, 48–60, 139; adolescence, 15–16; "Afternoon Tea," 162n25; appearance, 24–25, 52; *Art and Handicraft in the Woman's Building at the World's Columbian Exposition*, 81–83; "An Artist's Life in Rome," xiii; *Atalanta in the South*, 68; birth, 1–4; Books and Authors War Bond Rally, 138; Brown University Honorary Doctor of Letters, 138; California and the Southwest, 136; Chicago, 73–83; childhood, 8–12; "Civilization Will Survive," 138; Cornish Art Colony, New Hampshire, 106–8, 110; depression, 45, 116, 128; *Dr. Howe and His Famous Pupil, Laura Bridgman*, 109; drawing by Benjamin Curtis Porter, *pl. 8*; *The Eleventh Hour in the Life of Julia Ward Howe*, 117; Florida and the Caribbean, 134–35, 136–37; "Flower o' the May," 66–68; Golden Special, 125–26; "Golden Special," 162n25; Grand Tour, xi-xii, 29–41; *John Elliott, The Story of an Artist*, 129; lectures, xiii, xiv, 75, 85, 87, 120, 124, 153n7; *Julia Ward Howe, 1819–1910*, ix, xii, 118; *Lord Byron's Helmet*, xiii, 130–31; magazine articles, 104–5; *Mammon (Honor)*, 70; marriage, 61–62; *The May Dream*

Index 171

(ideal portrait by John Elliott), *pl. 36*; "Memories of 80 Years," 162n25; "Memories of the Civil War," 8, 162n25; *My Cousin, F. Marion Crawford*, 137; "The Navy at Newport," 133–34; *A Newport Aquarelle*, 50–52, 60; New York City, 108–9; The Papeterie, 119; *Phil Owens—A Life Sketch*, 70; *Phillida*, 71; *Phillida* (cover illustration), *pl. 29*; photograph at an exhibition, *pl. 13*; photograph at Art Association of Newport with Council, *pl. 37*; photograph at Art Association of Newport on 90th birthday, *pl. 33*; photograph at Lilliput by Carl Thorp, *pl. 30*; photograph by Bacharach, ix, *pl. 7*; photograph on "Golden Special" train, *pl. 5*; photograph speaking on WPRO Radio about Art Association of Newport, *pl. 35*; photograph with John Elliott, *pl. 32*; photograph with siblings, *pl. 4*; photograph with sister Laura, *pl. 2*; portrait by Adele Herter, *pl. 16*; portraits by Benjamin Curtis Porter, *pls. 9, 10*; portrait by Durr Freedley, *pl. 20*; portraits by John Elliott, *pls. 11, 12*; portrait by José de Villegas, *pl. 17*; portrait by Mabel Norman Cerio, *pl. 19*; portrait shown in *The Triumph of Time, pl. 27*; Pulitzer Prize, ix, 118; "Ralph Darrow's Tryst," 114; religious beliefs, 80; *Roma Beata*, 104; Roman letters, 104; Rome, 95–101; *The San Rosario Ranch*, 56–58, 69; *Sicily in Shadow and in Sun*, 113; stereopticon, *pl. 1*; *Sun and Shadow in Spain*, 113; *This Was My Newport*, xiv, 139; *Three Generations*, xii, 129, and mentioned in captions, *pls. 14, 15, 26, 34, 36*; *Two in Italy*, 104; *Uncle Sam Ward and His Circle*, xiv, 137; "What I Saw and Heard in Panama," 134; women's suffrage, xiii, 121–22

Emerson, Ralph Waldo, 11, 65
Emery, Mary M. (Mrs. Thomas), 118, 124
Ernst Studio, Newport, photograph of Art Association of Newport Council Members, *pl. 37*

Farwell, Rose, 85
Fearing, George Richmond, Mrs., 88
Field, Kate, 54
Fields, Annie, 11
Finzi, Eugene, 135
First World War, 125, 127, 131
Flagler, Henry, 134
Frazee, John, 12
Freedley, Durr, 137–38; portrait of Maud Howe Elliott, *pl. 20*
Froebel, Friedrich, 40
Fuller, George, x, 64–65
Fuller, Henry, 106
Fuller, Lucia Fairchild, 106, 158n16

Gabriel, Paul, 90
Gardner, Helen, 85, 99
Gardner, Isabella Stewart, 50, 53, 56, 62, 66, 86, 92, 99, 102, 111–12, 121
Gardner, John, 55, 60, 61
Garland, Marie, 136
Gauthier, José Maria, 27
Gibson, Charles Dana, 108, 112–13
Gilder, Helena de Kay, 62, 63
Gilder, Jeannette, 48
Gilder, Richard Watson, 48, 62
Gladstone, William, 30
Godey's Magazine, 66
Grant, Nellie, 21
Grant, Ulysses, 21, 31
Green Peace (house), Boston, 6, 7, 26
Grimes, Medora, 23
Griswold, John N. A. (house), 125,

160n30; photograph on lawn showing Council, *pl. 37*
Grosvenor Gallery, London, 31, 32
Guiney, Louise Imogene, 86
Gyra, Francis, 137, 138

Hague School, 90
Hall, Caroline Minturn ("Carrie"). *See* Birckhead, Caroline Hall
Hall, David Prescott, 20–21, 88
Hall, Florence Howe, 1, 6, 16, 19, 20–21, 42, 45–46, 88, 115–18, 121; *Dr. Howe and His Famous Pupil, Laura Bridgman*, 109; photograph with siblings, *pl. 4*
Hall, Henry Marion, 104, 132
Hallowell, Sarah, 82–83
Hall, Prescott, 13
Hall, Samuel Prescott, 129
Handy, A. D., Boston, *pl. 1*
Harte, Bret, 54
Hastings, Thomas, 110
Hawes, J. J., 109
Hawthorne, Nathaniel, 8, 59
Hawthorne, Sophia Peabody, 81
Hayden, Sophia, 82
Henschel, George, 44
Herford, Oliver, 108
Herter, Adele (Mrs. Albert), 137; portrait of Maud Howe Elliott, *pl. 16*
Herter, Albert, 137
Herter Brothers, 11, 74
Higginson, Frank, Admiral, 39
Higginson, Thomas Wentworth, 5, 54, 102
Holmes, Oliver Wendell, 11, 48, 102
Homer, Winslow, x, 78
Hosmer, Harriet, 17, 81
Houghton, Lord. *See* Milnes, Richard Monckton
Houston, Frances Lyons, 107
Howard, Frances Minturn, 130, 140

Howard, George, Earl of Carlisle, 31
Howe, Florence. *See* Hall, Florence Howe
Howe, Henry "Harry" Marion, 4, 21, 92, 109, 115, 116–18, 120, 125; photograph with siblings, *pl. 4*
Howe, Joseph, 10
Howe, Julia Romana. *See* Agnanos, Julia Romana
Howe, Julia Ward, ix, x, 26–27, 29–30, 32, 33, 38–40, 42–45, 53, 58–60, 82, 89–90, 100–1, 109, 113; art appreciation, 12–13, 16–18, 63; *The Battle Hymn of the Republic*, x, 9; biography of, ix; death, xii, 115–16; *From the Oak to the Olive; A Plain Record of a Pleasant Journey*, 16, 145n10; marital discord, 19; marriage, 2–3; *Passion Flowers*, 1–2; portrait by John Elliott, *pl. 25*; Saturday Morning Club, Boston, 119; women's suffrage, 18–19. See also *The Boatswain's Whistle*
Howe, Laura Elizabeth. *See* Richards, Laura Elizabeth
Howe, Maud. *See* Elliott, Maud Howe
Howe, Samuel Gridley, ix, x-xi, 2–6, 10, 103, 109, 130; abolition, 9; death, 26; efforts on behalf of Greek freedom, 16; letters about Maud Howe, 19–21; marital discord, 19; marriage, 2–3; photograph at work, *pl. 6*; photograph with granddaughter Alice Richards, *pl. 3*; silverpoint drawing by John Elliott after photograph by John Adams Whipple, *pl. 31*; temperament, 6
Howe, Samuel Gridley Jr., 9
Hubbard, Henry Vincent, 107
Hughes, Charles Evans, x, 125–26; in caption, *pl. 5*
Hunter, Anna Falconnet, 124
Hunt, Helen, 54

Hunt, Louisa Dumaresque Perkins (Mrs. William Morris), 18
Hunt, Richard Morris, 54, 118
Hunt, William Morris, x, 10, 17–18, 63; Newport Studio, 124
Hurlbert, William Henry, 48

Inness, George, x, 78
Isma'il, Pasha, Khedive of Egypt, 38
Israels, Josef, 90

James, Henry, 30, 66, 98–99, 113, 124
James, Henry Sr., 8
James, William, 124
Janvier, Thomas Alibone, 108
Jones, Frederick Rhinelander, 62
Jones, Mary Cadwalader, 62
Jones, William Safford, Reverend, 122

Karolik, Maxim, x
Keene, James, 56
Keene, John R., 149n9
Kemp, Frederick Shakerley, 35, 47, 91–92, 97
Kellor, Frances, 123, 125
Kendall, William Sergeant, 120, 123
Kernochan, J. Frederick, Mrs., 85
Ketterlinus, John, 134
Kimball, Clara, 102
Kimball, David, 102
King, Ethel Rhinelander (Mrs. Leroy), 123
King, Grace, 59

La Farge, John, x, 54, 62, 63, 78–79, 124
Lafayette Escadrille (First World War), 131
Lafayette, Marquis de, 8
Langley, Samuel Pierpont, 111
Langtry, Lily, xi, 31
Launitz, B. E., 12

Lawton's Valley, Portsmouth, Rhode Island, 4, 6, 7, 18, 19
Lazarus, Emma, 54
Leighton, Frederick, Sir, 41
Lent, Frank, 68–69, 154n8
Lilliput (house), Newport, Rhode Island, 127, 137
Lincoln, Abraham, 9, 10
Lindsay, Coutts, Sir, 31
Livermore, Mary, 72
Longfellow, Henry Wadsworth, 1, 5, 44, 48
Loring, Katherine, 103
Loudon, John, 98

The Macchiaioli, 34
MacKaye, Percy, 110, 125
MacVeagh, Wayne, 98
Mailliard, Annie Ward, 2, 42, 46
Mailliard, Joseph, 48
Mancini, Antonio, 111
Mann, Horace, 5
Mansfield, Richard, 88
Margherita of Savoy, Queen Consort of Italy, 105
Marquand, Henry Gurdon, 76, 118
Mason, Ellen and Ida, 85, 124, 132–33
McAllister, Julia, 38–39
McAllister, Ward, 23, 51
McKim, Mead and White, 89
Meredith, George, 47
Metropolitan Museum of Art, New York, 18
Miantonomi Park Memorial Commission, Newport, Rhode Island, 134
Miller, Joaquin, 59
Millet, Joseph, 69
Milnes, Richard Monckton, 1st Baron Houghton, 30, 53
Mitchell, John Ames, 108
Mitchell, Maria, 53

Monroe, Harriet, 82
Moore, Clement, 14
Morris, Harrison S., 104, 118, 120, 124, 137; photograph at Art Association of Newport with Council, *pl. 37*
Morris, William, 32, 78
Morse, Alice C., 82
Moscatelli, Vincenzo, 95, 98
Mount Auburn Cemetery, Cambridge, Massachusetts, xiv, 140
Mozier, Joseph, 17

National Academy of Design, New York, 12, 25
New Orleans Cotton Centennial, Louisiana (1884), 58–60
Newport Art Museum and Art Association, ix, xiv
Newport County Woman Suffrage League, 121
Newport Progressive League, 122
Nightingale, Florence, 8
Norman Bird Sanctuary, Middletown, Rhode Island, 23
Norman, Mabel. *See* Cerio, Mabel Norman
Norton, Charles Eliot, 102
Norton, Richard, 98
Oak Glen (house), Portsmouth, Rhode Island, xii, 19, 115, 116, 127
O'Keeffe, Georgia, 136, 161n22
O'Reilly, John Boyle, 93

Palmer, Bertha Honore (Mrs. Potter), 72, 74, 81–82, 85
Papeterie, The, 119
Paris, Exposition Universelle; 1867, 16; 1878, 35–36, 78
Parker, Theodore, 5, 6
Parnell, Charles, 30
Parrish, Maxfield, 112
Passy, Frederic, 32

Peabody, Elizabeth Palmer, 8
Peabody, Sophia. *See* Hawthorne, Sophia Peabody
Pell, Herbert, 138
Perkins, George Hamilton, 97
Perkins Institution for the Blind, xi, 3–4
Perkins, Isabel. *See* Anderson, Isabel Perkins
Perkins, Louisa Dumaresque. *See* Hunt, Louisa Dumaresque Perkins
Perkins, Mary, 50
Perkins, Thomas Handasyd, 18
Perry, Marsden, 125
Philadelphia Centennial Exhibition, 1876, 27–28
Picknell, William, 65
Pierce, Phineus, 92
Porter, Benjamin Curtis, 18, 66, 85; drawing of Maud Howe Elliott, *pl. 8*; *Portrait of a Lady with a Dog* (1876), 25, *pl. 9*; *Portrait of a Lady* (Maud Howe Elliott) (1877), 25, 36, *pl. 10*
Potter, James Brown, Mrs. (Cora Urquhart), 51
Pottier, Daniel, 63
Powel, Harford W. H., 123
Pratt, Joseph, Dr., 128
Pretyman, Jenny (Mrs. William), 74–75
Pretyman, William, 74–75
Price, Edith Ballinger, 139
Primrose, Archibald, 5th Earl of Rosebery, 30
Prince, Frederick O., 89, 92
Prince, Morton, 101, 102
Prince, Norman, 127
Progressive Party (Bull Moose Party), x, xiii, 122–23
Providence Progressive League, 123
Pulitzer, Joseph, 118

Ramos, José, Dr., 139–40
Reid, Whitelaw, 49

Rhode Island Progressive Committee, 122
Rhode Island Women's Progressive Party, x, 122
Rhys, Ernest, 71
Rice, Thorndike, 48
Richards, Alice Maud, 26, 88, 89, 90, 103; photograph with grandfather, Samuel Gridley Howe, *pl. 3*
Richards, Henry, 6, 20, 26
Richards, Laura Elizabeth, ix, 1, 3, 16, 17, 20, 24, 26, 37, 43, 45–46, 58, 83, 88, 94, 97, 108, 115–18, 132, 137; death, 139; *Julia Ward Howe, 1819–1910*, ix, xii, 118; photograph with siblings, *pl. 4*; photograph with sister Maud, *pl. 2*; Pulitzer Prize, ix, 118
Richards, Rosalind, 61, 103
Richards, William Trost, 54
Rideout, Alice, 83
Riis, Jacob, 123
Rives, Sara Whiting (Mrs. George), 123
Rogers, Randolph, 17
Rogers, William Barton, 54
Roosevelt, Theodore, x, xiii, 105, 111, 122
Root, John, Mrs., 85
Rosebery, Lord. *See* Primrose, Archibald
Royal Academy, London, 31, 41
Ruskin, John, 16, 31
Ryder, Albert Pinkham, 63–64, 108

Saint-Gaudens, Augustus, x, 62, 77, 107
Salvation Army, 93
Salvini, Tomasso, 43
Santo Domingo, 21–22, 26
Sargent, John Singer, 62, 66, 77
Sargent, Violet, 77
Sartorio, Aristide, 111
Saturday Morning Club, Boston, 119
Schliemann, Heinrich, Dr., 40

Sears, J. Montgomery, 89, 102
Sears, Sara Choate, 89, 102
Second World War, 138
Shaw, Julia, 140
Sherwood, Jean (Mrs. John B.), 74
Sims, Anna (Mrs. William S.), 133–34
Sims, William S., Admiral, 133
Sirani, Elisabetta, 33
Smith, Alfred, 7.
Smith, Joseph Lindon, 132
Smithsonian Institution, Washington, D.C., 110–12
Snell, George, 11, 18
Society of American Artists, New York, 63
Society of the Four Arts, Palm Beach, Florida, xiii, 137
Sothern, Edward Askew, 22
Staigg, Richard, 54
Stanley, Arthur, Dean of Westminster Abbey, 31
Stebbins, Emma, 17, 81
Stepniak, Sergio, 93
Sterner, Albert, 120, 123
Stetson, Charles Walter, 63, 64
Stevens, Paran, Mrs., 18–19, 51
Stillman, Marie Spartoli, 32, 98
Stillman, William, 32, 98
Stone, Charles Pomeroy, General, 38
Story, Julian, 48
Story, William Wetmore, 17, 33, 35–36
Stuart, Gilbert, x
Stuart, Jane, 109
Sturtevant, Helena, 120, 123, 124–25
Sturtevant, Louisa, 120, 123
Sumner, Charles, 5, 12, 21
Swasey, Jeannette, 120, 123
Swinburne, Elizabeth, 124
Symonds, John Addington, 100

Taft, William Howard, 122
Terry, Arthur, 33, 48, 101

Terry, Linda (Mrs. Roderick), 118, 120
Terry, Louisa Crawford, 2, 17, 32, 33, 42, 45, 100
Terry, Luther, 17, 33, 101
Terry, Margaret "Daisy." *See* Chanler, Margaret "Daisy" Terry
Terry, Roderick, 118
Thayer, Abbot, 78
Thomas, Ruth, 136
Thorp, Carl, photograph of Maud Howe Elliott at Lilliput, *pl. 30*
Thorvaldsen, Bertel, 12
Town and Country Club, Newport, Rhode Island, xiii, 53, 119
Twain, Mark, 54

Upham, Jabez Baxter, 11
Urquhart, Cora. *See* Potter, James Brown, Mrs. (Cora Urquhart)

Vanderbilt, Frederick William, Mrs., 85
Van Rensselaer, Mariana, 81
Villegas, José de, 48, 111; portraits of Maud Howe and John Elliott, *pls. 17, 18*
von Bloden, Wilhelm, 130
von Rabe, Anne, 32
von Rabe, Eric, Baron, 32
Vose, Seth, 18

Waring, Colonel Charles, 53
Ward, Samuel (grandfather of Maud Howe Elliott), 12–14, 23; house at Bellevue Avenue and Old Beach Road, 146n27
Ward, Samuel (uncle of Maud Howe Elliott), xiv, 22–23, 43–44, 48, 50, 52, 149n9; portrait by John Elliott, 60, 151n67, *pl. 15*
Warden, William, 134

Warner, Charles Dudley, 59
Watts, George Frederick, Sir, 31, 89
Weir, Julian Alden, x, 14
Weir, Robert, 14
Weld, William Fletcher, 97
Wells, Emmeline B., 46
Wendell, Barrett, 86, 102
West, Benjamin, 41
Wetherill, Rebecca, 27
Wetmore, Edith, 124, 133
Wetmore, George, Senator, 133
Wetmore, Maude, 133
Wheeler, Candace, 82–83
Whipple, Edwin, 8
Whipple, John Adams, 109; silverpoint drawing by John Elliott after photograph by, *pl. 31*
Whistler, James McNeil, 31, 79
White, Stanford, 62
Whitman, Sarah Wyman, 92
Whitney, Gertrude Vanderbilt, 124, 127
Whitney, William Collins, Mrs., 85
Whitwell, Sophia Louisa, 54
Wiggins, Laura (Betty) Richards, 117, 133
Wilde, Oscar, 52–53, 54
Williams and Everett, Boston, 65
Williams, Harold, 89
Williams, Helen, 85
Wilson, Woodrow, 123
Woods, Eliott, 110
World War I. *See* First World War
World War II. *See* Second World War
Wormeley, Katharine, 8
Wyndham-Quin, Windham, 4th Earl of Dunraven and Mount-Earl, 30

Yarnell, Emily (Mrs. Harold), 136
Yarnell, Harold, Admiral, 136
Yates, Edmund, 31